VINTAGE RATINGS

PENEDÈS P. 26

RIOJA P. 85

The Simon and Schuster pocket guide to

Spanish Wines

Jan Read

Simon and Schuster
New York

Key to symbols

r.	red	In (parentheses) means relatively unimportant
p.	rosé	
w.	white	
am.	amber	
cl.	*clarete*	
g.	*generoso*	
res.	*reserva*	
dr.	dry	
s/sw.	semi-sweet	
sw.	sweet	See p.12 for more information
sp.	sparkling	
pt.	*pétillant*	
★	everyday wine	
★★	above average	
★★★	excellent quality, highly reputed	
★★★★	grand, prestigious, expensive	
[★★]	usually good value in its class	
HARO	name in small capitals indicates a cross-reference	
D.O.	denominación de Origen—name and origin controlled	
3 ano.	bottled during 3rd year after harvest	
74, 75	recommended years which may be currently available	
DYA	drink the youngest available	
NV	vintage not normally shown on label	
★→★★★	restaurants recommended for good food	

Key to maps

1,000m

Editor David Arnold
Art Editor Linda Cole
Editor in Chief Susannah Read
Executive Art Editor Douglas Wilson
Production Sarah Goodden

Edited and designed by
Mitchell Beazley International Ltd.
87–89 Shaftesbury Avenue,
London W1V 7AD

Published by Simon and Schuster, Inc.
Simon & Schuster Building
Rockefeller Center
1230 Avenue of the Americas
New York, New York 10020
Simon and Schuster and Colophon are registered trademarks of Simon and Schuster, Inc.

Library of Congress Cataloging in Publication Data
Read, Jan.
The Simon and Schuster pocket guide to Spanish wines.
Includes index.
1. Wine and wine-making – Spain.
I Title. II. Title: Pocket guide to Spanish wines.
TP559.S8R395 1983
641.2'22'0946 83-598
ISBN 0-671-47194-5

Maps by Illustra Design Ltd., Reading
Typeset by Servis Filmsetting Ltd., Manchester
Printed in Hong Kong by Mandarin Offset International Ltd.

Contents

Spain

The regions shown on this map are those used for the chapters of this guide. The definitive boundaries for the individual provinces are shown on the regional maps at the start of each section.

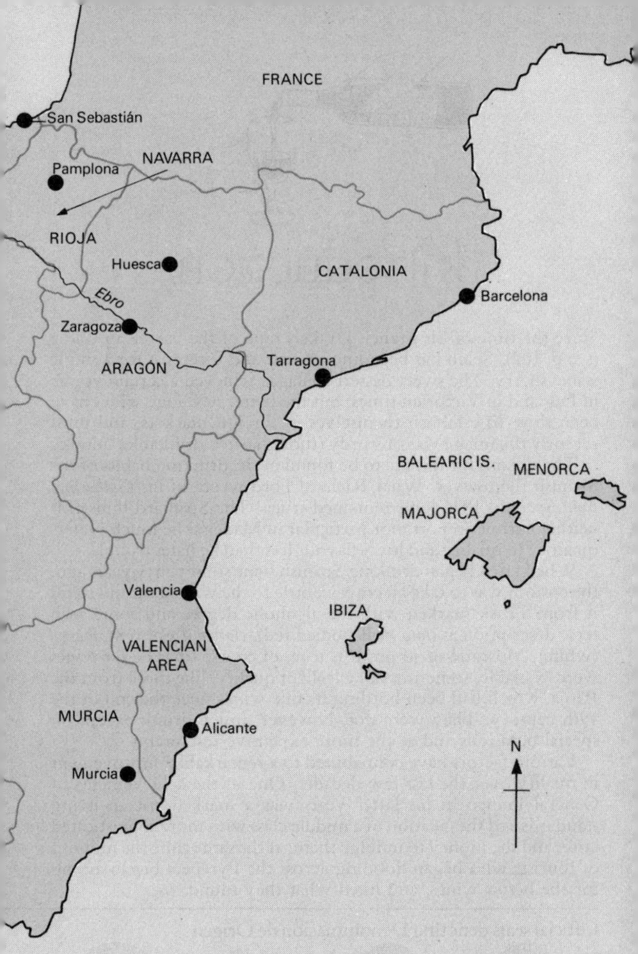

FRANCE
San Sebastián
NAVARRA
Pamplona
RIOJA
Huesca
CATALONIA
Ebro
Barcelona
Zaragoza
ARAGÓN
Tarragona
BALEARIC IS.
MENORCA
MAJORCA
Valencia
IBIZA
VALENCIAN AREA
MURCIA
Alicante
Murcia
N

CANARY IS.
LANZAROTE
TENERIFE
GRAN CANARIA

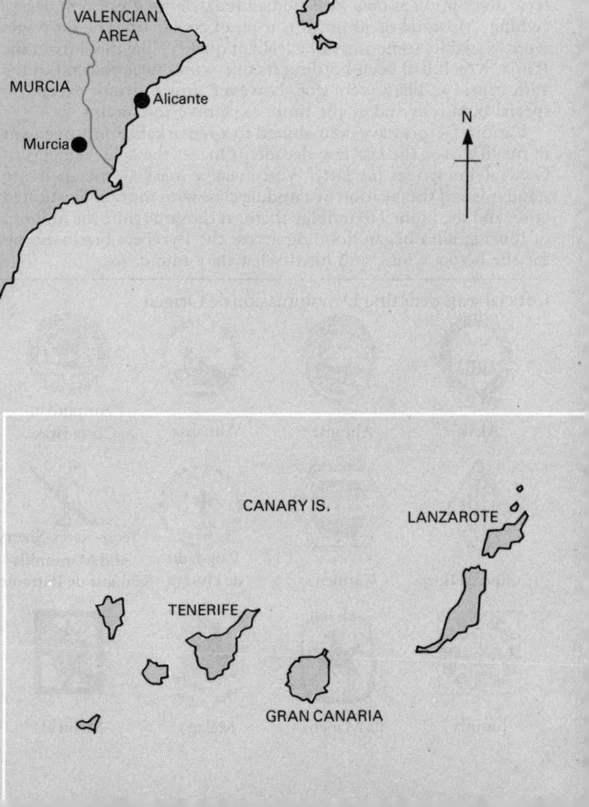

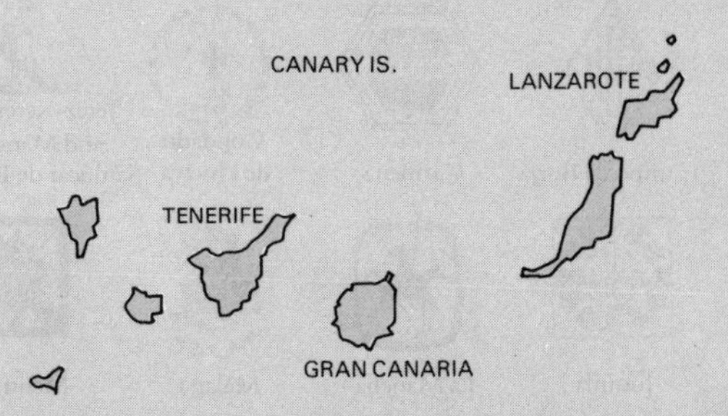

Introduction

Since the time of Sir Francis Drake's rape of the barrels in Cádiz (see p. 102), Spain has been known first and foremost for a single wine: sherry. The sweet dessert Málagas achieved a certain vogue in England in Victorian times, but the better beverage wines have been slow to establish themselves in foreign markets, and until recently the image was of sturdy (though often drinkable) 'plonk'.

The reasons for this are to be found in the drinking habits of the Spanish themselves. What Richard Ford wrote in his *Gatherings from Spain* in 1846 long remained true: "The Spaniard himself is neither curious in port, nor particular in Madeira; he much prefers quantity to quality and loves flavour less than he hates trouble . . ."

When I first began drinking Spanish wine some thirty years ago, the custom was to take an empty bottle to the wine shop and to fill it from a cask marked with the alcoholic degree and some such terse description as *tinto* (full-bodied red), *clarete* (light red), *blanco* (white), Moscatel or so on. It is true, of course, that better wines were available, sometimes of excellent quality, like those from the Rioja, which had been bottling its fine wines since the end of the 19th century. They were not, however, much drunk except on special occasions and at the more expensive restaurants.

Various factors have contributed to a remarkable improvement in quality over the last few decades. One of the achievements of General Franco in his latter years was a marked rise in living standards and the creation of a middle class with more sophisticated tastes and the money to indulge them; at the same time the millions of tourists who began flooding across the Pyrenees began asking for the better wines, and liked what they found.

Official seals denoting Denominación de Origen

Alella

Alicante

Almansa

Ampurdán-Costa Brava

Campo de Borja

Cariñena

Condado de Huelva

Jerez-Xeres-Sherry and Manzanilla-Sanlúcar de Barrameda

Jumilla

La Mancha

Málaga

Méntrida

Hand in hand with this, and starting with the Rioja in 1926, the Ministry of Agriculture began the demarcation of the different wine-growing areas, laying down strict regulations for the production of better quality wines sold under a *Denominación de Origen* and modernizing the cooperatives.

Over the last ten years there has been an increasing realization among the younger and more enlightened *bodegueros* that Spain's future as a wine producer lies in quality rather than quantity. While the bulk of the wine from the vast central plateau is cooperative-made and acceptable enough for everyday drinking, dozens of other regions are now producing characterful and individual growths, and perhaps no other country in Europe makes wine in such a variety of styles: there are the *pétillant* young wines of the north and north-west; a whole gamut of reds, whites and rosés; excellent sparkling wines produced in larger quantity than Champagne; apéritif and dessert wines such as sherry, Montilla and Málaga: and a cupboard-full of vermouths and liqueurs.

Exports of the better table wines have soared in recent years. For example, shipments of Rioja to the U.K. increased from 20,000 cases in 1970 to some 350,000 ten years later, and are still increasing; and the story is much the same in the U.S.A. and Northern Europe, indicating the growing appreciation of outstanding value, particularly in the medium-price bracket.

The arrangement of the A-Z listing in this volume differs somewhat from that of its companions in the series. This reflects the fact that in Spain individual labels and house styles are generally of greater significance than minor geographical areas, and the smaller producers tend not to bottle their wine but to sell to larger concerns or direct to local restaurants.

I have been helped by *bodegueros* and official bodies up and down Spain too numerous to mention individually, but should particularly like to thank that brilliant oenologist and leading exponent of Spanish wines, Don Miguel Torres Riera. Mr. John Hawes of Laymont & Shaw Ltd. has kindly made available to me his notes on Galician wines; and my wife, Maite Manjón, has made a major contribution to the sections on *Wine and food*, which I hope will add to the enjoyment of visitors to Spain.

Montilla-Moriles | Navarra | Penedès | Priorato | Ribeiro

Rioja | Rueda | Tarragona | Utiel-Requena

Valdeorras | Valdepeñas | Valencia | Yecla

How to read an entry

Entries are generally of two types: those descriptive of a region, and those relating to individual producers (*bodegas*) and their wines. The top line of entries referring to table wines gives the following information in abbreviated form:

1. The name of the producer
2. Whether the wine is bottled with a *Denominación de Origen* (D.O.). See **Laws and labels**.
3. The different types of wines—red, rosé, white, sparkling, *reserva*, etc.—made by the producer.
4. Their general standing as to quality, a necessarily rough and ready guide based on the following ascending scale:
   ★ everyday wine
   ★★ above average
   ★★★ excellent quality, highly reputed
   ★★★★ grand, prestigious, expensive
   So much is more or less objective. Additionally there is a subjective rating; a box round the stars of a wine which is in my experience particularly good value within its price range, be it luxury or everyday.
   Stars have not been used in the sections on MÁLAGA, MONTILLA-MORILES, SHERRY, SPARKLING WINES or SPIRITS, AROMATIC WINES & LIQUEURS. Here the producers often make such a vast range of wines or spirits that general judgements become more or less meaningless: one of a sherry house's *finos* may deserve three stars, while its *oloroso* is of merely two-star quality, and *vice versa.* Guidance to the quality of such wines will be found in the descriptive notes.
5. Vintage information: which were the more successful of the recent vintages that *may* still be available and which of the younger are ready for drinking and will probably improve with keeping. A consistent climate and Spanish bottling practice place far less importance on vintages than with French wines, and vintages are not given for the many wines which are made for current consumption.

The second line of each of these entries begins with:

1. The town or village in which the *bodega* is located.
2. The province, in brackets.
3. Where a *bodega* makes demarcated wines, the D.O. is specified, e.g. D.O. Penedès. This is not repeated for the many wines of Rioja and the sherry region, which all fall under their respective single D.O.s.

The information under *Wine and food* at the end of each section is primarily intended for visitors, and the dishes which are briefly described are those typical of the region. 'International cooking' proliferates in the tourist resorts and large cities of Spain, as elsewhere. Where wines are coupled with individual dishes, they are examples of what I myself might choose; but I do not believe in hard and fast rules about which wine goes with which dish, and suggest that all readers follow their individual preference.

Stars against restaurants indicate a scale of excellence roughly equivalent to that applied to the wines. The names of recommended hotels appear under the towns listed in the A-Z listing, and suggestions for travelling to and within the regions are made in the introductory sections.

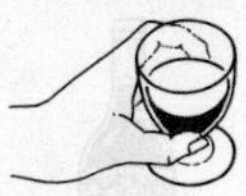

Anatomy of Spanish wine

Spain has more land under vines than any other country in Europe, but comes third, after Italy and France, in terms of production, which amounted in 1979 to 4.3 billion liters. The reasons for this low yield are various: much of the soil is barren; many of the vines are old and in need of replacement; and the vineyards are most often split up among small holders without the resources or expertise to combat maladies such as rot or mildew.

Criss-crossed by great chains of mountains, Spain is a country of wide geographical contrasts, ranging from the wet and mountainous north to the arid central plateau, with its bitter winters and hot summers, and Andalucía in the south, mild in winter and sun-baked for the rest of the year. It is a pattern giving rise to wines in great variety, and almost every region, apart from the Atlantic coast in the north, produces wines of sorts.

The best of the world's table wines are produced along a belt lying between 30–50° latitude in both hemispheres, and the best Spanish table wines come from the Rioja and Penedès, lying in the center of this zone but somewhat cooler than average because of their altitude. The Rioja is predominantly a producer of red wines; the Penedès makes both red and white (together with a great deal of sparkling wine), but is better known for its white. When faced with an unfamiliar Spanish wine list, it is usually a safe bet to order a red Rioja or white Penedès; experience takes one further.

The great central plateau of La Mancha, which produces a massive 35% of Spain's wines, is classified as semi-arid and produces wine in bulk rather than for bottling, most of it made in its 450 cooperatives for everyday drinking and blending. Ninety per cent of them are white, though the best, from Valdepeñas, made with a blend of black and white grapes, are red.

The coastal region of the Levante, bordering the Mediterranean to the east of La Mancha, produces earthy, full-bodied wines high in alcohol, both red and white, of which the most distinguished are the light and fresh rosés from Utiel-Requena.

Andalucía is more or less exclusively a producer of apéritif and dessert wines made in *solera* by the progressive blending of older and younger wines. Apart from sherry, the best known are the very similar wines from Montilla-Moriles near Córdoba and the classical dessert Málagas, so popular in Victorian times.

The future looks bright for the Spanish wine industry. As regards exports, the emphasis has for too long been on quantity rather than quality. This has largely been because the heat of the long summers in the central and southerly parts of the country produces very large amounts of sugar in the grapes, and traditional methods of fermentation have led to robust wines overstrong in alcohol. With the introduction of stainless steel vats, permitting fermentation at lower and controled temperatures, the picture is changing; and the Mediterranean countries (after all the cradle of wine-making in Europe) may yet be at an advantage over the wetter and colder areas of northern Europe. Certainly there is an awareness now among wine-makers of the importance of quality.

Laws and labels

Most of the better Spanish wines are bottled with a *Denominación de Origen* (D.O.), corresponding to the French *Appellation d'Origine Contrôlée* (A.O.C.) or Italian *Denominazione di Origine Controllata* (D.O.C.) and formulated in accordance with the rules of the Office International du Vin (O.I.V.).

The first regions to be so demarcated were the Rioja in 1926, Jerez in 1933 and Málaga in 1937. The complete list now embraces the following areas:

Alella
Alicante
Almansa
Ampurdán-Costa Brava
Campo de Borja
Cariñena
Conca de Barberá
Huelva
Jerez-Xéres-Sherry and
  Manzanilla-Sanlúcar
  de Barrameda
Jumilla
La Mancha
La Ribera del Duero
Málaga
Manchuela
Méntrida
Montilla-Moriles
Navarra
Penedès
Priorato
Ribeiro
Rioja
Rueda
Somontano
Tarragona
Terra Alta
Tierra de Barros
Utiel-Requena
Valdeorras
Valdepeñas
Valencia
Valle de Monterrey
Yecla

Each of these regions is controlled by a Consejo Regulador, a regulatory body under the presidency and vice-presidency of delegates appointed by the Ministries of Agriculture and Commerce and including representatives of the growers, the *bodegas* (wine-makers) and shippers. In 1972 the Ministry of Agriculture set up a central body, the Instituto de Denominaciones de Origen (INDO), to coordinate and to control the activities of the Consejos Reguladores in the field. Following the death of General Franco and the restoration of local autonomy to the four provinces of Catalonia, between 1978 and 1980 INDO transferred its functions in Catalonia to an agency of the revived Generalitat, the Instituto Catalán de Vino (INCAVI).

All Spanish wines must conform to the procedures and standards laid down in the *Estatuto de la Viña, del Vino y de los Alcoholes*, a lengthy government decree first promulgated in 1970 and applying to Spain as a whole. It defines the different types of wine and spirits and lays down rules for acceptable and unacceptable methods of viticulture and vinification, for chemical composition, and for the transport, distribution, sale and export of wines.

In addition to complying with the *Estatuto*, wines with *Denominación de Origen* must also be made in accordance with the further detailed provisions of a *reglamento* issued by the appropriate Consejo Regulador. Briefly, this defines the geographical area within which a demarcated wine may be made and grown, the permitted grape varieties and the density of plantation; and also sets limits of the amount of must that may be extracted from the grapes. Further regulations relate to viticulture; pruning; the vinification and maturation of the wine; and to its chemical composition, limits being set for alcoholic degree, volatile acidity, sugar content, dry extract, etc. Apart from *reglamentos* applying to a particular region, there are others, like that for the sparkling wines, applying to the country generally.

The Consejos maintain control laboratories in the different regions, and when a wine has satisfied its inspectorate there and in the field, the Consejo authorizes the printing of labels to cover the amount involved. Its guarantee often appears on the label in the form of a small pictorial emblem or stamp, some of which are shown on pp. 6–7.

Standards of excellence in the different demarcated regions vary greatly, and are highest in those, like the Rioja, Penedès and Jerez, with an established reputation for making fine wines. It is, indeed, something of a mystery why a region like Manchuela, without a single establishment for bottling the wines, was demarcated in the first place. Again, a few of the best *bodegas* in Spain, like Torres in the Penedès, do not market their wines under a *Denominación de Origen*, either because the region has not yet been demarcated or because they feel that their own label constitutes a better guarantee of quality.

Wines shipped to the Common Market countries are labeled to conform with standard EEC requirements, the information for an undemarcated wine being much briefer than that for wines with *Denominación de Origen* or, in the jargon of the Commission, 'Quality Wines PSR'. There is as yet no set form of Community labelling for fortified wines such as sherry or Málaga, but their labels must conform with the regulations of the country to which they are exported. It is worth examining a label to see how much wine you are buying, since many bottles contain 70 cl rather than the 75 cl preferred by the Commission.

Pending the entry of Spain into the EEC, light wines sold within the country are often labeled not with the vintage year, but with a description such as *3° año* or *5° año*, meaning that it was bottled during the third or fifth calendar year after the harvest and *not*, as commonly stated abroad, that the wine is three or five years old. Many *2° año* wines, bottled during the calendar year following the harvest (the 'second') are not, in fact, even a year old.

Spanish wine terms commonly appearing on labels are listed in the glossary.

Grape varieties

It would be a Herculean task to list all the grape varieties used in the production of the wines named in this book. In Galicia alone, there are 136 recognized types of vine. To add to the confusion, the same grape often goes under a different name in different regions of Spain: the Catalonian Tempranillo is the Ull de Llebre in the Rioja, and the Cencibel in Valdepeñas. For clarity and accuracy, the main grape varieties of each region are discussed in the general introductions, and the entry for each D.O. zone names the grapes used for those wines.

Glossary

1. Words used on wine labels

Abocado	Semi-sweet table wine.
Amontillado	A style of sherry made by ageing the *fino* wine.
Amoroso	A light dessert sherry.
Añejo, añejado por	Old, aged by.
(4)°ano etc.	Bottled in the (fourth) year after the harvest.
Blanco	White.
Bodega	Literally, a wine cellar, but used to describe a concern which may have grown, made, shipped or sold the wine. Without further qualification it normally means that the *bodega* has made and shipped the wine.
Brut, Brut natur	Extra-dry, used only of sparkling wine.
Cava	1. An establishment making sparkling wines. 2. A term used to describe such a wine made by the Champagne method.
Cepa	Literally, a 'vine'. Its use on labels is not precise, though the word is sometimes coupled with the name of a grape.
Clarete	Light red table wine.
Con crianza	Used on the back label, this indicates that the wine has been aged in oak in accordance with the *reglamento* of the Consejo Regulador (local regulatory body).
Cosecha	Vintage, e.g. Cosecha 1976
Cream	A sweet dessert sherry or Montilla
Criado por	Matured and/or blended by.
Denominación de Origen	The guarantee of the Consejo Regulador (regulatory body) for a demarcated area, often printed on the label in the form of a small facsimile stamp or drawing.
Dulce	Sweet.
Elaborado por	Matured and/or blended by.
Embotellado por	Bottled by.
Espumoso	Sparkling wine.
Fino	A pale, dry and delicate sherry or Montilla.
Generoso	An apéritif or dessert wine.
Gran reserva	Wine of good quality, aged in the case of *tinto* and *clarete* for at least two years in oak cask, followed by a minimum of three in a bottle. White or rosé *gran reservas* must be aged for a minimum period of four years, with at least six months in oak.

Gran-vas	Sparkling wine made by the *cuve close* method (see SPARKLING WINES).
Manzanilla	One of the driest of sherries, made at Sanlúcar de Barrameda.
Oloroso	A dark, fragrant, full-bodied sherry or Montilla.
Palo cortado	A rare and superior sherry or Montilla, with the nose of an *amontillado* and the body of an *oloroso*.
Pasada, pasado	Used to describe old and superior *fino* and *amontillado* sherries.
Raya	1. Term used in classifying musts for sherry. 2. A sherry or Montilla resembling *oloroso*, but not of the same quality.
Reserva	Wine of good quality, aged in the case of *tinto* and *clarete* for at least three years in total in oak cask and bottle (and usually for longer) with a minimum of one year in cask. White and rosé *reservas* must be aged for at least two years in total in oak cask and bottle, with a minimum of six months in oak.
Rosado	Rosé.
Seco	Dry.
Semi-seco	Semi-dry.
Solera	This denotes (or should denote) that the wine has been aged in a series of butts containing progressively older wine of different vintages (see SHERRY).
Tinto	Full-bodied red wine.
Vendimia	Vintage, e.g. Vendimia 1976.
Viña, Vinedo	Vineyard. Used rather loosely; the name 'Viña Zaco' does *not* mean that the wine originated exclusively from a vineyard of this name.
Vino	Wine (See also *Miscellaneous* below).

2. Miscellaneous

Agua	Water.
Agua de soda	Soda water.
Agua mineral	Mineral water:
con gas	sparkling
sin gas	still
Aguardiente	1. Alcohol of not more than 80° strength distiled from vegetable materials. 2. Colloquial name for *aguardiente de orujo*, akin to the French *marc*.
Anís	Aniseed-flavored liqueur resembling anisette.
Bodeguero	The person who owns or runs the *bodega*.
Café	Coffee.
Cerveza	Beer.
Chacolí	A green (young) wine from the Biscay coast.
Cold fermentation	Fermentation in stainless steel vats over long periods at low temperatures. See ANATOMY OF SPANISH WINE.
Comarca	Sub-district.
Coñac	Spanish brandy.

Crema	Liqueur:
de cacao	cocoa-based
de café	coffee-based
de menta	creme de menthe
de naranja	Curaçao
Flor	A film of yeasts which grows on the surface of some wines during maturation in *solera.* See SHERRY.
Ginebra	Gin.
Hielo	Ice.
Horchata	Milky-looking, non-alcoholic drink made from *chufas* or earth-nuts.
Leche	Milk.
Licor	Liqueur.
Limonada	Lemonade (fizzy).
Orujo	Slang name for *aguardiente.*
Parador	State tourist hotel of a good standard, often housed in building of historic interest.
Ponche	A herbalized brandy.
Queimada	A punch made from *aguardiente.*
Ron	Rum.
S.A.	Sociedad Anónima, an indication of a public company's limited liability, equivalent to Ltd., plc, or Inc.
Sangría	Cold wine-cup, made by adding sliced orange and lemon, together with ice and a dash of brandy, to red wine.
Sidra	Cider.
Sifón	Soda water.
Socio	A member of a wine cooperative.
Té	Tea.
Vermut	Vermouth.
Vino	Wine:
corriente	inexpensive everyday wine
de aguja	slightly sparkling, *pétillant*
de Jerez	sherry
de lágrima	sweet wine made from the juice which has emerged from the grapes without mechanical crushing
de mesa	table wine
de pasto	an ordinary table wine, often light
embotellado	a better wine, bottled at the *bodega*
gaseoso	cheap carbonated sparkling wine
generoso	an apéritif or dessert wine, such as sherry or Málaga.
rancio	an old white wine, maderized and sometimes fortified
verde	young wine, white or red, with a slight sparkle or *pétillance*
Zumo	Fruit juice:
de naranja natural	juice from freshly-crushed oranges

3. Ordering wines and drinks

May I see the wine list?	**La carta de vinos, por favor.**
I should like a bottle/half-bottle of . . ./a carafe/half-carafe of your house wine.	**Por favor traiga una botella/media botella de . . ./una jarra/media jarra de vino de la casa**

Where does your house wine come from?	**¿De dónde es el vino de la casa?**
Can you recommend a good local wine?	**¿Puede usted recomendar un vino bueno de la región?**
Yes, I would like a bottle.	**Sí, me gustaría una botella.**
I should like to drink a red/dry white/sweet white wine.	**Me gustaría beber un vino tinto/vino blanco seco/vino blanco dulce.**
Can you please chill the wine?	**¿Por favor puede usted enfriar el vino?**

The waiter, too, will have something to say, and will probably begin by asking if you would like an apéritif:
¿Quieren ustedes un apéritivo?
Depending upon whether you would like one or not, the answer is:

Yes, I should like a . . . and the lady a . . .	**Sí, por favor, un . . . para mí y un . . . para le senora.**
No, thank you.	**No gracias.**

After you have ordered the wine, he will ask you whether, as is usual in Spain, you want mineral water.
¿Quieren ustedes agua mineral?

Yes, I should like a bottle/half-bottle of still/sparkling	**Sí, por favor. Me gustaría una botella/media botella sin gas/con gas.**

At the end of the meal the waiter will ask you if you want coffee:
¿Quieren tomar café?

Yes, I/we would like black coffee/white coffee/coffee with a little milk.	**Sí, por favor, me/nos gustaría café solo/café con leche/café cortado.**

Except in expensive restaurants, if you want brandy or a liqueur at the table, you should ask for it:

I/we should like a brandy/liqueur. What sorts do you have?	**Me/nos gustaría tomar un coñac/licor. Qué marcas tienen?**
And to ask for the bill:	**La cuenta, por favor.**

Aragón

One would not make a special journey to Aragón on a wine tour of Spain. Nevertheless, its best-known district of Cariñena produced a sizeable 30.7 million liters of wine in 1979, much of it sold outside the immediate area for everyday drinking; and if you approach the Rioja from Barcelona and the Mediterranean coast, the fast A2 *autopista* will take you through Zaragoza and the heart of Aragón. Wines apart, Zaragoza is a major tourist destination.

In the early nineteenth century, Cariñena was one of the most sought-after Spanish wines, but today the bulk is made in cooperatives for early consumption or, because of its body and strength, for blending. In Aragón as a whole, the principal grape varieties are the black Garnacha tinta, Bobal, Cariñena and Juan Ibañez, and the white Garnacha blanca.

As in much of central Spain, the land is arid, lying mostly at a height of between 450–600m. (1,500–1,950ft.), and the climate is of the Mediterranean type. Many of the vineyards are situated around

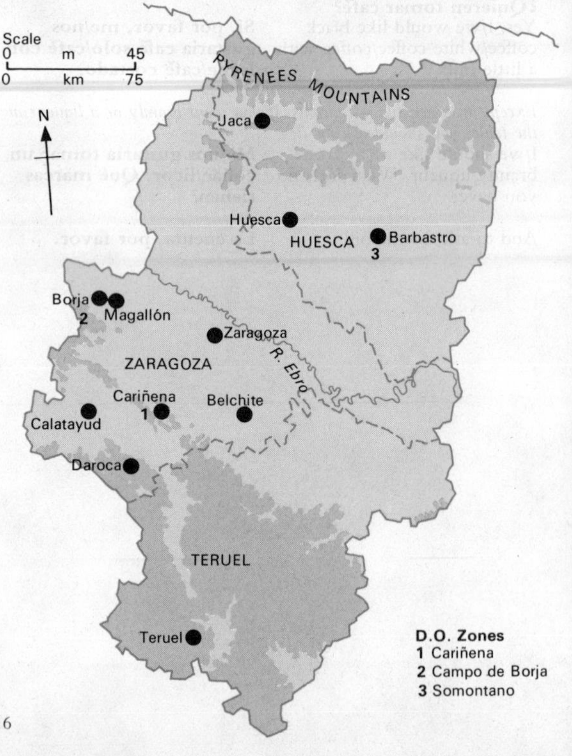

the valley of the Ebro, which crosses the region from NW to SE.
Aragón possesses 3 D.O. zones: Cariñena, and further N the more recently demarcated Campo de Borja and Somontano.

Belchite r. w. dr. ★
Small undemarcated area E of CARIÑENA making sturdy red and white wines.

Borja, Campo de D.O. r. ★
The region takes its name from the small town of Borja in the Ebro valley W of Zaragoza, the ancestral home of the Borgia family, whose castle still survives. Demarcated in 1977, it embraces 9,394ha (23,203 acres) of vineyards. The great bulk of the wine, made from the Garnacha tinta grape with smaller amounts of Bobal, is a very fully bodied red, more astringent and acidic than the wine from CARIÑENA and containing an average 15–16% alcohol, but sometimes a hefty 18%. For this reason it is often used for blending with less robust growths from other regions, much of it being sold in bulk to concerns in the Rioja and Catalonia.

Calatayud (r.) cl. ★
Undemarcated area in the W of Aragón making honest enough wine for everyday drinking, but without the depth or quality of CARIÑENA. The best is the *clarete*.

Cariñena D.O. r. (w. dr. or sw. g.) [★→★★]
A little to the S of Zaragoza, Cariñena, with 22,000ha (54,800 acres) under vines, is by far the most important wine-growing area in Aragón. The vines grow in calcareous clays, and the most predominant varieties are the black Garnacha tinta (57%) and white Viura (29.2%); oddly enough, the black Cariñena, which originated here, is much more widely grown in Catalonia and France. The typical wine is the red, of a purplish ruby color with a bouquet of violets, 13–17% in strength, full-bodied and deep in flavor, slightly astringent when young, but becoming smoother and silkier when aged for 2 years in cask. Cariñena also produces a white wine known as "Pajarilla" from the Viura and Garnacha blanca, and a fortified dessert wine made like Málaga.

Daroca r. ★
Undemarcated area in the far S of Aragón on the borders of Teruel, producing sturdy red wines with 13–16% alcohol.

La Magallonera, Bodegas D.O. r. ★
Magallón (Zaragoza). D.O. Campo de Borja. A small family concern, founded some 30 years ago by Andrés Ruberte, one of a well-known family of wine-makers. Its wines are among the best of the red heavyweights from the region, especially its "Pagos de Oruña" *tinto*.

San José de Aguarón, Cooperativa Vitícola D.O. r. [★]
Aguarón-Cariñena (Zaragoza). D.O. Cariñena. Founded in 1955 and numbering 500 members, the cooperative has large numbers of oak casks for ageing its well-made and typical wines, such as the red "Puente de Piedra".

San Valero, Cooperativa de D.O. r. (p. w. dr.) [★]
Cariñena (Zaragoza). D.O. Cariñena. Large cooperative on the Zarogoza–Teruel road in the village of CARIÑENA; makers of the reliable "Don Mendo" and "Monte Ducay".

Somontano D.O. r. ★→★★
This very recently demarcated region in the province of Huesca in the foothills of the Pyrenees produces wines completely different from the others of Aragón. Made from a profusion of different grape varieties, including the Alcañón, Macabeo (Viura), Garnacha tinta, Mazuelo and Parraleta, they are ruby-colored, faintly perfumed, light on the palate and slightly acid, with some 11–13% alcohol. At the turn of the century they were popular in France, and the best of the area's wineries, Bodegas Lalanne in Barbastro, is of French origin.

Soria, Bodegas Joaquin D.O. r. (p. w. dr.) cl. ★→★★
Cariñena (Zaragoza). D.O. Cariñena. Small family firm dating from 1840, with its own vineyards and cellars for ageing its thoroughly typical wines, especially the "Espigal" *clarete*, made with a blend of Garnacha tinta and Macabeo (Viura) grapes.

Valdejalón r. ★
Undemarcated area just W of Zaragoza. The predominant grape variety, the Garnacha tinta, produces wines high in alcohol and extract, more resembling those of BORJA than of CARIÑENA.

Vicente, Suso y Perez S.A. D.O. r. (p. w. dr.) res. ★→★★
Cariñena (Zaragoza). D.O. Cariñena. This large *bodega* is the best-known of the private concerns in CARIÑENA and the biggest exporter. It buys in the grapes from independent farmers and matures its wines in oak. "Don Ramón" *tinto* and *rosado*, "Comendador" *reservas*, and "Duque de Sevilla", "Mosen Cleto", and "Viña Tito" reds.

Zaragoza
Capital of the medieval Kingdom of Aragón, Zaragoza is rich in historic remains from Roman times onwards, including the Moorish Aljafería with its figured plasterwork and beautiful *artesonado* ceilings; but the city is dominated by the many-domed Basilica del Pilar, looming above the long bridge across the Ebro, which contains the oldest Marian sanctuary in Europe. The Festival of El Pilar in October is the most important date in Spain's religious calendar.

The best hotels are the 5-star Corona de Aragón and 4-star Goya.

WINE & Food

Aragón is sometimes called the *Zona de los Chilindrones*, in recognition of the famous sauce made with onions, tomatoes and peppers, and served with chicken and lamb. The young lamb from the mountains is excellent, and S of Zaragoza in the direction of Teruel the miles of gardens and orchards produce some of the best fruit in Spain: peaches, plums, apricots, apples, cherries and strawberries. The vegetables, too, including the white Aragonese cabbage and cardoon, are first rate.

The sturdy red wines go well with simple dishes and country fare, but, as in other of the lesser regions, with a more sophisticated meal, you may well wish to vary them with a good red Rioja or white Catalan wine.

Bacalao al ajoarriero
Dried salted cod with garlic, paprika and chopped parsley.

Migas de pastor
These crisp-fried breadcrumbs are often served as a starter. Some devotees eat them with hot chocolate or with grapes, and they are also served as a side dish.

Pollo al chilindrón
Chicken with chilindrón *sauce, made from tomatoes and peppers.*

Sopas de ajo
Garlic soups with lemon and seasoning are a great speciality of Aragón.

Teresicas
Small pastries made with butter, flour and yeast and fried in olive oil.

Ternasco asado
Roast baby lamb with white wine, lemon and seasoning.

Restaurants

Huesca (at Esquedas on the Tarragona road) ★ *Venta del Sotón.*

Zaragoza ★★ *La Casa del Ventero* (sophisticated regional and Lyonnais dishes); ★ *Los Borrachos* (elegant and comfortable, good fish and game); ★ *Mesón del Carmen* (typically Aragonese).

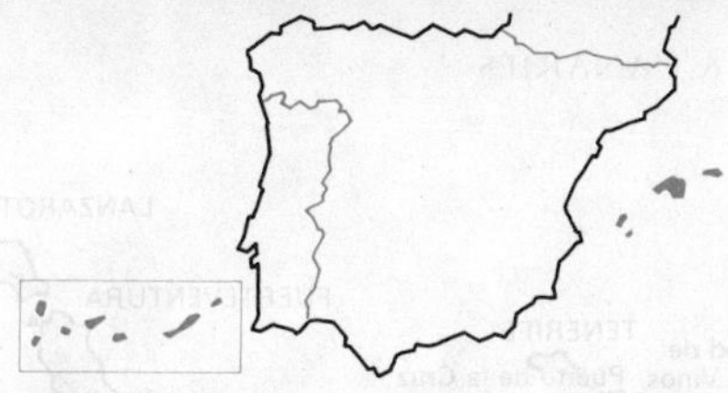

Balearics & Canaries

Both these groups of islands, the green and fertile Balearics with their mild Mediterranean climate and sandy beaches, and the volcanic Canaries in the wastes of the Atlantic off the coast of North Africa, are favorite tourist resorts for sun-starved northern Europeans. On balance they consume more wine than they make, so that familiar names from the mainland figure more on their wine-lists than the local growths.

Before the devastations of phylloxera there were about 27,000ha (80,000 acres) under vines in Majorca, the main producer in the Balearics, but in the principal vineyard areas of Binisalem and Felanitx, the area has now shrunk to 4,260ha (10,650 acres). Tourism aggravated this decline – it proved more profitable to sell the land for holiday villas, and the young people left the villages to work in the hotels of Palma and Pollensa.

The soils of the Balearics are mainly ferruginous clays, and the vines are grown in small plots interspersed with olives and almonds. Most of the grapes are native to Majorca, the typical varieties being the Manto Negro, Callet, Fogoneu and Fogoneu Francés. Apart from the superior growths of José L. Ferrer, most of the wines are reds or rosés made by the cooperatives or small proprietors for current consumption.

In the Canaries, famous for its sack in the 16th century, wine production is now confined to the islands of Tenerife, La Palma and Lanzarote. The soils are volcanic, and the principal grape varieties are the white Listán blanco and Malvasía (Malmsey), and the red Listán. The wines are acceptable enough for vacation drinking, but because demand exceeds supply, there is an unfortunate tendency to blend them with wine from the mainland; one of the few wines with real character is a white Malvasía from Bodegas Mozaga, halfway to a dessert wine.

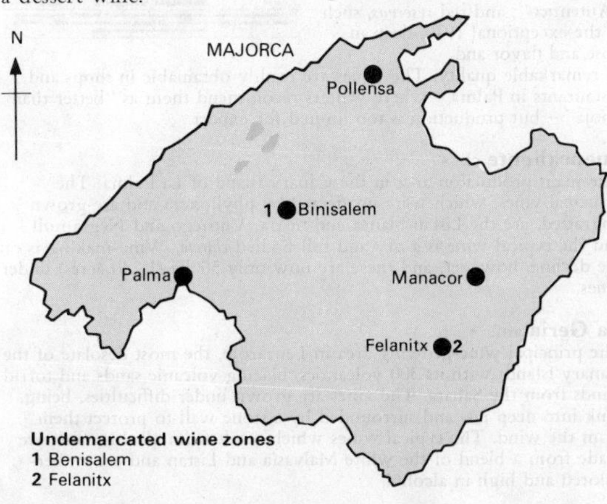

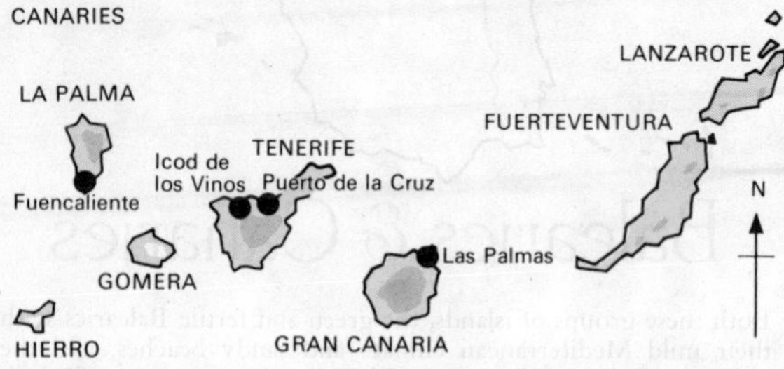

Binisalem r. ★→★★
With 1,708ha (4,260 acres) under vines, Binisalem is the main wine-growing area in central Majorca although the area under vines has shrunk to a fraction of its former size. Of the three grape varieties, Manto Negro is better than Callet and Fogoneu, and produces full-bodied reds of 14–16% strength with pronounced bouquet and a high amount of extract.

Felanitx p. ★
In the SE of the island, Felanitx, with 2,552ha (6,370 acres) under vines, is the largest of the Majorcan wine areas, although not producing a wine to match those of José L. FERRER in BINISALEM. The typical grape is the Fogoneu, usually vinified so as to give rosés of 9–11%. Much of the wine is made in the cooperative at Felanitx serving some 400 small proprietors, and there are also four distilleries in the town producing grape spirit and alcohol.

Ferrer, José L., Bodegas r. (w. dr.) res. ★★→★★★
Binisalem (Majorca). José L. Ferrer, a wealthy enthusiast and informed oenologist, and also owner of one of the best hotels in Palma, owns 150ha (370 acres) of vineyards planted with the Manto Negro and makes the only wines of distinction from the Balearics, and certainly the name to look for on local restaurant wine lists. They include a "Blanc de Blancs"; the young, fresh and fruity red "Autentico"; and red *reservas*, such as the exceptional 1970, deep in nose and flavor and of remarkable quality. The wines are readily obtainable in shops and restaurants in Palma – where waiters recommend them as "better than Rioja" – but production is too limited for export.

Fuencaliente cl. ★
The main production area in the Canary island of La Palma. The principal vines, which were unaffected by phylloxera and are grown ungrafted, are the Listán blanca and negra, Vijiriego and Negramoll, and the typical wine is a dry and full-bodied *clarete*. Wine-making is on the decline, however, and there are now only 500ha (1,240 acres) under vines.

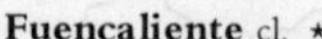

La Geria am. ★
The principal wine-growing area in Lanzarote, the most desolate of the Canary Islands with its 300 volcanoes, blazing volcanic sands and torrid winds from the Sahara. The vines are grown under difficulties, being sunk into deep pits and surrounded by a stone wall to protect them from the wind. The typical wines which result from all this effort are made from a blend of the white Malvasía and Listán and are amber-colored and high in alcohol.

Icod w. dr. ★
Icod, in the island of Tenerife, has 520ha (1,390 acres) of vineyards planted with the white Listán blanca and Malvasía. It makes white wines of 11–13% with good aroma but little fruit.

Las Palmas
The largest town in the Canaries, with a population of 350,000, Las Palmas is dramatically situated on Grand Canary beneath an extinct volcano and possesses good beaches, a colorful promenade and a bustling port with regular ferry services to the other islands. Of its many hotels, serving a large tourist industry, the best are the 4-star Cristina, Santa Catalina and Reina Isabel.

Manacor p. ★
Sizeable wine-growing area near FELANITX in Majorca, making very similar rosé wines from the Fogoneu grape.

Mozaga, Bodegas w. sw. ★→★★
Maker of the best wines from the Island of Lanzarote, the "Malvasía seco". The grapes are picked when well ripe, lightly crushed and aged in oak for 2–3 months after vinification. The wine is further aged in bottle in cellars excavated beneath the lava.

Orotava, Valle de la w. dr. ★
Small wine-growing area situated between TACORONTE and ICOD in the island of Tenerife. It produces dry white wines very similar to those of Icod.

Palma de Mallorca
Palma is one of the most beautiful cities of the Mediterranean, with its wide bay and surrounding beaches and the 13th-century cathedral dominating the port. The narrow streets in the center are full of elegant shops, good restaurants and old houses with secret, shaded patios. Nowhere in Majorca is very far from Palma, so it is a good base for visiting the wine areas. There are dozens of hotels, ranging from the luxurious 5-star Son Vida, Fénix Sol and Nixe Palace to more modest establishments.

Tacoronte r. ★
Tacoronte, with 1,200ha (2,980 acres) under vines and an annual production of 1.5 million liters, is the most intensively cultivated of the wine areas in Tenerife. By far the most important grape is the black Listán negra, producing spicy red wines with body and a fairly high degree of alcohol.

WINE & Food

The Balearics, famous for the invention of mayonnaise (from Port Mahón), have a varied regional repertoire. As might be expected, they excel in seafood and rich fish soups. The appetizing *coca mallorquina*, traditionally made in outdoor ovens fired by wood, much resembles the Italian *pizza*; *tumbet* is a variation on *ratatouille*; most typical of the excellent charcuterie are the delicate white *butifarra* and soft red *sobrasada*; there is a good Mahón cheese; and do not miss the fluffy *ensaimadas*, halfway between bun and pastry, for breakfast. Although the Canaries have a few regional specialities, these do not amount to a cuisine; like the Canary wines, you may find it difficult to find them in holiday hotels, where the menus and wine lists are mainland Spanish, if not the international style provided for tourists. Apart from pretty basic cooperative-made wine, the one local label to look for in the Balearics is that of José L. Ferrer.

Balearics

Acelgas con pasas y piñones
Spanish variety of spinach, paler in color and sweeter than the English, boiled and served with sofrito, *a sauce made with pine kernels, raisins, toasted bread and garlic.*

Berenjenas rellenas estilo balear
Eggplants stuffed with ground beef, chopped ham, onions, eggs, breadcrumbs and garlic.

Caracoles con sobrasada
Snails cooked with ham, onions, tomatoes, garlic, olive oil, milk, brandy and white wine. They are served with sobrasada, *the soft and spicy Majorcan pepper sausage, and green vegetables.*

Sopa de pescador Formentor
Rich fish soup made with garlic, onions, tomatoes, olive oil and parsley.

Tumbet
A Majorcan egg and vegetable pie made with potatoes, red peppers, onions, zucchini and tomato sauce.

Canaries

Buñuelos de dátiles
Sweet fritters made with flour, orange juice, Cointreau, sugar, eggs and dates.

Gofio
Popular form of bread eaten all over the Canaries in country districts and made in the shape of a big ball from a mixture of flour with water or milk.

Mojo
Sauce prepared with olive oil, vinegar, hot paprika, cumin seeds and chillis.

Papas arrugadas
New potatoes, boiled in their skins in sea water or much-salted water, then baked in a hot oven and served with mojo *sauce.*

Restaurants

Felanitx, Majorca ⋆ *Violet* (isolated, but worth the visit).

Inca, near Binisalem, Majorca ⋆ *Celler C'an Amer* (one of the best for typical Majorcan dishes).

Las Palmas, Grand Canary *Acuario* (best in the city, fresh shellfish from a tank).

Palma de Mallorca ⋆ *Ancora* (local ingredients imaginatively prepared).

Teguise, Lanzarote *Las Salinas* (international food, local dishes in the buffet).

Tacoronte, Tenerife *Las Cuevas de Tacoronte* (good local food and wines).

Catalonia

The resourceful and industrious Catalans claim that they make wines in a greater variety of styles than any other region of Spain, instancing the fine table wines from the Penedès; its sparkling wines (separately described under SPARKLING WINES) which account for 90% of Spanish production; the maderized *rancio*; and the old *solera*-made dessert wines of Tarragona, so much resembling Málaga or sweet *oloroso* sherry. All these, plus some of the best brandy in the country and a gamut of vermouths and liqueurs, both indigenous varieties and foreign brands made under licence, give substance to that claim.

Comprising the provinces of Gerona (Girona), Barcelona, Lérida (Lleida) and Tarragona, with an area about the size of The Netherlands or Belgium, Catalonia's landscape is rugged and broken – it has been described as a flight of stairs rising from the

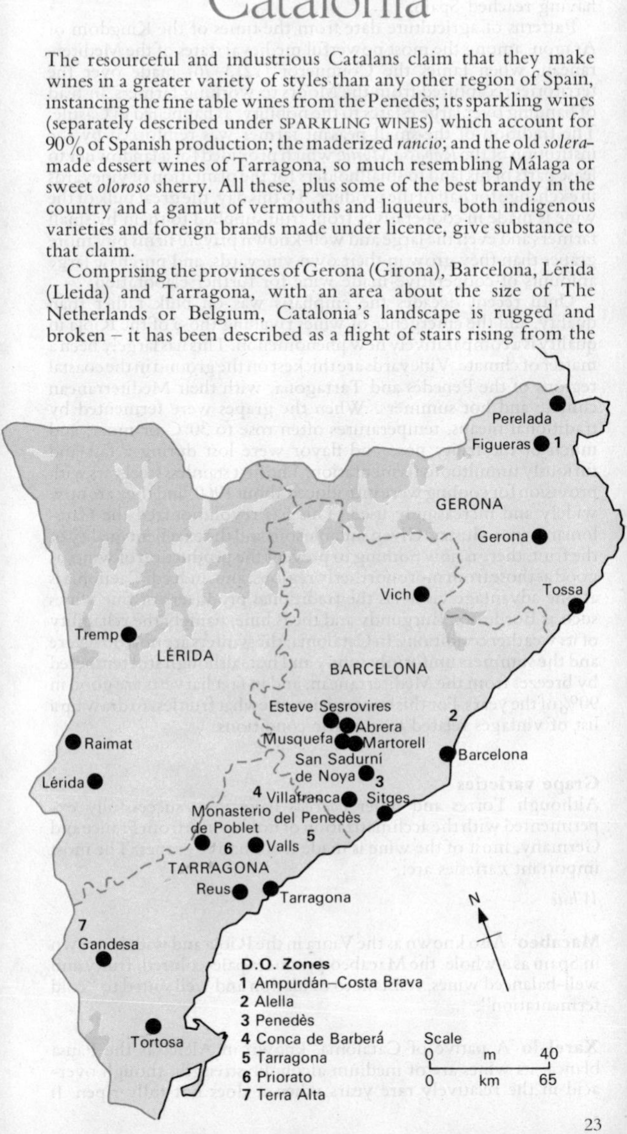

Perelada
Figueras 1
GERONA
Gerona
Vich
Tossa
Tremp
LÉRIDA
BARCELONA
Esteve Sesrovires
2
Abrera
Musquefa
Martorell
Raimat
Barcelona
San Sadurní de Noya
3
Lérida
4 Villafranca del Penedès
Sitges
Monasterio de Poblet
5
6
Valls
TARRAGONA
Reus
Tarragona
N
7
Gandesa
Tortosa

D.O. Zones
1 Ampurdán–Costa Brava
2 Alella
3 Penedès
4 Conca de Barberá
5 Tarragona
6 Priorato
7 Terra Alta

Scale
0 m 40
0 km 65

coastal plain of the Mediterranean towards the peaks of the Pyrenees and its associated spurs to the S. In the more mountainous areas the slopes must be terraced to allow a foothold for the vines, a system still employed in upland areas such as Priorato, and you need not leave the *autopista* from Barcelona through the Penedès to see disused terraces, constructed during the late 19th century, when every available patch of ground was pressed into service to supply wine to a France desolated by phylloxera, the epidemic not at that time having reached Spain.

Patterns of agriculture date from the times of the Kingdom of Aragón, among the most powerful medieval states of the Mediterranean, when James the Conqueror (1213–76) made over the territories recaptured from the Moors to working farmers, instead of handing over large estates to the nobility, as happened in Castile. The tradition of the small peasant farmer was reinforced by the institution of the *Rabassa Morta*, which provided for a landowner to lease parts of his land to smallholders for the plantation of vineyards in exchange for half of the produce. To this day, the great bulk of the wine is made in cooperatives from fruit supplied to them by small farmers and even the large and well-known private firms buy more grapes than they grow in their own vineyards, and purchase large amounts of cooperative-made wine for further elaboration.

Until recent decades the emphasis was on bulk rather than quality, and the emergence of wines rivalling those of the Rioja in quality is a comparatively new phenomenon. This has largely been a matter of climate. Vineyards are thickest on the ground in the coastal regions of the Penedès and Tarragona, with their Mediterranean climate and hot summers. When the grapes were fermented by traditional means, temperatures often rose to 30°C or more, and much of the fruity nose and flavor were lost during a fast and furiously tumultuous fermentation. The first stainless steel vats with provision for cooling were introduced about 1960, and they are now widely and increasingly used. This has revolutionized the Catalonian wine industry. Given suitable soils and the excellent quality of the fruit, there is now nothing to prevent the production of wines as good as those from more northerly regions; and, indeed, Catalonia is at one advantage vis-à-vis the traditional producers of fine wines such as Bordeaux, Burgundy and the Rhine, namely the reliability of its weather conditions. In Catalonia, the winters are not too severe and the summers uniformly sunny and hot, although still tempered by breezes from the Mediterranean, and in fact harvests are good in 90% of the years. For this reason, it is somewhat fruitless to draw up a list of vintages related to climatic conditions.

Grape varieties

Although Torres and other *bodegas* have very successfully experimented with the acclimatization of noble vines from France and Germany, most of the wine is made from native grapes. The most important varieties are:

White

Macabeo Also known as the Viura in the Rioja and widely grown in Spain as a whole, the Macabeo produces pale-colored, fruity and well-balanced wines, resistant to oxidation and well suited to "cold fermentation".

Xarel-lo A native of Catalonia, known in Alella as the Pansa blanca, its wines are of medium alcoholic strength, though over-acid in the relatively rare years when it does not fully ripen. It is one of the grapes much used for making sparkling wines in the Penedès.

Parellada (or Montonec) Grown exclusively in the higher areas of the Alto Penedès and Conca de Barberá, its musts are low in alcohol (9–11%) and high in acidity. Again much used for making sparkling wines, it is the Parellada which gives the exceptionally fresh and fruity bouquet to still wines like the Torres "Viña Sol".

Garnacha blanca Also grown in the Rioja, it is extensively cultivated in Terra Alta and the Camp de Tarragona, yielding wines high in alcohol with little acid.

Malvasía This is the well-known Malmsey, of Greek origin, but grown for centuries in Spain. Its musts are fruity and of medium strength and, as also in Madeira, where Malmsey is the name given to the sweetest wine, when fortified and aged give rise to dessert wines like those of Sitges.

Pansé Grown in the Camp de Tarragona, Conca de Barberá and Ribera d'Ebre, it matures late and prolifically, but the wines are coarse and high in alcohol.

Pedro Ximénez Much grown in Andalucía, where it is used for sweet wines, and in Montilla, where it makes dry, the Pedro Ximénez is grown in small amounts in Priorato and Terra Alta, where its musts are mixed with those from other varieties.

Black

Cariñena Originally a native of Aragón, the Cariñena produces wines of 11–12% strength, robust, rich in color and extract, but without a very distinctive nose.

Garnacha peluda A mutant of the Garnacha tinta, cropping more regularly and with similar characteristics.

Garnacha tinta Another native Spanish grape, very widely grown in the Rioja and other parts of Spain. Its wines are high in alcohol (11–14%), full-bodied, fruity and deep in color, but oxidize rapidly, soon turning a brick-red when aged in wood.

Monastrell A native grape, also widely grown in the central regions of Spain. The yield is small, but its wines are deep in color, of considerable elegance, and mature well.

Ull de Llebre (Ojo de Liebre) This is the well-known Tempranillo of the Rioja or Cencibel of Valdepeñas which produces wines of 11–13% with good acïd balance, distinctive fruity nose and good ageing properties.

Sumoll Once widely cultivated in the Penedès, the Sumoll, which produces aromatic but very tart wines, is now being phased out.

Catalonia now possesses seven Denominaciones de Origen, of which control has recently passed from INDO (Instituto de Denominaciones de Origen) to INCAVI (Instituto Catalán de Vino), an agency of the Generalitat, the autonomous governing body of Catalonia revived since the death of General Franco. The areas, with their annual production figures are: Penedès (130 million liters); Alella (1.5 million liters); Tarragona (70 million liters);

Priorato (1.5 million liters); Ampurdán-Costa Brava (10 million liters); Conca de Barberá (2.5 million liters); and Terra Alta (2.4 million liters).

Vintages, as has been explained, are remarkably consistent, and the only really poor one in recent years was 1972. The following chart for the Penedès gives some idea of the variation:

Year	Red wines	White wines
1969	fair	very good
1970	very good	fair
1971	good	fair
1972	poor	poor
1973	very good	good
1974	good	fair to good
1975	good	very good
1976	very good	good to very good
1977	good to very good	very good
1978	very good	good
1979	fair to good	good
1980		good

Provided you have a car, it is not difficult to plan a visit to the Catalan wine-growing areas, since four of them (Ampurdán-Costa Brava, Alella, Penedès and Tarragona) lie along the axis of the A17 *autopista* from the French border to Barcelona and its southward extension (the A7) to Tarragona and Valencia. Conca de Barberá, Priorato and Terra Alta, in the hills of the hinterland, are less easy of access and require fairly time-consuming side trips, but there are notable consolations in the rugged and well-wooded countryside, the hill-top castles and in the great monasteries of Montserrat and Poblet, so closely associated with the development of viticulture in the region. Catalonia also boasts the pleasant coastal resorts and the splendid cliff scenery of the Costa Brava; and it would be a single-minded devotee of wines who did not pause in Barcelona to visit Gaudí's astonishing cathedral of La Sagrada Familia or its magnificent museums and galleries, or in Tarragona to see the remarkable Roman remains.

Large *bodegas*, like Torres, welcome visitors without appointment, arranging guided tours and instructive tastings of their wines; and even in the smallest cooperative you will be able to taste and buy the wine, and will receive a friendly welcome – if you can muster enough Spanish to communicate. If in doubt about your reception, ask the porter at the hotel to telephone beforehand.

Catalan food is interesting and varied, though sometimes more than substantial in country hotels and restaurants. The names of hotels in or near the wine-growing areas are given in the A–Z listing.

The Catalans take their regained autonomy seriously. Under Franco it was forbidden to speak in Catalan – now it is a point of pride to do so. Many signs and place names are now in Catalan, which is more like a separate language than merely a dialect, though the Castilian equivalent is often added. This also applies to menus, although these sometimes appear exclusively in Catalan in smaller restaurants. The waiter or proprietor will, however, always explain in Castilian.

Alella D.O. (r. p. am.) w. dr. or sw. ★★
Traditions of wine-making in this small region date from Roman times, but it is now threatened by urban expansion from Barcelona to its S, and of the 1,400ha (3,490 acres) under vines in 1967 only 400ha (990 acres) survive, producing mostly white wine. The grape varieties approved by the Consejo Regulador are: for the white wines, Xarel-lo

(or Pansa blanca), Pansa rosada and Garnacha blanca; and for the reds, Tempranillo (Ull de Llebre), Garnacha tinta and Garnacha peluda. Many of the vineyards, all of them small and none exceeding 1.5ha (3.7 acres) are owned by professional people dedicated to preserving the wine industry. The vines are planted on granitic slopes sheltered from the prevailing E wind, one of which, with a northerly aspect, produces wine of high acidity; while the wine from the other more southerly slope is rather sweeter.

Alella Vinícola, Bodega Cooperativa D.O. (r. p. am). w. dr. or sw. ★★
Alella (Barcelona). D.O. Alella. This well-equipped cooperative, founded in 1906 and numbering 153 members, makes the bulk of the wine from Alella, all of it, in accordance with the regulations of the Consejo Regulador, aged for at least two years with a minimum of one in oak. It is sold as "Alella Legítima" in hock-type bottles under the brand name of "Marfil" ("Ivory"), and the wines range in alcohol content from 11.5% to 13.5%. The white "Marfil blanco" is characteristically fresh and fruity, but the drier "Marfil seco", with more astringency, though less round and fragrant, is a better accompaniment to food. The red "Marfil tinto" is soft and fruity.

Altar wine
Altar wine, made without chemical additives especially for the celebration of Holy Communion, is a speciality of Tarragona and particularly of DE MULLER S.A., suppliers to Popes Pius X, Benedict XV, Pius XI, Pius XII and John XXIII. It is often made with the Macabeo from the CAMP DE TARRAGONA, alcohol being added to the musts so as to produce a sweet white *generoso* of some 15%. Recently De Muller, which runs to a special *bodega* with stained glass windows, has been making drier wines, more to the taste of a younger generation of priests. It is exported all over the world from Tarragona in resin-coated steel drums.

Ampurdán S.A., Cavas del D.O. r. p. w. res. sp. ★→★★
Perelada (Gerona). D.O. Ampurdán-Costa Brava. Situated in the village of Perelada near Figueras, on the verges of the Pyrenees, this is the sister ship of the well-known sparkling wine concern of the Castillo de Perelada (see SPARKLING WINES). Its worthwhile still wines include the 3-year-old red "Tinto Cazador", "Rosado Perelada", and a good red "Reserva Don Miguel", aged for 1½ years in cask and 5–6 in bottle. The dry and *pétillant* white "Pescador" is made in *cuves closes* pressurized to only a quarter of the normal extent; and the *bodega* also produces a *cuve close* sparkler, the subject in 1960 of the famous "Spanish Champagne" case, brought by the French Champagne companies in England and known in France at the time as "the Second Battle of the Marne".

Ampurdán-Costa Brava D.O. r. p. w. dr. ★→★★
One of the more recently demarcated regions, abutting the Pyrenees in the province of Gerona and inland from the holiday coast. A problem for the growers is the prevailing N wind, the *tramontana*, which blows for some 100 days in the year, at velocities of up to hurricane force. For this reason the vines are staked. The area under vines is some 5,000ha (12,450 acres), and the main vine varieties are the black Garnacha tinta and Cariñena, and the white Xarel-lo. Some 70% of the wine, made mostly in cooperatives, is rosé, but the region is now producing a fresh young *vi novell* in the manner of Beaujolais nouveau. Some 200,000 liters of this were made in 1981.

l'Anoia, Comarca de r. (p.)
Undemarcated area bordering the PENEDÈS to the W.

Aquila Rossa S.A. D.O. r. p. w. dr. or sw. g. ★→★★
Vilafranca del Penedès (Barcelona). D.O. Penedès. Sizeable firm founded in 1888, making reliable red, white and rosé "Montgros" and also a range of vermouths.

d'Artes (Bages), Comarca (w. dr.) sp.
Undemarcated area to the NW of Barcelona.

Bach, Masia D.O. r. p. w. dr. or sw. res. ★★→★★★
Sant Esteve Sesrovires (Barcelona). D.O. Penedès. Shortly after the First World War a couple of elderly bachelor brothers from Barcelona, who had made a fortune by supplying uniforms to the Allied armies, built themselves a flamboyant Florentine-style mansion in the Penedès and started a small winery. It grew, like Topsy, and when it was recently taken over by the great sparkling wine firm of Codorníu (see SPARKLING WINES), embraced vast cellars and 8,500 oak casks with a total capacity of 3.1 million liters. The *bodega* maintains its high reputation, and Angel Escude, who has been its director and oenologist for many years, makes good red and dry white wines and a velvety red *reserva*; but the wine for which it is best known is the luscious and oaky "Extrísimo Bach", one of the best white dessert wines from Spain.

Baix Ebre-Montsià, Comarca de (r.) w. dr.
Undemarcated area in the extreme S of the province of Tarragona, bordering the Ebro delta.

Baixa Segarra (Les Garrigues), Comarca de la r. w. dr.
Undemarcated area to the N of the demarcated region of CONCA DE BARBERÁ.

Barcelona
Barcelona, the capital of Catalonia and second city of Spain, takes its name from the Cathaginian general Hamilcar Barca, but was founded long before his time, probably by the Phoenicians. Apart from being an excellent and centrally located base for visits to the wine areas of Catalonia, it is a city of outstanding interest. Do not miss the old city, with its Roman remains, its Gothic cathedral, the Palace of the Generalitat (the governing body of Catalonia), and the flower-decked Ramblas; or again, the many buildings by that master of Art Nouveau, Antonio Gaudí, foremost among them the extraordinary unfinished cathedral of La Sagrada Familia. There are many outstanding museums and galleries, including those devoted to Primitive Art, Picasso and Miró.

Once every 2 years, in mid-March, Barcelona is of special interest to gastronomes, when it mounts the Salón Internacional de la Alimentaria, one of the largest international wine and food fairs, with exhibits from every Spanish wine firm of consequence. It is a city long famous for its high culinary standards, and in recent years its restaurateurs have been leading exponents of the *nouvelle cuisine*. Of its many comfortable hotels, reasonably priced establishments with high standards are the Colón, near the cathedral, the Regente and the old-fashioned and thoroughly traditional Oriente in the Ramblas.

Bombonas
These large, loosely stoppered pear-shaped glass carboys are used for making the traditional, sherry-like Catalan RANCIO wine in an open-air CAMPO DE AÑEJAMIENTO.

Bosch-Guell S.A., Bodegas D.O. r. p. w. dr. ★★
Vilafranca del Penedès (Barcelona). D.O. Penedès. Family firm founded in 1886 and making good still wines: "Blanco selecto Rómulo", "Clarete fino Rómulo" and "Rosado seco Rómulo".

Camp de Tarragona D.O. r. w. dr. or sw. ★
Large sub-denomination of the D.O. TARRAGONA occupying much of the center of the province and embracing the towns of REUS, Valls, and TARRAGONA itself. Its vineyards are the most extensive of the Tarragona region, but in recent years farmers have found that hazelnuts are a more profitable crop, and the plantations, amounting to some 70% of arable land in some areas, have been making severe inroads. Most of the wines are sturdy whites made from the Macabeo (Viura) and Xarel-lo, known locally as the Cartuxà, but the Cooperativa de Valls makes small quantities of a smooth, ruby-colored wine from the Ull de Llebre (Tempranillo) and Trepat – do not look for it, however, since the

whole production is pre-empted by the Mossos d'Esquadra, the security force of the Catalan Generalitat.

Campo de añejamiento
Name given to the open-air plots where the maderized Catalan RANCIO is made in BOMBONAS by a method corresponding to that of a rough and ready *solera* (see SHERRY). *Campos de añejamiento* are also to be found in other parts of Spain, as in La Seca near Valladolid (see OLD CASTILE-LEÓN).

Caralt, Conde de D.O. r. p. w. dr. or sw. res. sp. ★★→★★★
San Sadurní de Noya (Barcelona). D.O. Penedès. Long known for its sparkling wines made by the Champagne method, this old family firm is now part of the RUMASA group, sharing premises with SEGURA VIUDAS (see SPARKLING WINES) and RENÉ BARBIER. Apart from sparkling wine, it now produces a range of sound still wines: "Conde de Caralt" *tinto, rosado, blanco seco, blanco suave,* etc. The red *reservas,* like the light and soft 1971, with its faint hint of cedarwood at the end, are wines of considerable sophistication.

See also SPARKLING WINES.

Castell del Remei r. p. w. dr. res. ★★→★★★
Penelles (Lérida). Old-established firm with its own vineyards in the undemarcated *comarca* (sub-district) of Penelles-La Noguera in the extreme W of Catalonia near Lérida. It has for long grown small amounts of Cabernet Sauvignon and Semillon, and its wines, which have won many medals in international exhibitions abroad, are matured for long periods in oak casks. They include a "Reserva blanco", "Reserva tinto", a younger "Castell de Remei rosado" and the "Extra Cep Semillon 1920" and "Extra Cep Cabernet 1921".

Compañía Vinícola del Penedès (C.V.P.) D.O. r. p. w. dr. res. ★→[★★]
Vilafranca del Penedès (Barcelona). D.O. Penedès. Associated with Mascaró, makers of excellent sparkling wines, brandy and liqueurs, C.V.P. makes a range of red, rosé and white wines: "Sello Real tinto"; "Caballo Loco tinto"; "Viña Franca blanco"; "Viña Fierro tinto"; and "Castillo de Liz rosado". The older red wines are somewhat disappointing and have not aged graciously. Best is the fruity young white "Viña Franca", not bought from cooperatives like some of the reds, but vinified in the *cavas* of Mascaró, and with the typically fresh and fragrant nose of the Parellada, the outstanding local white grape.

Conca de Barberá D.O. (r. p.) w. dr.
This hilly region, bordering the Penedès to the W, is one of those fairly recently demarcated by INCAVI (Instituto Catalán de Vino), the regulatory body set up by the Generalitat on its restoration. Its 9,900ha (26,600 acres) of vineyards produce an annual average of 250,000 liters of wine, most of it white and for everyday drinking, made from Parellada and Macabeo (Viura) grapes. Its Parellada grapes are also much in demand for making sparkling wines in the *cavas* of SAN SADURNÍ DE NOYA. A little red and rosé is also made from the Ull de Llebre, Sumoll and Trepat, but the only concern to bottle any wine (in Reus, outside the region) is the great cooperative combine, the UNIÓN AGRARIA COOPERATIVA.

An interesting development in the region has been the purchase of the 12th-century Castle of Milmanda and its surrounding vineyards by Bodegas TORRES, after investigation had shown that the soils were exceptionally well suited for growing Cabernet Sauvignon and Pinot Noir, and plantation is now in full swing.

Conca de Tremp, Comarca de la r. w. dr. (p.)
Undemarcated area to the far NW of Catalonia in the province of Lérida, better known for its reservoirs and hydroelectric schemes than its wine. The better wines are made by Bodegas Valeri Vila and sold as the red, white and rosé "Castell d'Orcau".

Coniusa r. p. w. (sp.) ★→★★
Raimat (Lérida). The *comarca* of El Segria, in the W of Catalonia near

Lérida, was famous for its vineyards in medieval times, but wine-making had long fallen into abeyance when Don Manuel Raventós Domenech, of the sparkling wine firm of Codorníu, bought the Castle of Raimat some years ago and embarked on extensive replanting of the area with selected vines from the Penedès and abroad. Raimat now produces sound but unexciting wines: the light red "Can Rius"; the sturdier red "Can Clamor"; a "Can Abadia" with a pleasant Tempranillo nose, matured for 2 years in oak and 1 year in bottle; and also white and rosé wines. As a dependency of Codorníu, Raimat also produces some sparkling wine.

Dalmau Germans y Cía. D.O. r. w. dr. or sw. am. gen. ★→★★
Tarragona. D.O. Tarragona. The firm began blending and exporting wines as long ago as 1830, and like many of the large houses in Tarragona it is mainly concerned with bulk shipments abroad. It does, however, bottle some of its better wines exclusively for the home market, notably the "Selecto blanco seco", "Casta Dorada blanco suave" and "Añejo selecto tinto".

De Muller S.A. D.O. r. p. w. dr. or sw. am. gen. ★→★★★★
Tarragona. D.O. Tarragona, Priorato, etc. This is the most prestigious wine firm in Tarragona. Founded in 1851, it is still in family hands, its President being the Marqués de Muller y de Abadal. Its picturesque old cellars in the port area of Tarragona have a total capacity of 4 million liters and house more oak casks than all the other concerns in Tarragona put together; it was also the first firm in Spain to use refrigeration techniques. If its Tarragona table wines, sold under the label of "Solimar", are not up to PENEDÈS standards, its fortified and *solera*-made wines, reminiscent of very old and round olorosos and Málagas, are outstanding. They include the "Moscatel añejo", "Aureo", "Moscatel rancio", "Pajarete" and others. De Muller has for long been a principal supplier of ALTAR WINE to the Vatican and also maintains a small *bodega* in SCALA DEI, producing several fortified wines of note including a velvety, full-bodied "Priorato de Muller", used as a basis for the splendid dry Priorato "Dom Juan Fort Solera 1865" and the sweet "Priorato Dulce Solera 1918".

Falset, Comarca de D.O. r. w. dr. ★
Sub-denomination of the D.O. Tarragona to the SW of the region. Its cooperative-made wines are high in alcohol, the reds velvety and with agreeable astringency, and the sturdy whites soon tending towards maderization.

Freixedas, Bodegas J. D.O. r. p. w. dr. res. sp. ★→★★
Vilafranca del Penedès (Barcelona). D.O. Penedès. Founded in 1897, this large-scale exporter owns 80ha (198 acres) of vineyards at Cugat Sesgarrigues, but buys in most of its grapes and wine. Apart from sparkling wine, it makes the red, white and rosé "Santa Marta" and a 5-year-old *reserva*.

Freixenet S.A. D.O. r. p. w. dr. sp. ★★
San Sadurní de Noya (Barcelona). D.O. Penedès. Much better known for its sparkling wines, Freixenet has recently begun making fresh white, rosé and red wines labeled as "Viña Carossa". See also SPARKLING WINES.

Gandesa, Cooperativa Agrícola de D.O. (r.) w. dr. res. ★→★★
Gandesa (Tarragona). D.O. Terra Alta. Founded in 1919, this is the oldest of the cooperatives in the recently demarcated region of TERRA ALTA and now has a capacity of 2.8 million liters. It bottles 25% of its wines, of which the best are the robust, but characterful "Gandesa Blanc Gran Reserva" and "Gandesa Blanc Especial". In 1938, during the Spanish Civil War, the cooperative found itself in the firing line, but this was not allowed to interfere with production, and a year later the remains of two of General Franco's Moorish guards were found in one of its vats!

Hill, Cavas D.O. r. p. w. dr. s/sw. or sw. res. sp. ★★→★★★
Moja-Vilafranca del Penedès. D.O. Penedès. The Hill family emigrated

from England to the Penedès in 1660, planting a small vineyard and establishing a *bodega* much expanded by Don José Hill Ros in 1884. The firm now makes wines by the Champagne process and a large range of still wines, including red, white and rosé "Viña San Manuel"; "Extra Rosé"; the semi-sweet "Oro Penedès"; and a good red "Penedès reserva".

INCAVI

Following the death of General Franco and the restoration of local autonomy to the 4 provinces of Catalonia, between 1978 and 1980 the Instituto Nacional de las Denominaciones de Origen transferred control of the demarcated regions and oenological stations in Catalonia to an agency of the revived Generalitat, the Instituto Catalán de Vino. Under the energetic direction of Jaume Ciurana, it has since demarcated the new regions of CONCA DE BARBERÁ and TERRA ALTA and sub-divided the D.O. TARRAGONA.

León S.A., Jean r. w. dr. res. ★★★

Plá de Penedès (Barcelona). Owned by a Los Angeles restaurateur of Spanish descent, this tiny *bodega* was one of the first to plant foreign vines in the Penedès and, unusually for Spain, grows all its own grapes. The vineyards now extend to 10ha (25 acres) planted with Chardonnay and 100ha (247 acres) with Cabernet Sauvignon. Annual production amounts to 10,000 bottles of Chardonnay and 200,000 of Cabernet Sauvignon, the bulk of them exported to the U.S.A., though a little of the wine is available in Spain. Both are excellent wines, though the Chardonnay, which is fermented in oak casks, rather than "cold" in stainless steel, is perhaps not quite as fresh as some.

López Beltrán y Cía S.A. r. p. w. dr. or sw. res. ★→★★

Tarragona. Large family firm founded in 1862, but now installed in modern premises. It both exports bottled wine on a large scale and supplies the home market: "Don Beltrán blanco selección", "Don Beltrán rosado", "Don Beltrán tinto".

Mollet de Perelada, Cooperativa de D.O. r. p. w. dr. gen. ★→★★

Perelada (Gerona). D.O. Ampurdán-Costa Brava. Simón Serra, the French-trained oenologist of this sizeable cooperative with a storage capacity of some 2.8 million liters, is making very fresh red, white and rosé "*Vi Novell*" after the style of Beaujolais Nouveau, of which the most attractive is perhaps the red. The cooperative also makes a very full and fruity dessert wine from Garnacha blanca grapes, fermented with their skins for a few days before addition of grape spirit, and small quantities of a good sparkling wine.

Monistrol, Marqués de r. dr. or sw. p. w. pt. dr. or sw. res. ★★→★★★

This old family concern outside San Sadurní de Noya in the PENEDÈS has recently been taken over by Martini & Rossi. It has been making excellent sparkling wine since 1882 and still wines since 1974. The best are the refreshing and incipiently *pétillant* young "Vin Natur blanc de blancs", made with 60% Parellada and 40% Xarel-lo, bottled only 2 months after the grapes are picked; a fruity rosé: and a smooth, velvety red *reserva*, aged for 3–4 years in oak *barrica* and 1½ in bottle. See also SPARKLING WINES.

Montserrat, Monastery of

On the NW fringe of the PENEDÈS, the Monastery of Montserrat is an essential stop for any visitor to the area. The precipitous hill to which it clings, with its massive outcrops of rounded, weatherworn rock, is so extraordinary as to have inspired Wagner's *Parsifal*, and appropriately enough the splendid boys' choir is the oldest musical conservatory in Europe. In medieval times its vineyards, along with those of POBLET, were among the most important in Catalonia. The Virgin of Montserrat, whose blackened wooden image is preserved in the monastery, is the patron saint of Catalonia, and the monastery, founded in the 11th century, is the object of mass pilgrimages, catering for its pilgrims and the many tourists in huge restaurants with panoramic views across the Penedès.

Penedès D.O. r. p. w. dr. s/sw. or sw. am. g. res. ★→★★★★
The Penedès, with its 25,000ha (62,300 acres) of vineyards, is a limestone region SW of Barcelona best known for its sparkling wines, but the best of its still wines rival those of the Rioja.

The region slopes upwards from the Mediterranean coast to a height of some 700m. (2,290ft.) in the hills of the interior. The temperate climate and adequate rainfall are ideal for growing grapes. There are three sub-regions: the hotter Bajo Penedès near the coast is best suited for black grapes: the Medio Penedès, at an average altitude of 200m. (670ft.), produces some 60% of the wine from the area as a whole, much of it made from the white Xarel-lo and Macabeo and used for sparkling wines; and the typical grape of the cooler and hillier Alto Penedès is the white Parellada, used both for the dry, fragrant and refreshing white wines and also for sparkling *cava* wines, widely produced in the area (see SPARKLING WINES).

The Consejo Regulador, the offical regulatory body, whose standards are rigorous, approves the following types of native grape: the white Macabeo (or Viura), Xarel-lo, Parellada (or Montonec), and Subirat-Parent; and the black Cariñena, Monastrell, Garnacha tinta, Samsó and Ull de Llebra (or Tempranillo). In addition to these, Bodegas TORRES has successfully acclimatized a variety of noble grapes from abroad in the hills of the hinterland.

Owing to the favorable climate, vintages are remarkably consistent, the best of the last decade being, for the white wines, 1974, 1975, 1976, 1978, 1979 and 1980; and for the reds, 1970, 1971, 1973, 1974, 1975, 1976, 1977, 1978 and 1980. The only really disastrous year during this period was 1972.

The best base for visiting the Penedès is VILAFRANCA DEL PENEDÈS where there is one of the best wine museums in the world. Many visitors prefer to stay in one of the more comfortable hotels of the pleasant coastal resort of SITGES, half-an-hour's drive from Vilafranca, or in BARCELONA, an hour away by the *autopista*.

Apart from *bodegas* with individual entries, other concerns which bottle wine under their own label are:

Aleget, J.
Almuzara, A.
Compañía Internacional de Grandes Vinos S.A.
Ferret, J.
Juve y Camps. S.A.
Lavernoya, Cavas
Llopart, J.
Lluch, Jaime
Martorell Vinícola
Masia Puigmolto
Masia Vallformosa S.A.
Miret, Hacienda
Pujadas, Pedro
Parato Vinicol S.A.
Sancho, Bodegas Manuel
Sogas, José María
Torello
Vilafranca, Bodega Cooperativa de

See also SPARKLING WINES.

Penelles (La Noguera), Comarca de r. w. dr. sp. ★
Tiny undemarcated area in the W of Catalonia near Lérida, best known for the wines of the CASTELL DEL REMEI.

Pinord, Bodegas D.O. r. p. w. dr. or sw. g. ★→★★
Vilafranca del Penedès. D.O. Penedès. Family firm making a large range of wines which are marketed under labels including "Reynal", "Chatel", and "Chatedon".

Poblet, Monastery of
Famous Cistercian monastery dating from the 12th century in the hills of CONCA DE BARBERÁ, and the burial place of the Kings of Aragón and Catalonia. During the Middle Ages it was the abbeys and monasteries which most fostered viticulture, and along with those of the monastery of MONTSERRAT, the vineyards of Poblet were vital in keeping wine-making traditions alive in Catalonia. Today an interesting feature of Poblet is the magnificent arched wine cellars.

Pontons
Vineyard area at a height of 700m. (2,250ft.) in the Alto PENEDÈS, developed by Bodegas TORRES for growing the native Parellada and also the Riesling, Gewürztraminer and Chardonnay vines from the cooler climes of northern Europe. Hailstorms, so damaging to vines, are dispersed by a system of rockets charged with silver iodide, and the results are so promising that other producers are now moving into the area.

Porrón
This conical-shaped glass drinking vessel with spout and handle, now sold in debased form in souvenir shops up and down Spain, has been used for centuries in Catalonia. When in use, the spout does not touch the lips, so that the *porrón* serves the practical purpose of enabling a party of drinkers to enjoy their wine without the need for glasses.

Priorato D.O. r. (w. dr.) am. ★→★★
A small, mountainous enclave, with 3,700ha (9,200 acres) of vineyards and its own D.O., within the much larger D.O. TARRAGONA. The name means "Priory" and derives from that of the ruined monastery of SCALA DEI.

The grapes are grown in small plots or on terraces in the volcanic soils of the steep hillsides, a decayed lava with high silica content, which, in combination with the hot summer sun, produces good, very fully bodied wines with high alcohol content. Authorized grapes for the red wines are the Garnacha tinta, Garnacha peluda and Cariñena; and for the whites, the Garnacha blanca, Macabeo (Viura) and Pedro Ximénez.

The most typical wine is red, almost black in color with a huge amount of extract, containing up to 18% of alcohol and much in demand for blending. The other speciality is a golden yellow RANCIO.

Apart from the Cellers de SCALA DEI and DE MULLER, there is only one producer which bottles and labels its wines: the UNIÓN AGRARIA COOPERATIVA (cooperative union) with cellars in Reus outside the demarcated area.

The best base for visiting Priorato is TARRAGONA on the coast.

Rabassa Morta
The historic form of land tenure in Catalonia, according to which a proprietor leased land to a farmer on condition that he planted it with vines, and that the landowner should share the produce with the farmer, whose right to cultivate the land expired only with the death of the first-planted vines. After the onset of phylloxera in 1876 and replanting with grafts, the life of the vines became much shorter, and the institution fell into disuse. It is now usual for small farmers to own their land.

Raimat, Castillo de
See CONIUSA.

Rancio
A maderized or oxidized white wine, popular in various parts of Spain, but particularly so in Catalonia. *Rancios* vary enormously in character and quality from the tart and sour product of a peasant *bodega* or local cooperative, where the wine is left to oxidize without sufficient hygiene, to the perfected wines of DE MULLER in Tarragona. These are sweetened with *mistela* (a must in which fermentation has been checked by the addition of alcohol) or *arrope* (boiled down must), and aged in *solera*. They can be magnificent, resembling in their different styles very round and old *oloroso* sherries. Another type is made in large glass carboys, known as BOMBONAS, and left partially unstoppered and open to the sun and wind, as at Bodegas TORRES, whose fortified "Dry Solera" is very palatable and distinctly sherry-like. What all *rancios* have in common is a deep golden yellow color, a sherry-like nose, more or less marked, and a high degree of alcohol.

René Barbier S.A. r. p. w. dr. or sw. res. [★★] →★★★
This company, like the CONDE DE CARALT, with which it shares cellars at the *cavas* of the sparkling wine firm of SEGURA VIUDAS near San

Sadurní de Noya in the PENEDÈS, is now part of the great RUMASA combine. Its "Kraliner" is a lively and fresh young white wine, and the "Tinto 1978" a fruity, medium-bodied red for everyday drinking. The *bodega* also makes a velvety red *reserva* with marked bouquet.

Reus
Important wine town of some 60,000 inhabitants W of Tarragona. It is here that the great cooperative combine, the UNIÓN AGRARIA COOPERATIVA maintains its central establishment for blending, maturing and bottling wines from outlying cooperatives. There are also many private firms engaged in elaborating both wines and vermouth.

Ribera d'Ebre, Comarca Vitícola Especial r. w. dr. ★
Sub-denomination of the D.O. TARRAGONA adjoining the D.O. TERRA ALTA in the extreme SW of the province of Tarragona. The wines resemble those of FALSET but are rather more acid. It makes some good dessert wines, especially those from its leading bodega, Pedro ROVIRA.

Robert, Bodegas g. ★★
Sitges (Barcelona). One of the few small bodegas still making the classical white dessert SITGES from Malvasía and Moscatel grapes.

Rovira S.A., Pedro D.O. r. p. w. dr. or sw. g. res. ★→★★
Old-established firm with cellars at Móra la Nova in the Ribera d'Ebre, a *comarca* (sub-district) of the D.O. TARRAGONA, and at Gandesa in the D.O. TERRA ALTA. Sturdy beverage wines typical of the areas and *solera*-made apéritif and dessert wines. The firm also has a branch in VILAFRANCA DEL PENEDÈS.

San Cugat del Vallés, Monastery of
Between Barcelona and Montserrat, San Cugat, with its beautiful Romanesque cloisters, was one of the great religious houses which did so much to foster viticulture. Among its muniments is a deed recording the gift of a vineyard to the monastery in 927.

San Miguel de las Viñas, Cofradía de
Catalan order of *tastevins*, celebrating its functions at the historic old castle of San Martí near Vilafranca del Penedès. Its light-hearted inauguration ceremony, conducted to the strains of a band in traditional costume, includes drinking from a PORRÓN and distinguishing blindfold between a white and a rosé wine – much more difficult than it sounds – on pain of continuing the tasting indefinitely.

San Sadurní de Noya (Sant Sadùrní d'Anoia)
Township in the E of the PENEDÈS towards MONTSERRAT, where most of the *cavas* making sparkling wines are situated. Now that firms such as MONISTROL, CARALT, RENÉ BARBIER and FREIXENET are diversifying, it has also become a center for making still wines.
See also SPARKLING WINES.

Scala Dei, Cellers de D.O. r. res. [★★]
Scala Dei (Tarragona). D.O. Priorato. Housed in a picturesque old stone building near the ruined monastery, the Cellars are equipped with stainless steel fermentation vats, underground *depósitos* coated with epoxy resin, oak *barricas* and a modern bottling line allowing for the topping up of bottles with carbon dioxide. The *bodega* has a capacity of 950,000 liters and an annual output of 111,000 bottles; and Jaume Mussons makes some of the best of the full-bodied Priorato, almost black in color, with a deep blackberry flavor and containing some 14.5% alcohol, ageing his wines for 18 months in oak and further in bottle.

Scala Dei, Monastery of
When visiting the *bodega*, it is worth walking the 10 minutes to the great roofless monastery, choked with trees and aromatic vegetation, a victim of Mendizábal's anti-clerical reforms of about 1830. According to legend, it was founded when angels were seen ascending and descending a ladder into the heavens, and the theme of the ladder is embodied in the seal of the Consejo Regulador for Priorato.

Serra Vinos, Jaime D.O. p. w. dr. or sw. ★→★★
Alella (Barcelona). D.O. Alella. Private firm making some of the small amount of Alella not produced by the BODEGA COOPERATIVA: "Alellasol blanco seco", "Alellasol blanco semi" and "Alellasol rosado".

Sitges
The Subur of the Romans, Sitges, on the coast S of Barcelona, is now a pleasant and relatively unspoilt seaside resort with a palm-fringed promenade, though bursting at the seams in summer. Its famous dessert wine, made by allowing Malvasía and Moscatel grapes to wrinkle on the branch before picking, the addition of grape spirit to the must and long maturation in oak, is now made only in minuscule amounts.

Sitges celebrates a picturesque harvest festival in early September, with a harvest queen, decorated floats, the solemn pressing and blessing of the first fruits, and a fountain flowing free wine.

A good base for visiting the PENEDÈS, the best of its many hotels are the 4-star Calipolis and Terramar, and the 3-star Antemare, both on the sea-front.

Tarragona
The Imperial Tarraco of the Romans, Tarragona is a city rich in historic remains, including massive walls built by the Romans on a much earlier foundation of monolithic blocks, an aqueduct and forum, and a fine Gothic cathedral. It is an important wine city specializing in the blending of wines, both from the surrounding region and other parts of Spain, and their bulk export. Among the dusty streets around the port, the great *bodegas de exportación* are thick on the ground. It is most reputed for the Tarragona *clásicos*, sweet dessert wines, both red and white, containing up to 23% alcohol – it was a cheap *clásico*, sold as "Tarragona" and also known by the less complimentary names of "poor man's port" and "red biddy", that was once so popular in English pubs. Another important activity in the town is the elaboration of vermouths and liqueurs.

Tarragona is a good base for visits to the outlying regions, and the most comfortable hotels are the 4-star Imperial Tarraco and 3-star Astari and Lauria.

Tarragona D.O. r. w. dr. am. ★→★★
Tarragona, the largest demarcated region in Catalonia, with some 25,000ha (62,640 acres) under vines and an average annual output of 70 million liters, is divided into the sub-regions of CAMP DE TARRAGONA, FALSET and RIBERA D'EBRE. Its beverage wines, made mainly in cooperatives, tend to be sturdy and high in alcohol, and thus very suitable for blending, but lack the delicacy of those from the PENEDÈS to its N.

Apart from *bodegas* with individual entries, other concerns which blend, mature and bottle wine, usually cooperative made, under their own labels are:

Amigó Germans y Cía.	José Oliver S.A.
Cochs S.A.	Ramón Mestre Serra
Joan Solé Bargalló	Tapias S.A., Cellers
(Cellers Catalano-Aragonesas)	Vinos Padró S.L.

Terra Alta D.O. r. w. dr. ★→★★
The newly demarcated Terra Alta, with 16,000ha (39,700 acres) under vines and an average annual output of 24 million liters, lies in mountainous country in the extreme SW of Catalonia, bordering the province of Teruel. It makes robust but characterful wines, white and red, the best from the Cooperativa Agrícola de GANDESA and Pedro ROVIRA S.A.

Torres, Viñedos r. p. w. dr. s/sw. sw. g. res. ★★→★★★★ Red: 70, 71, 73, 74, 75, 76, 77, 78, 80 White: 74, 75, 76, 78, 79, 80 Vilafranca del Penedès (Barcelona). The Torres family has been making and selling wine in the PENEDÈS since the 17th century. It is now the most reputed firm in Catalonia to make still wines, exporting them all over the world – exports to the U.S.A. alone top a million bottles annually – and under its President, Don Miguel Torres Carbó, is still very much a family concern.

His son, Don Miguel Torres Riera, with a French degree in oenology, has been responsible for introducing a variety of foreign vines to the Penedès, grown, in addition to native vines, on its 400ha (990 acres) of vineyards. Like almost all Spanish *bodegas*, it also buys grapes from independent farmers. The foreign varieties include the white Chardonnay, Gewürztraminer, Riesling, Sauvignon blanc; and the red Cabernet Sauvignon, Cabernet Franc, Petit Syrah and Pinot Noir; and vines accustomed to a cooler habitat are grown in the hills of the hinterland.

Torres has also been responsible for technical innovations. All its wines are made in temperature-controled stainless steel vats, the whites by "cold fermentation". Typical of these are the various styles of the dry, fresh and fruity "Viña Sol", "Gran Viña Sol" and "Waltraud" and also the semi-dry "Esmeralda", made with a blend of Gewürztraminer and Moscatel d'Alsace. Its red wines spend less time in oak casks – usually 1½–2 years – and correspondingly more time in bottle than those from the Rioja, and are therefore less "oaky" in nose and flavor. Reds such as the "Tres Torres" and the fruity and full-bodied "Gran Sangre de Toro" are made with native grapes, but the pride of the Torres stable, velvety, smooth, intensely fruity and long in finish, is the "Gran Coronas Black Label", made with Cabernet Sauvignon and Cabernet Franc. At the Gault-Millau "Olympiad" held in Paris in 1979, the 1970 vintage was judged by a short head to be better than the then less fully developed 1970 Château Latour. Torres also makes a RANCIO and excellent brandy, and has recently acquired vineyards and a winery in Chile. None of the wines carry a D.O., as Torres does not believe in the system.

Unión Agraria Cooperativa r. p. w. dr. or sw. res. ★→★★ Reus (Tarragona). This vast combine, founded in 1962, handles wines from all 180 cooperatives in the province. It sells large quantities of wine to private firms for further elaboration and bottling. More select growths, such as the "Priorat seco especial", "Priorat dulce" and "Priorat Centrum" from the Cooperativa de Gratallops, are matured in the central cellars at Reus, and then bottled and sold under their own label. Among its many other labels are the red and white "Tarragona Unión"; red, white and rosé "Yelmo"; the dry, semi-dry and rosé "Collar Perla", "Collar Zafiro" and "Collar Rubí"; and also *reservas*.

Vilafranca del Penedès
Vilafranca, a small town off the *autopista* between Barcelona and Tarragona, is the center of the still-wine industry in the PENEDÈS and the home of many of its best-known *bodegas*. It also makes some sparkling wine by the Champagne process and is the headquarters of the Spanish offshoots of Cinzano and Cointreau.

Apart from the *bodegas*, the great point of interest is the Wine Museum, installed in a 13th-century palace of the Kings of Aragón, and one of the best in the world. The exhibits begin with tableaux illustrating wine-making from ancient times onwards; and there are numerous examples of amphorae, Greek, Carthaginian and Roman. The main hall houses every type of agricultural implement, press and barrel, many of them originating from old *bodegas* in the region. There are also pictures and drawings, drinking glasses and PORRONES. The visit ends in a small bar, where local wines may be sampled. Closed Monday.

The Museum is also the headquarters of the old-established Academía de Tastavins de Sant Humbert, a wine faternity devoted to maintaining the traditions and quality of the Penedès wines.

Vilafranca possesses a number of pleasant restaurants (see WINE AND FOOD), but boasts only a single modern but basic hotel, rather grandiloquently named the Pedro III El Grande.

Vinícola Ibérica, La r. p. w. dr. or sw. g. ★→★★

Tarragona. One of the oldest-established firms in the port area of TARRAGONA, buying, blending and maturing wines from different parts of Spain for bulk export. It possesses a direct pipeline from the center of the *bodega* to the quay, and among its specialities are a bottled *sangría* (better made fresh with red wine, fizzy lemonade, oranges and lemons, and a dash of Spanish brandy) and the traditional fortified "Tarragona", or "poor man's port".

WINE & Food

Catalonia has a long-established tradition of gastronomy; and the raw materials, especially the fish, shellfish and fresh vegetables, are first-rate. There are 5 famous sauces: *ali-oli* (the *aïoli* of Provence), and the piquant *picada, chanfaina, sofrito* and *romesco*. Appetites are hearty, and in the smaller regional restaurants even the soups and starters are meals in themselves. Some of the more sophisticated restaurants of places like Barcelona and the province of Gerona have been much influenced by the *nouvelle cuisine*.

Bolets

Field mushrooms, often cooked on a charcoal grill with garlic and parsley.
★★ Torres "Viña Sol", ★★ C.V.P. "Viña Franca" or other dry white.

Butifarra catalana

White sausage, resembling boudin blanc, *eaten raw, cooked on its own or used in other dishes.*

Calcotada

Made only in the spring, this is prepared by slicing tender spring onions in half and grilling them over a wood fire. They are served with a sauce resembling romesco.
★★ Monistrol "Vin Natur Blanc de Blancs" or other light dry white.

Conejo con caracoles

Young rabbits stewed with snails, herbs, cinnamon, almonds and biscuit crumbs.
One of the lighter red wines from René Barbier, Hill, Caralt, Torres, etc.

Costillas con ali-oli

Grilled ribs of lamb served with ali-oli.
A medium-bodied red such as ★★★ Torres "Magdala".

Crema catalana

The local variation on cream caramel or "flan", made with egg yolks, milk and cinnamon and topped with a brittle layer of caramel.
★★★ Bach "Extrísimo".

Embutidos de Vich

The mountain town of Vich in the Pyrenees near the French frontier makes a variety of excellent charcuterie, *including* chorizos *(pepper sausage),* morcilla *(blood sausage),* butifarra *(white sausage) and* jamón serrano *(highly cured ham). Apart from the* morcilla, *which must be cooked, the others are often eaten as apéritifs and are valuable adjuncts to a picnic.*

Escudella i Carn d'olla
This most typical of Catalan dishes is served in 2 parts: first the escudella, *a meaty soup with pasta; and then the* carn d'olla, *a rich stew containing veal, chicken, salt and ground pork, blood sausage, egg, breadcrumbs and vegetables both fresh and dried.*
A full-bodied red, such as ★★ "Cartoixa Scala Dei" or the less potent ★★ Bach "Tinto".

Espinacas a la catalana
Boiled spinach with pine kernels and raisins.
Try one of the lighter *rancios.*

Habas a la catalana
Vegetable dish containing fresh broad beans, butifarra negra *(Catalan black sausage) and belly of pork, together with spring onions, fresh mint, bay leaf and parsley.*
★★ Monistrol rosé or ★★ Torres "De Casta".

Langosta a la catalana
Stewed lobster with onions, carrots, garlic, herbs, parsley, saffron, pepper, sweet paprika, chocolate, nutmeg and brandy.
This obviously calls for a wine of character such as the ★★ Torres "Gran Viña Sol Green Label", with its body and hint of oak.

Mel y mató
Fresh cream cheese with honey.
★★ Torres "San Valentin" or other sweet or semi-sweet wine.

Menja blanc
A dessert made from ground almonds, cream, kirsch and lemon.
Ideally, ★★★★ De Muller "Moscatel Muy Viejo, Solera 1926".

Pan con tomate y jamón
Catalan country-style bread rubbed with fresh tomatoes, oil and salt. It appears at the beginning of the meal and is sometimes served with slices of cured ham.
Any full-bodied Mediterranean-type dry white.

Panellets
A sweet made with almonds, sugar and eggs, or alternatively with pine kernels in the form of a marzipan.

Parrillada de pescado con salsa romesco
Mixed grill of fish served with the typical Catalan romesco *sauce and mayonnaise.*

Perdiz a la catalana
Partridge stewed with herbs and lemon.
★★★ Torres "Gran Coronas" or ★★★ Monistrol "Gran Reserva".

Pollo en chanfaina
Chicken stewed with eggplants, green peppers, tomatoes, wine and herbs, and served with croûtons.
★★★ Bosch-Guell "Clarete" or other light red.

Postre de músico
Mixed plate of almonds, raisins, hazelnuts, walnuts, figs or other dried fruit.

Rape a la Costa Brava
Angler fish cooked with fresh peas, red pimientos, mussels, saffron, garlic, parsley and white wine, with a little lemon.
★★ Cavas del Ampurdán "Pescador".

Sopa catalana con albondiguillas
Chicken broth containing small meat balls and flavored with cinnamon, garlic and chervil.
★★★ Dry sherry.

Sopa de mejillones catalana
A soup made with mussels and flavored with tomatoes, aguardiente, *garlic,*

parsley and cinnamon.
★★ Torres "Dry Solera", a dry sherry or Montilla, or a spicy white from Valencia, Jumilla or Alicante.

Tortilla de butifarra y mongetes
A hearty omelette containing Catalan sausage and served with haricot beans, first boiled and then fried.
★★ Alella "Marfil tinto", ★ Perelada "Tinto Cazador" or other honest-to-goodness red.

Zarzuela de mariscos
Literally a "variety show", this most famous of Catalan dishes is a mixture of shellfish and firm white fish in a sauce made with saffron, garlic, white wine and parsley.
With seafood such as this the Spaniards often drink red rather than white wine, and the choice is between a good medium-bodied red, such as a ★★ Caralt or René Barbier tinto, or a dry white like the ★★★ Torres "Gran Viña Sol" with sufficient character to stand up to the rich assortment of flavors.

Restaurants

Barcelona is full of good restaurants, and recommendations include: ★★★ *Jaume de Provença* (for connoisseurs of Catalan and *nouvelle cuisine* dishes); ★★ *Agut d'Avignon* (near the Cathedral, fashionable, good value for what it is, Spanish and international cooking); ★★ *Neichel* (leading and sophisticated Barcelona exponent of the *nouvelle cuisine*); ★★ *Reno* (old-established and as good as ever); ★ *Florian* (small and inventive with attractively priced young wines); ★ *Casa Costa* (in the port area, fresh seafood, Catalan style).

Cambrils near Tarragona ★ *Can Gatel*; ★ *Casa Gatell*; ★*Eugenia* (all specializing in fish and seafood).

Figueras ★★★ *Ampurdán* (in the Motel Ampurdán outside Figueras; highly sophisticated restaurant started by Josep Mércader, founder of the new Catalan cuisine); ★ *Hotel Durán* (good Catalan food and long list of Ampurdán wines).

Lérida ★ *Forn de Nastasi.*

S'Agaro ★★ *La Gavina* (sophisticated international cooking in this most elegant and expensive of Costa Brava hotels).

Sitges ★ *Mare Nostrum*; ★ *El Greco*; ★ *Vivero.*

Tarragona ★ *Meson del Mar*; ★ *Sol Ric.*

Vilafranca del Penedès ★ *Airolo*; *Casa Juan.* Outside, on the road to Sitges: *Celler de Penedès*; *Masia Segarulls* (both simple restaurants with typical and substantial Catalan fare).

Extremadura
& the South-west

The Extremadura lies between the two Castiles and Portugal in the SW of Spain. It suffered from mass depopulation after the expulsion of the Moors in the 13th century, and again in the 16th, when thousands of Extremeños joined in the conquest of the New World.

It remains an empty and sparsely populated area, and in its high *sierras*, clothed with cork-oak, beech and chestnut, sheep are more numerous than humans. Cultivation of vines is somewhat spora-

D.O. Zones
1 Huelva
2 Tierra de Barros
Others
3 Montánchez
4 Cañamero

Jarandilla
CÁCERES
Cáceres
Guadalupe
Cañamero
4
Montánchez
3
Medellín
Mérida
Badajoz
BADAJOZ
Almendralejo 2
Salvatierra de los Barros
HUELVA
1
Huelva
Lepe
Bollullos del Condado
Coto Doñana
N
Scale
0 m 45
0 km 75

dic, the most densely planted area being in the recently demarcated Tierra de Barros around Almendralejo in the province of Badajoz. Here, the summers are hot and the rainfall low, with an annual average of only 370mm. (15in.). The principal grape is the Cayetana blanca with an astonishingly high yield, 36hl/ha, of a neutral white wine of low acidity. Of the annual output of some 160 million liters, 80% goes to Jerez, Asturias and Galicia for blending, the remainder being consumed locally or distiled.

Two small areas in the Extremadura, Cañamero and Montánchez, produce *flor*-growing wines of marked individuality; but to taste them you will have to visit the region, which is, although usually ignored by vacationers, one of great scenic and historical interest, with its forgotten towns of Medellín and Trujillo, the birthplaces of Cortés and Pizarro, the splendid monastery of Guadalupe and, above all, Mérida, with its little-known and marvelous Roman monuments.

Outside Extremadura, the other wine-growing area in the far SW is the demarcated region of Huelva, again with nostalgic historical associations, since it was from Palos, near the city of Huelva, that Columbus first sailed for the Americas. It is known for its decent white table wines, but more especially for *generosos* in the various styles of sherry, which would be more familiar if they had not for so long been sent to Jerez de la Frontera for blending.

It is difficult to list more than a handful of *bodegas* which actually bottle the wine, since so much of it, especially from the Extremadura, is made by small proprietors for consumption in local bars and restaurants, or sold in bulk by the cooperatives for blending outside the region.

Almendralejo
The main wine town of the newly demarcated region of TIERRA DE BARROS in the province of Badajoz. Its dusty main street is crowded with *bodegas* and distilleries.

Badajoz
Province of Extremadura flanking the Portuguese frontier and lying between those of Cáceres to the N and Huelva to the S. The principal wine-growing area is that of TIERRA DE BARROS.

Bodega Cooperativa Vinícola del Condado D.O. w. dr. g. ★→★★
Bollullos del Condado (Huelva). D.O. Huelva. The best of the cooperatives in the D.O. HUELVA, making white table wines and *generosos* in the style of sherry.

Bollullos del Condado
The most important of the wine towns in the D.O. HUELVA with numerous *bodegas* making white table wine and sherry-like *generosos.* It is also a center for distilling the *holandas* used for making brandy (see SPIRITS, AROMATIC WINES & LIQUEURS).

Cáceres
Province of Extremadura bordering Portugal and to the N of Badajoz, whose most characterful wines are CAÑAMERO and MONTÁNCHEZ. The other wine-growing areas are those of Miajados, W of Guadalupe, and Jerte, Hervás, Cilleros and Ceclavin, scattered around the historic old towns of Jarandilla and Plasencia in the N of the province. In the main, their wines are *tintos* and *claretes*, but Cilleros on the Portuguese border makes a sturdy white, characteristically turbid and of 15% strength.

Cañamero D.O. w. dr. ★★
The small hill town of Cañamero, a few miles SW of GUADALUPE, is famous for a *flor*-growing white wine much sought after by Spanish *aficionados.* The soils consist of clays layered with slate and quartzite and

the vineyards extend to some 1,000ha (2,470 acres). 80% of the grapes are made up of the white Alarije, Bomita, Airén and Marfil; the red varieties are the Garnacha tinta, Morisca, Palomino negro and Tinto fino. The wines are made in the cement vats of the small *bodegas* and develop a film of yeasts on the surface in the manner of sherry. The wine is thereafter aged in oak casks and becomes turbid after some 14–18 months, but subsequently clears. The wines are yellow in color, becoming paler with age, round and smooth on the palate with a fragrant, sherry-like nose, and of some 15% strength.

Cevisur, Bodegas D.O. w. dr. ★
Tierra de Barros (Badajoz). D.O. Tierra de Barros. One of the few small family firms typical of those companies which do exist in the region which bottles a representative wine, the white "Viña Extremeña".

Condado de Niebla
Ancient domain of the Guzman Counts, who occupied it after its reconquest from the Moors, and now the heart of the wine-growing area of HUELVA.

Galan, Bodegas r. w. dr. ★→★★
Tiny *bodega* in the village of MONTÁNCHEZ, N of Mérida, making the typical and slightly turbid *flor*-growing wines, which it bottles under the name "Trampal" and sells, in very limited quantities, as far afield as Madrid.

Guadalupe
High in the mountains NE of Mérida, the little town of Guadalupe clusters around a monastery founded by Alfonso XI in 1340 in thanksgiving for his victory over the Moors at Salado. It later became the shrine of the Conquistadores and was enriched by generations of princes and grandees; among its many treasures is a magnificent series of paintings by Zurbarán. The bars of Guadalupe are the best place to sample the *flor*-growing CAÑAMERO; it is also the house wine at the comfortable Parador Nacional Zurbarán, facing the monastery and housed in a 15th-century hospice for pilgrims.

Hijos de Francisco Vallejo D.O. g. ★★
Bollullos del Condado (Huelva). D.O. Huelva. Family firm making honest and representative wines of the *generoso* type.

Huelva D.O. ★→★★
The province of Huelva lies in the SW corner of Spain between the Portuguese frontier and the Atlantic. The demarcated region covers 18,622ha (46,550 acres) and in 1979 produced some 95 million liters of wine, of which 15 million liters were white table wine and 13 million liters *generosos* of the sherry type, most of the rest going for distillation. The region has always been overshadowed by its more famous neighbors, Jerez and Montilla, and the best of its *generosos* were sent to Jerez for blending until the region was demarcated in 1964 and the practice was outlawed. The soils are chalky and of the same general type as those of Jerez, though darker in color. In the past, 90% of the vineyards were planted with the white Zalema, but this is being replaced by Palomino, Mantúa, Garrido fino, Pedro Luis and Pedro Ximénez.

The *solera*-made *generosos* are of the same general types as those of Jerez – *fino, amontillado, oloroso*, etc. – but lack the finesse of the best sherry. The white table wines average 11.5–14% and are acceptable enough for everyday drinking, without any great distinction.

Jarandilla cl. ★
The *claretes* from Jarandilla, in the N of the province of Cáceres, were once rated among the best in Spain and were the prime favorites of the Emperor Charles V during his last years at the nearby Monastery of Yuste.

Lepe
Small town W of Huelva near the Portuguese frontier, famous because its wines were the precursors of sherry and were mentioned by Chaucer.

Mérida
Once the tenth city of the Roman Empire, Mérida, in the W of the province of Cáceres, is the best placed and most interesting town from which to visit the wine-growing areas of Extremadura. Its Roman remains, including a theater, a circus, an amphitheater, and a triumphal arch, as well as bridges, aqueducts and tesselated pavements, are among the most impressive in Europe. Both of its hotels, the 4-star Parador Nacional Via de la Plata and 3-star Emperatriz, are housed in historic buildings and offer regional wines and cooking.

Montánchez r. w. dr. ★→★★
This small village, high in the hills above Mérida, is remarkable for making a red wine which grows a *flor* in the manner of sherry. The wines, both red and white, are aged in earthenware *tinajas* (see NEW CASTILE-LA MANCHA) for about a year after vinification, when the yeasts appear on the surface. They emerge slightly turbid with a pronounced and aromatic sherry-like nose, and the "red" is in fact more of an orange color. Of 13–14.5% strength, they are usually drunk as apéritifs and may be sampled in the bars of Mérida.

Pulido Romero, Bodegas José r. p. w. dr. [★→★★]
Sizeable *bodega* in Medellín, the birthplace of Hernán Cortés, and maker of the better than average "Castillo de Medellín" in an area where most wine is either peasant-made for local consumption or produced in cooperatives for bulk shipment and blending.

Ruiz, Bodegas w. dr. [★★]
Cañamero (Cáceres). The only *bodega* of any size to bottle the individual *flor*-growing white CAÑAMERO. It may be sampled at the Parador or in the bars of nearby GUADALUPE.

Salas Acosta, Bodegas Miguel D.O. g. ★★
Bollullos del Condado (Huelva). D.O. Huelva. Family firm making some of the best of the sherry-like wines from the region.

Tierra de Barros D.O. r. w. dr. ★→★★
The newly demarcated Tierra de Barros, with 44,996ha (112,450 acres) under vines and centering on ALMENDRALEJO in the province of Badajoz, has the somewhat dubious distinction of making the cheapest wine in Spain, even exporting some of it to La Mancha! Some 75% of the grapes are Cayetán blanca, producing dry white wines, neutral in character without much acid and of 12–13.5%, whose main use, apart from current consumption, is for blending. The little village of Salvatierra de Barros on the verges of Portugal does, however, make small amounts of an aromatic and intensely colored red wine, prized by Spanish connoisseurs.

When General Junot sacked the Monastery of Alcántara in 1807 and ordered its medieval manuscripts to be used for making cartridges, one was salvaged and sent to the famous chef Escoffier, who commented that "it was the only positive advantage which France reaped from the [Peninsular] War". It contained the first directions for the use of truffles, still abundant in the region, and for making *pâté de foie gras.* Its pheasant Alcántara-style remains a classic recipe, but today the region is perhaps best known for its remarkable charcuterie – *chorizo* (pepper sausage), *jamón serrano* (cured ham) and the rest.

As regards the wines, the difficulty is to find the local growths in the better hotels and Paradors, which offer the standard list of Riojas. Nevertheless, the house wine at the Parador in Guadalupe is a thoroughly typical white Cañamero; at the Hotel Emperatriz in Mérida there is some choice of the better Extremaduran wines; and in hotels and restaurants generally, the carafe wine (when available) will probably be a sturdy red or white from Almendralejo.

Cochifrito
Lamb cooked and served in an earthenware dish with onions, garlic, paprika, freshly ground pepper, parsley and lemon juice.

Coliflor al estilo de Badajoz
Cauliflower, boiled and divided into florets, dredged in egg and breadcrumbs and then fried crisp in olive oil.

Ensalada de boquerones
Fresh anchovies, marinated in olive oil, vinegar, garlic, parsley and seasoning and eaten raw.

Frito típico extremeño
Kid fried with garlic, parsley, black pepper and bay leaves.

Huevos a la extremeña
A sauce is first made with olive oil, onions and fresh tomatoes, and to it are added boiled potatoes, chorizo, *ham and seasoning. The eggs are broken on the top and the dish finished in the oven.*

Huevos serranos
Large tomatoes, halved, scooped out and stuffed with chopped ham, then topped with fried eggs, sprinkled with grated cheese and browned in the oven.

Riñonada
A dish made with a mixture of lamb's kidneys and sweetbreads.

Solomillo de cordero
Lamb marinated with salt, pepper, olive oil and red wine, and cooked slowly with the liquid in a casserole.

Restaurants

Badajoz ⋆ *El Sotano* (best restaurant in the Extremadura; 4-year-old wines from Almendralejo).

Guadalupe ⋆*Hospedería del Real Monasterio* (typical dishes at moderate prices).

Huelva ⋆ *Los Gordos* (start with the Jabugo ham and continue with the mixed fried fish).

Jarandilla de la Vera *Parador Nacional Carlos V.*

Mérida *Hotel Emperatriz* (good range of regional wines); ⋆ *Parador Nacional Vía de la Plata* (the Parador has won various gastronomic awards for its cooking).

Galicia

Galicia, in the far NW of Spain, bounded to the S by Portugal and to the W and N by the Atlantic, comprises the provinces of La Coruña, Lugo, Pontevedra and Orense, of which only the two last produce significant amounts of wine. With its green hills, its chestnut forests, its unspoilt sandy coves and wide *Rias* (deep salt-water inlets like fjords), it is a romantic part of Spain. Its wines, too, will appeal to wine romantics; but the visitor may well come back disappointed, because so few of them are bottled commercially or are easily obtainable – except by Galician *cognoscenti.*

The granitic soils and wet climate are very similar to those of northern Portugal; and methods of viticulture, especially in the more westerly coastal districts, are strikingly alike, with high-climbing vines being trained away from the damp ground on chestnut stakes or grown in the form of a pergola along wires stretched from granite pillars. The wines often undergo a prolonged secondary or malo-lactic fermentation, which leaves them with a subdued and refreshing *pétillance.*

Many of the grape varieties are the same or akin to those of the

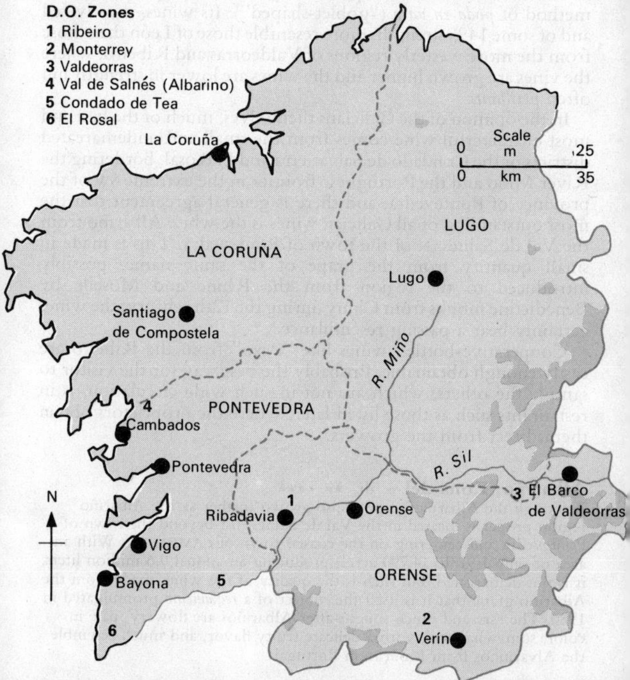

D.O. Zones
1 Ribeiro
2 Monterrey
3 Valdeorras
4 Val de Salnés (Albarino)
5 Condado de Tea
6 El Rosal

Vinho Verde area of Portugal, such as the Albariño (Alvarinho), Dona Branca, Espadeiro and Treixadira (Trajadura), so that it is hardly surprising that there should be a strong family resemblance between the wines from both sides of the Miño (or Minho) river. Having said as much, it must be pointed out that the Portuguese, with their numerous well-organized cooperatives and sophisticated private *adegas* (wineries), are much better organized and more scientific in their methods than the Galicians, and their wines are a great deal more consistent.

There are only six cooperatives in the whole of Galicia, and, even in two of the demarcated areas (Valdeorras and Monterrey), few private firms which bottle the local wine. The great bulk of them continue to be made in the simplest of *bodegas* by small proprietors, who sell them in the immediate vicinity. On balance, Galicia consumes more wine than it produces; and what has added to the natural difficulties of cultivating vines on the steep, terraced hill slopes is a persistent emigration from the region, especially to South America. In face of this, some of the larger private firms have taken to "stretching" the local wine, often flowery and fruity in flavor but distinctly acidic, with neutral white wines from La Mancha.

In a definitive study of the wines, *Os Viños de Galicia*, Xosé Posada has listed and described no less than 136 grape varieties grown in the area. The more important of them are mentioned in the A–Z listing in connection with the different regions. Of these, 3 have been demarcated, all in the province of Orense to the SE: Ribeiro, Valdeorras and Monterrey.

In Monterrey, the most easterly, the vines are grown low, *a la castellana*, as in most other parts of Spain, and are pruned by the method of *poda en vaso* ("goblet-shaped"). Its wines, mostly red and of some 14% strength, more resemble those of León than those from the more westerly regions of Valdeorras and Ribeiro, where the vines are grown higher and the wines are lower in strength and often *pétillants*.

In the opinion of the Galicians themselves, much of the best and most characterful wine comes from the small and undemarcated districts of the Condado de Salvatierra and El Rosal, bordering the River Miño and the Portuguese frontier in the extreme SW of the province of Pontevedra; and there is general agreement that the most outstanding of all Galician wines is the white Albariño from the Val de Salnés, N of the town of Pontevedra. This is made in small quantity from the grape of the same name, possibly introduced to the region from the Rhine and Moselle by Benedictine monks from Cluny during the 12th century; the wines certainly bear a passing resemblance.

Cooperative-bottled wines like "Pazo" from the Ribeiro are easily enough obtainable. Probably the best way for the visitor to sample the others, which are not in such wide circulation, is in restaurants such as those listed later, where the proprietors obtain them direct from the growers.

Albariño, Zona del w. dr. ★★→★★★
Although the Albariño grape is also grown further SE the Albariño region proper is located in the Val de Salnés just beyond the town of Pontevedra and centering on the coastal town of CAMBADOS. With an area of only 1,918ha (4,790 acres) producing an annual 9.6 million liters, it is not demarcated, but such is the quality of the wines made from the Albariño grape that it is itself the subject of a *reglamento* promulgated in 1980. The rare and much sought-after Albariños are flowery, pale in color, somewhat acid, with a delicate fruity flavor, and much resemble the Alvarinhos from Monção in Portugal.

"Albariño de Fefiñanes" w. dr. ★★★
This most famous of Albariños is made by the Marqués de Figueroa in a tiny *bodega* equipped with modern German presses and occupying a wing of the historic Palace of Fefiñanes on the outskirts of Cambados. Delicate, dry and fruity, it is not, however, *pétillant* like most Albariños, since all of his wines are aged in oak casks for 2 years, and the *reservas* for 6. It is therefore a deeper yellow, fuller in flavor and less acid than the typical wines from the area.

"Albariño del Palacio" w. dr. pt. ★★→★★★ DYA
Despite its name, this wine, made by a brother of the Marqués de Figueroa, is not from the Palace. Pale, flowery, extremely dry and somewhat acid, it is elegant and markedly *pétillant*.

Amandi cl. ★
According to tradition, the *claretes*, made exclusively from the Mencía grape, produced by this small village in the province of Lugo, were once favorites with Caesar Augustus, who drank them with his spiced lamprey.

Barco de Valdeorras, Cooperativa de D.O. r. w. dr. ★→★★
El Barco (Orense). D.O. Valdeorras. Apart from supplying wine in bulk, the cooperative bottles sizeable amounts of very drinkable dry red and white wine. Available in the U.K. and possibly soon to be shipped to Chicago, it is without *pétillance* and is sold as "Valdeorras tinto", "Valdeorras blanco" and "Moza Fresca".

Cambados
Small seaside town NW of Pontevedra and the only place of any size in the Zona del ALBARIÑO. The Parador del Albariño, near the sea in a garden shaded by eucalypts, is the pleasantest of places to stay and to sample the famous Albariños with the local shellfish and regional dishes.
Cambados celebrates an annual *Fiesta del Albariño* in mid-August, at which the wines are judged by expert tasters and are also available to the public.

Chaves, Bodegas w. dr. pt. ★★→★★★ 80, 81 DYA
Barrantes-Cambados (Pontevedra). Small family firm with its own vineyards and a *bodega* equipped with modern stainless steel fermentation and storage tanks and refrigeration equipment for precipitating tartrates. Most of its annual 30,000 bottles of good *pétillant* Albariño go to local hotels and restaurants, but its "Castel de Fornos" is one of the very few Galician wines available in the U.K.

Cosecheros del Vino del Ribeiro D.O. r. w. dr. ★
Ribadavia (Orense). D.O. Ribeiro. Bottlers of representative Ribeiro wines under the labels of "Ouro" and "Agarimo".

Gallega, Bodegas r. w. dr. cl. ★
Los Peares (Lugo). Because of emigration and of the difficult terrain in the steep valleys of the Miño and Sil, wine production in this area of Lugo has greatly declined, and the "Tres Rios" from this *bodega*, once produced locally, is now a blend of wines from León and La Mancha.

Larouco, Cooperativa de D.O. r. w. dr. ★
Larouco (Orense). D.O. Valdeorras. The cooperative bottles limited amounts of dry red and white Valdeorras, without *pétillance*, under the label "Silviño".

Miño, Condado de
See SALVATIERRA, CONDADO DE.

Miño, River
The Miño, rising to the N of Lugo, is the principal river of Galicia, flowing S through Orense and finally forming the northern border of Portugal, where it is known as the Minho.

Monterrey D.O. r. p. w. dr. ★
Small demarcated wine area in the S of the province of Orense,

centering on the valley of the River Támega and bordered by Portugal. It is sub-divided into the districts of Verín, Monterrey, Castrelo and Oimbra. Sheltered by the Sierra de Larouca, the vines grow low *a la castellana* and produce the strongest of Galician wines, of up to 14% strength. 70% of the wine is red and made from the Alicante negro, Garnacha, Tintorera (Mencía), Tinta fina, Tinta de Toro and Monstelo. The main white grapes are the Godello, Dona Branca and "Xerez" (Palomino). The most important producer is the Cooperativa de MONTERREY.

Monterrey, Cooperativa de D.O. r. p. w. dr. ★
Verín (Orense). D.O. Monterrey. The cooperative, founded in 1963, is, astonishingly, the only concern in the demarcated zone of Monterrey, in the S of Galicia near the Portuguese border, to bottle its wines. It makes fresh young red, rosé and white wines labeled as "Monterrey", and also a 2-year-old "Castillo de Monterrey".

Orense
Orense is the most southerly of the provinces of Galicia, bounded by Pontevedra to the W and Portugal to the S. It embraces the demarcated regions of RIBEIRO, VALDEORRAS and MONTERREY as well as some smaller undemarcated areas. Orense itself is not the most attractive of Galician towns, and it is pleasanter to stay in VERÍN or on the coast.

"Pazo" (r. p.) w. dr. ★→★★ DYA
One of the biggest-selling and most frequently encountered branded Galician wines; see BODEGA COOPERATIVA DE RIBEIRO.

Pontevedra
Province in the SW of Galicia, bordered by the R. Miño and Portugal to the S and by the Atlantic to the W. Its green and hilly coastline is deeply penetrated by the picturesque *Rías*, on one of which stands the port of Vigo. It is in this region that the high-climbing vines, trained on wires stretched between granite pillars, come into their own. Its wine-growing areas include EL ROSAL and the Condado de SALVATIERRA (also known as the Condado de Tea) along the Miño river in the S, and the Zona del ALBARIÑO in the Val de Salnés further N.

There is a Parador, housed in an old baronial house, in the historic old town of Pontevedra, and another at the frontier post of Tuy on the Portuguese border. The 4-star Parador Nacional Conde de Gondomar, S of Vigo on the coast, is one of the most luxurious in Spain. Situated in extensive grounds on a peninsula overlooking the Atlantic, its beaches, swimming pool, tennis courts and yachting basin make it an ideal place to combine a vacation with visits to the wine-growing areas.

Queimada See SPIRITS, AROMATIC WINES & LIQUEURS.

Ribeiro D.O. r. p. w. dr. pt. ★→★★
The most important wine-growing area in Galicia, situated in the W of the province of Orense in the basin of the River Avia. At a height of 100–300m. (330–1,000ft.) and with some 5,000ha (12,460 acres) under vines, it produced 37.3 million liters of wine in 1979. It is subdivided into three districts: Ribeiro de Avia, the oldest and most traditional area, making excellent white wines from Gomariz and reds from Beade, Regada and Costeira; Ribeiro del Miño, also producing good red and white wines; and Ribeiro de Arnoia, with its light and fragrant growths. The best of the white grapes are the Treixadura, Torrentés, Godello, Macabeo, Albilla and Loureiro, the Godello in particular giving the wines a fresh and fragrant nose. The best and most perfumed of the red wines are made from the Sonsón.

By far the largest producer is the Bodega Cooperativa de RIBEIRO. Other concerns not separately listed which bottle their wines are:
Alanis, Bodegas ("Alanis" and "Miñama")
Lorenzo, Bodegas Eloy ("Villa Paz")
Rivera, Bodegas ("Rexo" and "Antoxo")
Rofemar, Bodegas ("Saudade")
Ulloa, Marqués de ("Fino extra blanco")

Ribeiro, Bodega Cooperativa de D.O. r. p. w. pt. ⋆→⋆⋆
Ribadavia (Orense). D.O. Ribeiro. Situated in Ribadavia at the confluence of the Miño and Sil rivers, this is by far the largest cooperative in Galicia, with some 1,600 members. It is equipped with 300 concrete *depósitos* of up to 30,000 liters each, and modern equipment for vinifying, refrigerating and bottling the wine, and produces some 7 million liters annually with storage capacity for another 4 million.

The best of its wines, made with selected grapes, are sold under the label of "Pazo" (meaning a baronial house). The white is flowery, dry and not too acid, without much sparkle, and has won prizes in international exhibitions. The red is definitely *pétillant*, dry and astringent to a degree, and resembles the red *vinhos verdes* from over the border. The cooperative also bottles cheaper and less delicate wines under the labels of "Xeito" and "LAR".

Rodrigón
A post, usually made of chestnut, used for training the vines clear of the damp ground, especially in the more westerly districts of Galicia.

El Rosal (r.) w. dr. pt. ⋆
Small undemarcated area to the extreme SW of the province of Pontevedra near the mouth of the River Miño. Its high-growing vines produce an annual average of 1.5 million liters of wine, 65% of it white from the Albariño, Loureiro and Treixadura grapes – all familiar in the Minho across the border. The wines are *pétillant* and generally similar in type to the Portuguese *vinhos verdes*, but are made unscientifically by a host of small proprietors. For this reason, they are not as consistent, nor is its Albariños of the same quality, as those from CAMBADOS further N.

Rúa, Cooperativa de D.O. r. w. dr. ⋆
Rúa (Orense). D.O. Valdeorras. The cooperative sells most of its output in bulk, but bottles smaller quantities of red and white wine under the label of "Rúa".

Salvatierra, Condado de w. dr. cl. ⋆→⋆⋆
Also known as the Condado de Miño or Condado de Tea, this small undemarcated district, with 2,320ha (6,700 acres) under vines and an average annual output of 125,000 liters, lies in the S of the province of Pontevedra, flanking the R. Miño. The main grape varieties are the black Caiño, Brancellao, Espadeiro and Alicante; and the white Treixadura and Albariño. Connoisseurs of Galician wines consider that, with the Zona del ALBARIÑO, it produces the best and most typical wines of the whole region. They are typically *pétillant*, and the reds, which have been compared with clarets, predominate; but the difficulty is to find them, since none are bottled on a commerical scale.

Santiago de Compostela
Santiago lies to the NE of the Zona del ALBARIÑO, less than an hour's drive from CAMBADOS. It is the only city in Galicia with direct flights from Madrid, Barcelona and abroad; it possesses an old university, but most importantly it is the shrine of St. James the Apostle, the patron saint of Spain, whose remains are buried there, and from the 11th century onwards it has been the object of pilgrims from the length and breadth of Europe. Its cathedral is one of the most impressive in Spain, and the Hotel Reyes Católicos, installed in a 16th-century palace in the magnificent cathedral square, is among the most famous in the country.

Socalco
Name given to the steep hillside terraces in Galicia, sometimes so difficult of access that the peasants set up simple presses to vinify the wine *in situ*.

Tea, Condado de
See SALVATIERRA, CONDADO DE.

Tutor
Another name for the RODRIGÓN, a wooden post for supporting high-growing vines.

Val de Salnés
See ALBERIÑO, ZONA DE.

Valdeorras D.O. r. w. dr. ★→★★
The most easterly of the wine-growing areas of ORENSE, Valdeorras lies in the mountainous valley of the River Sil and comprises 3 sub-regions, those of Rúa-Petín, Larouco and El Barco de Valdeorras, each possessing its own cooperative. 90% of the white wine is made from the "Xerez" (a variety of the Palomino) and 80% of the red from the Garnacha de Alicante. The white wine is of 11–12%, clean and a little drier than that from Ribeiro; the red is cherry-colored, fragrant and of 11–12%.

By far the largest producer of bottled wine is the Cooperativa de BARCO DE VALDEORRAS.

Verín
Wine town in the SE of the province of Orense. The comfortable Parador Nacional de Monterrey, on a hill above the town and facing the Castle of Monterrey, offers local wines and food.

Vino de aguja
Term used to describe wines, like many of those from Galicia, with a slight *pétillance* resulting from a secondary malo-lactic fermentation. They are also known in Spain as *vinos verdes* – to the annoyance of the Portuguese, who have registered the description *vinho verde* or "green wine" with the O.I.V. (Office International du Vin).

WINE & Food

Galicia is famous for its *mariscos* or shellfish, which include mussels, lobsters, scallops, prawns, scampi in all shapes and sizes, clams, cockles, oysters, *percebes* (an edible barnacle) and *nécoras* (a species of spider crab). In seaside places you will often find *marisquerías* which serve nothing else, pricing the portions by weight. There are strong affinities with the cooking of northern Portugal, especially in the soups, rich fish stews and highly spiced tripe, hearty fare appropriate to the long wet winters.

As regards wine to go with this rich and nourishing assortment of dishes, the Galicians by preference drink a white Albariño with shellfish, which is perfectly matched by the acidity of the wine. The astringency of the red wines is a good counter to the richness and full flavor of the more substantial dishes.

Caldeirada gallega
Akin to the French bouillabaisse, *this is served in two parts: first the broth with slices of toast, and then the fish.*

Caldo gallego
A nourishing potage *made with ham bones and haricot beans.*

Callos a la gallega
Tripe with chick-peas, pig's trotters, paprika, chorizo *and hot seasoning.*

Centollo relleno/Changurro relleno
The meat from a spider crab is removed and boiled, then added to a mixture of cooked hake, onion, parsley, garlic and lemon juice. This is filled back into the shell, topped with breadcrumbs and grated cheese and browned in the oven.

Empanada gallega
Savory tart containing a variety of meat or fish with tomatoes, onions and chorizo. Xouba, *for example, is filled with small sardine-like fish; and* Raxo *with loin of pork.*

Filloas
Thick, fluffy pancakes, usually rolled and filled with jam.

Lacón con grelos
Ham bones cooked with chorizo *and sprouting turnip tops.*

Lamprea a la gallega
Lamprey prepared with shallots, garlic, olive oil, vinegar, sweet paprika, cinnamon and white wine.

Merluza al hinojo
Hake cooked with fennel.

Pato al estilo de Ribadeo
Duck cooked with turnips, orange segments, carrots, boiled chestnuts, porkmeat, white wine, anís *and a* bouquet garni.

Rape al queso
Angler fish baked with grated cheese.

Salsa zalpiscada
Sauce made with hard-boiled eggs, onion, garlic, vinegar, olive oil and seasoning. It is served with fish and shellfish.

Tarta de almendras
Almond tart.

Tarta de Puentedeume
A tart made with almonds, sugar and yolks of egg.

Vieiras al Albariño
Scallops marinated in Albariño wine, then seasoned with parsley, garlic and nutmeg, and sprinkled with breadcrumbs before being browned in the oven or under the grill.

Restaurants

Cambados ** *O'Arco* (near the Palace of Fefiñanes; shellfish, regional dishes and Albariño wines).

Orense * *Sanmiguel* (regional food, Ribeiro and Condado wines).

Pontevedra ** *Casa Solla* (seafood and Albariño wines).

Santiago de Compostela ** *Vilas* (regional cooking and wines); * *Chita* (well-prepared regional food, Ribeiro and Albariño house wines).

Vigo ** *El Mosquito* (especially for fish and shellfish); ** *Puesto Piloto Alcabre* (beach restaurant, fish and regional dishes, Albariño and Condado house wines).

Villagarcia de Argosa, near Pontevedra *** *Chocolate* (best restaurant in Galicia, with splendid wine list).

Málaga

Sweet wines from Málaga were already famous in Roman times, and reached the zenith of their popularity during the 19th century, when the largest exports were to North America. In common with other sweet dessert wines, their popularity has declined, and the explosive development of the tourist industry along the Costa del Sol has taken its toll of vineyards and *bodegas*. In 1829 production amounted to some 17.5 million liters, whereas in 1979 the amount of wine qualifying for Denominación de Origen was only 8.2 million liters. Nevertheless, Málaga at its best remains a glorious wine; and not all of it, in fact, is sweet.

The grapes are grown in two areas of the surrounding hills, one to the N of the city and neighboring the D.O. Montilla-Moriles, and the other to the E. Because of the mountainous terrain, especially in the eastern area of Axarquia, where access to the small vineyards is often only by way of rough tracks, most of the wine is vinified on the spot; but it must be matured in one of the large *bodegas* of Málaga itself to qualify for Denominación de Origen.

In the sheltered S of the area, the climate is mild, warm and predictable; in the N there are sharp frosts in winter and the summers are short and very hot. Most of the rainfall is in winter, and is usually torrential while it lasts – conditions ideal for vines and for "sunning" grapes destined for dessert wines.

In days past, there was a profusion of vine varieties, including the Moscatel, Pedro Ximénez, Airén, Moscatel Morisco, Romé, Jaén blanco, Jaén tinto and Jaén doradillo. However, in 1876 Málaga was one of the first areas in Spain to suffer from phylloxera – probably introduced direct from America – and many of the old varieties have disappeared. Today, the Consejo Regulador authorizes only the Pedro Ximénez and Moscatel for new plantations.

The must is usually fermented in cement containers resembling the earthenware *tinajas* of Montilla or Valdepeñas (see NEW

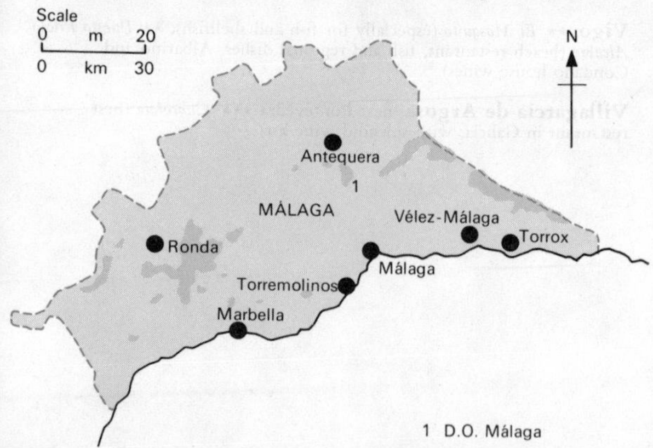

CASTILE-LA MANCHA), but larger, cylindrical in shape and reinforced with steel rods. On its arrival by road tanker in Málaga it is blended according to type, refrigerated to precipitate tartrates and then matured in *soleras* like those of Jerez (see SHERRY), the older wine being "refreshed" with the younger. Although some of the grapes are so sweet as to leave residual sugar in the must after fermentation is complete, an *arrope*, or syrup, made by boiling down unfermented must, is often added.

There are many different styles of Málaga, separately described in the A–Z listing. The most common is the *dulce color*, dark amber in color, full-bodied and sweet (sometimes cloyingly so) right through to the end; but there are others, more resembling tawny port, with a bitter-sweet flavor and dryish finish.

A number of the leading *bodegas* and their wines are separately described; the full list of firms which export wines with Denominación de Origen is:

Barceló S.A., Hijos de Antonio
Barceló S.A., Luis
Campos Sanchez, Manuel
Campos Sanchez, Rafael
Flores Hermanos S.A.
García Gomara S.L.
Garijo Ruiz, José
I.B.A. S.A.
Larios S.A.
López García, Salvador
López Hermanos S.A.
López Madrid, Antonio
Montealegre S.L., Bodegas
Mory & Cía., S.A., Juan
Pedra-Za Olmedo S.L., Augustín
Pérez Texeira S.A.
Rein Segura, Guillermo
Romero S.L., Casa
Sanchez Ajofrin S.L., José L.
Sanchez Sanchez y Cía., Juan
Scholtz Hermanos S.A.
Suárez Villalba, Hijos de José
Tinoco, Bodegas
Vinicola Andalucía S.A.

Antequera

The old town of Antequera lies N of Málaga on the winding uphill road to Córdoba and Sevilla and on the southern fringe of one of the two main vineyard areas of the D.O. MÁLAGA. This northern area, at a height of some 500m. (1,650ft.) is a limestone region, and the predominant grape is the Pedro Ximénez.

The Albergue Nacional de Carratera, government-run but simpler than a Parador, is nevertheless a pleasant place to spend a night in the area, and the cooking in its restaurant is both inventive and local.

Arrope

A syrup used in certain Málagas, made by evaporating down unfermented must in a copper pan, and adding alcohol to prevent subsequent fermentation. A dark treacle color, it tastes of caramel.

Axarquia

The second and larger of the vineyard areas of the D.O. Málaga, to the E of the city and stretching back from Vélez-Málaga and Torrox near the coast into the mountains, which rise sharply to a height of some 2,000m. (1,650ft.). The soils are a mixture of decomposed slate and a limestone clay, and its 12,773ha (31,320 acres) of vineyards are planted with 90% Moscatel. There are three bands: some 4,000ha (9,600 acres) near the coast, used mainly for growing dessert grapes; an intermediate zone of 7,000ha (17,100 acres) producing raisins; and a higher and more northerly strip of some 2,000ha (4,850 acres) where most of the grapes are vinified. There is some overlap in the usage of the fruit, and about 10% of the total crop is converted into wine.

Barceló S.A., Luis

Málaga. D.O. Málaga. A firm specializing in *vinos quinados* (see SPIRITS, AROMATIC WINES & LIQUEURS), tonic or medicated wines popular in Spain and containing quinine extract.

Barceló S.A., Hijos de Antonio

Málaga. D.O. Málaga. Large family firm founded in 1876 and the biggest exporter of Málaga wines, to Europe and North and South America. The wines are marketed under the name "Bacarles" and include "Cream", "Lágrima", "Moscatel", "Gran Vino Sanson", "Gran Vino de Honor" (Pedro Ximénez), "Muscat Minerva", the very old "Muscat Los Frailes" and another typically rich and sweet Pedro Ximénez wine, the "Gran Málaga Solera Vieja". The firm also produces *vinos quinados* (see SPIRITS, AROMATIC WINES & LIQUEURS) and has begun making table wines in the Ribera del Duero and the Rioja.

Baumé scale
As Málagas are sweet wines, one needs to refer to degrees Baumé, a measurement of the sugar content of wines. As a guide, 2° Baumé corresponds to 20.3g/liter of sugar; 4°, to 54.6g/liter; 6°, to 91.4g/liter; 8°, to 144.6g/liter; and 10°, to 169.8g/liter.

Blanco Seco
The least known of the styles of Málaga, this is made by fermenting out Pedro Ximénez musts to completion. Yellow or pale gold in color according to age, it resembles certain Montillas and is dry and aromatic with the nutty flavor of a good *amontillado* (see SHERRY) and of 15–22% strength.

Borge
One of the main vineyard areas of the AXARQUIA to the NE of Málaga, with 1,175ha (2,900 acres) under vines.

Cono
A large wooden vat, so called because of its truncated conical shape, in which the wine is first stored when it is brought down to Málaga.

Dulce color
The most familiar style of Málaga, sweetened with ARROPE, to which it owes its dark amber color, the hint of treacle in the nose and high Baumé degree of 8–12°. The alcohol content ranges from 14–23%.

Lágrima
The word means a "tear" and is used to describe the choicest and most luscious of the wines, made with the juice which emerges from the grapes without the use of mechanical means and simply as a result of the pressure from the grapes at the top of the load. It therefore comes from the pulp nearest the skins of the ripest grapes, and is vinified separately from the *yema* (or "yolk") obtained by further light pressing. The wines are old gold in color, very fully bodied, with an aromatic *oloroso* nose and long sweet finish. The degree Baumé is 6–10° and the alcohol content between 14–23%.

Lágrima Cristi
Sweeter variant of LÁGRIMA, of 8–12° Baumé and 15–18% strength.

Larios S.A.
Málaga. D.O. Málaga. A household word in Spain for its gin, Larios also makes good Málagas, especially the aromatic, fruity and honey-like "Colmenares Moscatel".

Málaga
The city of Málaga lies on the coast at some distance from the vineyards in the hills behind it, but to qualify for Denominación de Origen the musts have either to be vinified in one of its *bodegas* or, as is more usual, brought there for blending and maturation. Its historic buildings are not of great interest, and at first sight it seems that little remains of the romantic city sung of by Lorca only 50 years ago. The inexorable pressure of tourism has ringed it with high-rise vacation apartments and squeezed out the old *bodegas* into a peripheral no-man's land. But the port remains, and, behind the port, a network of narrow streets clustering around the market, some closed to traffic with restaurant tables on the pavement and dark, cavernous bars where one may settle down to serious tasting of Málagas in all their variety. Most of its hotels are geared to the package holiday industry, and since the demise of the splendid Miramar the quietest place to stay is at the Parador Nacional de

Gibralfaro, set amongst pines and eucalypts on a hill rising abruptly above the center.

Mollina
The most important of the vineyards in the northern zone, beyond ANTEQUERA, with 732ha (1,790 acres) under vines.

Moscatel
As the name implies, a style of Málaga made solely with Moscatel grapes, from the AXARQUIA. The color varies according to age from golden yellow to light golden brown, and the wines are soft and sweet, with a deep and fruity Moscatel nose. Degree Baumé varies from 6–13° and alcohol content from 15–20%.

"Mountain Wine"
Soubriquet for Málaga in its Victorian heyday. You can occasionally find silver wine labels with this name in antique shops.

Pajarete
A dry or semi-dry style of Málaga, amber or dark amber in color with a reddish cast. It contains 15–20% of alcohol, and Baumé is 2–6°.

Pedro Ximénez
A style of Málaga made solely with Pedro Ximénez grapes from the northern zone. When fully mature it is a dark treacly color with yellow rim and intense *oloroso* nose, and is full-bodied and very soft with a bitter-sweet finish. The degree Baumé is from 6–13° and the alcohol content 16–20%.

Pérez Texeira S.A.
Málaga. D.O. Málaga. The most outstanding wine from this *bodega* is the "Lágrima Viejo", made with musts obtained without mechanical pressing of the grapes.

Romé
These wines, made from the Romé grape, may be either red or gold in color with a degree Baumé of 2–8° and 15–20% of alcohol.

Semi-dulce
As the name indicates, one of the drier styles of Málaga, either golden yellow or ruby in color. The wines are bitter-sweet, with a full dry finish and deep *oloroso* nose. The degree Baumé ranges from 2–4° and the alcoholic strength from 16–23%.

Scholtz Hermanos S.A.
Málaga. D.O. Málaga. One of the best and most famous of the *bodegas*, the firm was founded in 1807, but changed its name in 1885 when it passed into German control, reverting to Spanish ownership after World War II. The vinification plant is at MOLLINA, but the wine is brought to the *bodega* itself to be matured. This was formerly in the center of the city, but now occupies modern premises on the outskirts with capacity for making 2 million liters of wine annually, of which half is exported. Among its 18 or so styles of wine are the dry "Seco Añejo 10-year-old", "Moscatel Palido", "Málaga Dulce Negro" and "Lágrima 10-year-old", but the best known is the "Solera Scholtz 1885". The date is of no particular significance, and it is in fact made with 10% of a near black Solera 1787 Pedro Ximénez "Lágrima Bisabuelo", 10% "Montilla Añejo", and 80% "Amontillado Viejo". Old gold in color, with overtones of good tawny port and *oloroso*, it is a complex and intensely fruity wine, with a bitter-sweet taste and long dry finish, and of 18% strength.

Tintillo
A red Málaga of 6–10° Baumé containing 15–18% of alcohol.

Vélez-Málaga
Principal town in the wine-growing area of AXARQUIA, E of Málaga and just back from the coast towards the hills. The pleasantest place to stay is at the Parador in Nerja, beautifully situated above the shore.

WINE & Food

On gastronomic maps of Spain, Andalucía is often labeled the *zona de los fritos* or "region of fried food", and high on the list of such dishes must come the fries of mixed fish, equally good around Málaga or in Cádiz and the sherry region. The shellfish is varied and abundant; and another great speciality are the *gazpachos* or cold soups, always containing garlic and a little olive oil and vinegar, but made with a variety of vegetables, chopped or puréed.

Málaga is not, of course, for drinking with a meal, but afterwards; the *blanco seco* is an unusual variant on *amontillado* as an apéritif.

Ajo blanco con uvas de Málaga
A cold soup made with almonds, garlic, vinegar and olive oil, together with white grapes, skinned and without pips.

Dulce malagueño
A sweet made with semolina, yolks of egg, sugar, raisins and membrillo, *a quince paste.*

Frito de pescados a la andaluza
A mixed fry of small fish, sometimes dipped in seasoned flour or maybe dredged in egg and breadcrumbs, and are then fried in hot olive oil. Fish such as chanquetes *(akin to whitebait),* boquerones *(fresh anchovies), or inkfish cut into rings are also fried and served by themselves.*

Moraga de sardinas Motril
Fresh sardines with salt, olive oil, white wine, lemon juice, parsley and garlic.

Raya en pimentón
Skate cooked with sweet paprika.

Salsa andaluza
Sauce made with pumpkins, tomatoes, pepper and garlic.

Sopa al cuarto de hora
A soup so called because of the cooking time of 15 minutes, and containing chopped ham, clams, hard-boiled eggs, onion, parsley, garlic and bread.

Sopa de almendras de Ronda
A sweet soup containing pounded almonds, sugar, a stick of cinnamon and grated lemon peel, with thin slices of bread.

Tarta helada
Sweet made with layers of sponge cake and ice cream.

Tortilla al Sacramonte
Omelette originating from the gypsy quarter of Granada and containing lamb's brains, sweetbreads, fresh peppers, potatoes and toasted breadcrumbs.

Restaurants

Antequera *Albergue Nacional de Carretera* (inventive Andalucian food).

Málaga ⋆ *Escorpio* (near the Parador, sophisticated French-style cuisine with local ingredients); *Casa Pedro* (on the shore, mixed fried fish and first-rate shellfish).

There are also scores of good restaurants, some outstanding, in places like Marbella and Torremolinos, in the Costa del Sol resorts.

Montilla-Moriles

Montilla-Moriles, one of the hottest and sunniest parts of Spain, lies in hilly country S of Córdoba. It makes wines of the sherry type matured in *solera*, and until it was demarcated in 1945 much of its wine was in fact shipped to Jerez for blending. Large quantities of sweet Pedro Ximénez wine are still, legitimately, supplied to the sherry *bodegas* for making sweet *olorosos* and cream sherries.

The best of its soils is the chalky white *albero* resembling the *albariza* of Jerez; but by far the most predominant grape is not the Palomino, but the Pedro Ximénez, picked here when fully ripe, but while still waxy white, and fermented to completion without sunning. Other grapes, used in smaller amounts, are the white Airén, Baladí and Moscatel. The yield from the low-pruned vines is small, and with 18,245ha (45,000 acres) under cultivation, 75% of the area of vines of Jerez, the region produces only 50% of the volume of the sherry area.

The main difference between the making of sherry and Montilla is that in Montilla-Moriles the must is fermented in the pear-shaped earthenware *tinajas*, also typical of MÁLAGA and La Mancha (see NEW CASTILE-LA MANCHA). When the wine "falls bright", some months after completion of its secondary fermentation, it is transferred to a *solera*, operated in almost exactly the same fashion as those in Jerez, except that the musts are so rich in sugar that they produce wines a little higher in alcohol and rarely require fortification.

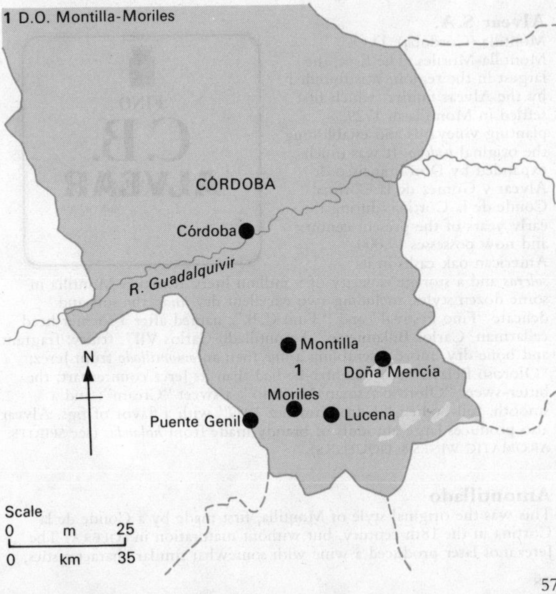

1 D.O. Montilla-Moriles
CÓRDOBA
Córdoba
R. Guadalquivir
N
Montilla
1
Doña Mencía
Moriles
Puente Genil
Lucena
Scale
0 m 25
0 km 35

As in Jerez, the musts are classified by the cellar master and emerge as one or other of the styles familiar in Jerez: *fino, amontillado, palo cortado, oloroso*, etc. (see the A–Z listing for details). The style for which the region is best known is the light, aromatic and very dry *fino*, which is made from the first pressing of the grapes and develops a vigorous *flor*. The *olorosos* are made from a must obtained by a second and firmer pressing.

It should be mentioned that some years ago the sherry shippers brought a legal action in England, contesting the use of the terms *fino* and *amontillado* as descriptions of Montilla – ironically, as it happens, since, in the first place, the Jerezanos borrowed the name "amontillado" from Montilla. For this reason, Montilla on sale in the U.K. is often labeled "fine dry", "medium" and "cream".

Although the wines are of excellent quality and very competitively priced, Montilla has experienced some difficulty in selling them abroad in competition with the more firmly entrenched sherries; and three of the best-known firms, Cobos, Cruz Conde and Montialbero, closed down in 1981 – sadly, because Cobos was for long rated among the best of Montillas.

The largest of the firms, Alvear, exports some 25% of its production, and Montecristo, a firm within the RUMASA group, some 50%. The most important foreign markets are Britain, with 62%, and the Netherlands, with 29% of exports.

As the Montillas are a distinct, identifiable style of wine as well as a geographical area, the headline symbols are omitted in this chapter.

Albero
The best of the soils, containing between 30–60% chalk. It is most widespread in the *sierras* of Montilla and Alto Moriles, where most of the large *bodegas* have vineyard holdings. Production is higher in the lower-lying areas, but the wines are not of the same alcoholic degree or quality.

Alvear S.A.
Montilla (Córdoba). D.O. Montilla-Moriles. The firm, the largest in the region, was founded by the Alvear family, which first settled in Montilla in 1729, planting vineyards and establishing the original *bodega*. It was much expanded by Don Francisco de Alvear y Gómez de la Cortina, Conde de la Cortina, during the early years of the present century and now possesses 17,000 American oak casks in its *soleras* and a storage capacity of 5 million liters. It makes Montilla in some dozen styles, including two excellent dry *finos*, the soft and delicate "Fino Festival" and " Fino C.B.", named after a former head cellarman, Carlos Billanueva; "Amontillado Carlos VII", fruity, fragrant and bone dry, more resembling a *fino* than an *amontillado* from Jerez; "Oloroso Pelayo Seco", lighter-bodied than its Jerez counterpart; the bitter-sweet "Oloroso Asman Abocado"; a sweet "Cream"; and a smooth, full-bodied "Pedro Ximénez 1927" with a flavor of figs. Alvear also produces large amounts of brandy made from *holandas* (see SPIRITS, AROMATIC WINES & LIQUEURS).

Amontillado
This was the original style of Montilla, first made by a Conde de la Cortina in the 18th century, but without maturation in SOLERA. The Jerezanos later produced a wine with somewhat similar characteristics,

but aged it in *solera*; and the *bodegueros* from Montilla subsequently followed suit. *Amontillados* from Montilla are of 16–22% strength, amber-colored, full on the palate and with a pungent, nutty nose.

Aragón y Cía S.A.
Lucena (Córdoba). D.O. Montilla-Moriles. Well known firm whose wines include the "Moriles 47", "Pacorrito", "Boabdil", "Moriles" *palo cortado* and "Araceli" Pedro Ximénez.

Benavides
Its vineyards are among the best in the Moriles area.

Carbonell y Cía S.A.
Córdoba. D.O. Montilla-Moriles. This large company, also one of the largest producers of olive oil in Spain, makes its wines in the demarcated region of Montilla-Moriles, but matures them in the *soleras* of its *bodega* in Córdoba. Among its labels are: "Moriles", "Serranía" and "Monte Corto" *finos*; "Moriles Superior" *amontillado fino*; "Flor de Montilla" *amontillado pasado*; "Néctar" *oloroso* and a "Pedro Ximénez".

Córdoba
A little to the N of the D.O. Montilla-Moriles, Córdoba is the headquarters of some dozen firms which maintain *bodegas* and *soleras* in the city for maturing their wines.

For 300 years, until the Caliphate disintegrated in 1031, Córdoba was the capital of Moorish Spain; and the Great Mosque, now the cathedral, resembling nothing so much as a cool grove of palm trees with its myriad arches and columns, was the most important in Western Islam and second only in size to that of Mecca. Other Moorish survivals are the 14th-century Alcázar or fortified palace, with its mosaics and gardens, and the Judería or ancient Jewish quarter, a maze of narrow alleys, criss-crossing at random and providing shelter from the sun.

About half-an-hour's drive from Montilla, Córdoba, with its historic interest and restaurants, is the obvious base for a visit to the region. It possesses a number of good hotels, including the 4-star Gran Capitán and Meliá Córdoba, and the 3-star Maimónides opposite the Mosque; but perhaps the quietest and most relaxing resting place is the spacious and comfortable modern Parador Nacional de la Aruzafa, looking down on the city from the N.

Firms with bodegas in Córdoba making D.O. Montilla-Moriles and not separately listed, are:

Alarcón Constant, Antonio
Campos de Córdoba S.A.
Carmen Flores S.A.
Miguel Velasco Chacón S.A.
Moreno S.A.
Quintela Luque, Bodegas
Ramiro Rodriguez, Alfonso
Raya Raya y Hnos., F. Jesús
Sanchez Aroca S.A.

Doña Mencia
Village to the SE of Montilla with 3 concerns making D.O. wines:

Crismona S.A., Bodegas
Luque S.A., Bodegas
Miguel Lama S.A.

El Bombo
One of the best vineyard areas near MORILES.

El Naranjo
Another favored vineyard area near MORILES.

Fino
Pale and dry with a greenish tint, slightly bitter, and light and fragrant on the palate, the unfortified *fino*, containing between 14–17.5% alcohol, is the best known of the styles of Montilla.

Gálves
Village in the Sierra de Montilla renowned for its vineyards.

Gracia Hermanos S.A.
Montilla (Córdoba). D.O. Montilla-Moriles. Family firm making traditional and good quality Montillas, now available in the U.K. under the labels of "Kiki Pale Dry", "Montiole Medium Dry" and "Ben Hur Rich Cream".

La Tercia
Well-known vineyard area near Moriles.

Lucena
Pleasant little town SE of Montilla and halfway between Córdoba and Antequera. Apart from wine, it produces olive oil and is known for its decorative metalwork. In addition to ARAGÓN Y CÍA, Lucena numbers 7 other bodegas making D.O. wines:

Aguilar Ecija, Laureano
Castroviejo y del Campo S.L.
Mora Chacón S.A.
Mora Cuenca, Ma. del Carmen
Mora Romero, José
Moran Cabrera, José
Torres Burgos S.A.

Monte Cristo S.A.
Montilla (Córdoba). D.O. Montilla-Moriles. Large company, now within the RUMASA group, whose products are well known abroad as they account for some 60% of British imports of Montilla and also exporting to the U.S.A.: "Dry", "Medium", "Pale Cream" and "Cream".

Montilla
Together with the nearby village of MORILES, this quiet hill town, the Munda Betica of the ancients and birthplace of Gonzalo de Córdoba, the Great Captain, numbers among its attractions the charming early 18th-century house of the Alvear family, with its splendid arcaded patio. Montilla is the wine center of the region, and possesses some 20 *bodegas* making D.O. wines. Apart from those listed separately and the well-known firms of Cobos and Montialbero, which have sadly closed, these are:

Bellido y Carrasco S.A.
Cía. Vinícola del Sur S.A.
Conde de la Cortina S.A.
Cooperativa Agrícola Ntra. Sra. de la Aurora
Espejo S.A., Bodegas
José Jaime Ruz S.A.
Laguna Naranjo, Enrique
Luque Ruz Bodegas
Marquez Panadero S.A., Bodegas
Mendez y Cobos S.A.
Miguel Baena S.A.
Montimor S.A.
Montisol S.A.
Ortiz Ruiz y Ortiz, Luis
Pérez Barquero y Manjón, Carmen
Robles Carbonero, Francisco
Tomas García S.A.

There is a 3-star hotel, the Don Gonzalez, just outside Montilla on the road to Antequera.

Montulia S.A., Bodegas
Montilla (Córdoba). D.O. Montilla-Moriles. Long-established and well-known maker of some dozen styles of Montilla, including "Montilla J.R. Fino", *amontillado*, Pedro Ximénez, and an excellent *palo cortado*. The firm also makes brandy and *anís*.

Moriles
Although famous for its wines, Moriles remains only a tiny village on a by-road some 20km (12 miles) S of MONTILLA. Although it lies at the center of some of the best vineyards in the region, there are only 2 *bodegas* in Moriles itself:

Fernándo Varo y Hnos.
F. Ojeda Lopez, Antonio y J. Y. F. Ojeda Corpas

Navarro S.A., Bodegas
Montilla (Córdoba). D.O. Montilla-Moriles. Sizeable exporter among whose wines are "Navarro Amontillado", "Montilla Fino Solear Especial", "Moriles Fino", "Fino Andaluz", "Solera Fina", "Solera Flor", "Oloroso", "Pedro Ximénez", and also "La Aurora", "Viejo Navarro", "Selecto Navarro" and "Solera 1830".

Oloroso
Style of wine resembling its counterpart from Jerez (see SHERRY), with 16–18% of alcohol, rising to 20% when very old, mahogany-colored, full-bodied, soft and highly aromatic; it can be either dry or with a hint of sweetness.

Palo cortado
Of 16–18%, this is a style combining the nutty bouquet of *amontillado* with the unmistakable flavor of *oloroso*.

Pedro Ximénez
A sweet wine with high alcoholic degree, taking its name from the vine, made in part with sunned grapes, of dark ruby color and containing at least a massive 272g/liter of sugar.

Pérez Barquero S.A.
Montilla (Córdoba). D.O. Montilla-Moriles. Another of RUMASA's acquisitions in Montilla. Its wines are available in the U.K. as "Don Roger" fine dry, medium dry, pale cream and cream.

Pozo Baena, Juan de
Córdoba. D.O. Montilla-Moriles. One of the firms which maintains *soleras* in Córdoba for maturing its wines, which include "Filigrana Moriles", "Filigrana Montilla", "Los Timbales", "Oloroso Viejo" and "Pedro Ximénez".

Puente Genil
Small town SW of Montilla. As well as its wines, it also enjoys fame as the chief producer of *membrillo,* the quince paste so popular in Spain. It is the headquarters of 6 *bodegas*:

Conde de los Moriles, Bodegas
Cooperativa Vitivinícola de la Purísima
Delgado Hermanos S.L.
Melero Muñoz, Damaso
Hijos de Enrique Reina S.R.C.
Varo Campos, Antonio

Raya
A style of Montilla similar to OLOROSO, but with less flavor and bouquet.

Ruedo
This is not a Montilla proper, but a dry, pale and light white wine containing about 14% of alcohol and made without maturation in a *solera*.

Los Ruedos de Montilla
Its grapes are among the best from the Sierra de Montilla.

Solera
An assembly of 500-liter butts used for maturing the wine. As in Jerez (see SHERRY), the butts are loosely stoppered and arranged in "scales" containing progressively older wine, and when wine is drawn off for shipment or bottling, the final "scale" is "refreshed" with younger wine. A Montilla *solera* usually contains five "scales" for the *finos* and four for the *olorosos.* The *soleras* are operated almost exactly like those in Jerez, except that the musts are brandied only in occasional years when they are low in alcohol.

Tinajas
The large, pear-shaped earthenware vessels used for fermenting the wine. The tops are left open during the first stages of fermentation and later covered with wooden lids. Once the wine clears after completion of the secondary fermentation, it is racked and transferred to a SOLERA for maturation. In the larger, more modern *bodegas, tinajas* are being replaced with bigger cylindrical vessels of reinforced cement.

See also NEW CASTILE-LA MANCHA and MÁLAGA.

Zona del Albero
Name given to the area around MORILES, whose soils are particularly rich in the chalky ALBERO.

WINE & Food

With local variations, the food from the Córdoban area and Montilla-Moriles is that of Andalucía as a whole, and many of the typical dishes are described under JEREZ and MÁLAGA. Although Córdoba is not near the coast like the other two regions, the restaurants serve a variety of shellfish, and mixed fries of fish are also popular. It is usual to begin with a glass of chilled *fino* Montilla, often served with *aceitunas aliñadas* or king-sized olives, and to continue drinking it throughout the meal.

Brazo de gitano
Popular sweet made with eggs, flour and jam, and resembling a Swiss roll.

Callos a la andaluza
Tripe stewed with calf's feet and chick-peas.

Caracoles a la andaluza
Snails cooked with garlic, toasted almonds, sweet paprika, tomatoes, onions, white pepper and lemon.

Huevos a la flamenca
Eggs cooked in an earthenware dish with onions, ham and sliced tomato, and decorated with prawns, slices of chorizo, *asparagus tips and red pepper.*

Membrillo
A sweet quince paste, served on its own as a sweet or with cheese.

Perdices a la torera
"Bullfighters' partridge", garnished with ham, anchovies, green peppers and tomatoes.

Polvorones
A dry, powdery sweetmeat, a speciality of Estepa, just W *of Montilla-Moriles, made with flour, pork fat, caster sugar and cinnamon, and often served with sherry or Montilla.*

Rabo de toro
Popular Córdoban stew of oxtail with vegetables.

Revuelto de aspárragos trigueros
Scrambled eggs with young asparagus.

Salmorejo
A thick Córdoban variation of gazpacho *(see* SHERRY*), made with garlic, olive oil and breadcrumbs, but without peppers or tomatoes.*

Salsa de patatas
A sauce from the Sierra Morena, N *of Córdoba, made with fried purée potatoes, peppers, bay leaf, cumin, olive oil and seasoning, and served with fish.*

Ternera con alcachofas a la cordobesa
Veal served with artichokes and cooked with Montilla and seasoning.

Tocino de cielo
A sweet popular throughout Andalucía and made with eggs and sugar flavored with a vanilla pod.

Restaurants

Córdoba ★★★ *El Caballo Rojo* (facing the Mosque, sophisticated Andalucian cooking); *Almudaima* (Cordoban cooking, which hardly rises to the charming surroundings); *Pepe "El de la Judería"* (small bullfighters' haunt in the old Jewish quarter with delicious and reasonably priced *tapas*).

Montilla *Las Carmachas* (formerly owned by the Cobos family and known for its regional cooking, this restaurant is undergoing a period of readjustment under new management).
See also MALAGA/Antequera.

Navarra

Navarra, to the W of Catalonia and extending from the Pyrenees to the Ebro basin, was a kingdom in its own right until it fell to Ferdinand the Catholic in 1512. At one time it extended over the Pyrenees, hence the alternative spelling of "Navarre" for the portion now lying in France.

It is a province with wide variations in climate between the sub-humid conditions of the mountainous N and the dry, Mediterranean-like climate of central and southern Spain which is felt in the Ebro in S Navarra. The soils are in general chalky, with deposits of silt and gravel along the river valleys, and are well suited to viticulture.

The wine-growing districts extend S from the provincial capital, Pamplona, and were demarcated in 1967. The D.O. Navarra is further sub-divided into the *comarcas* of Baja Montaña, Valdizarbe, Tierra de Estella, Ribera Alta and Ribera Baja, with a combined area of 27,359ha (67,100 acres) under vines and an output in 1979 of 83 million liters of wine. The small area of the Rioja Baja spilling

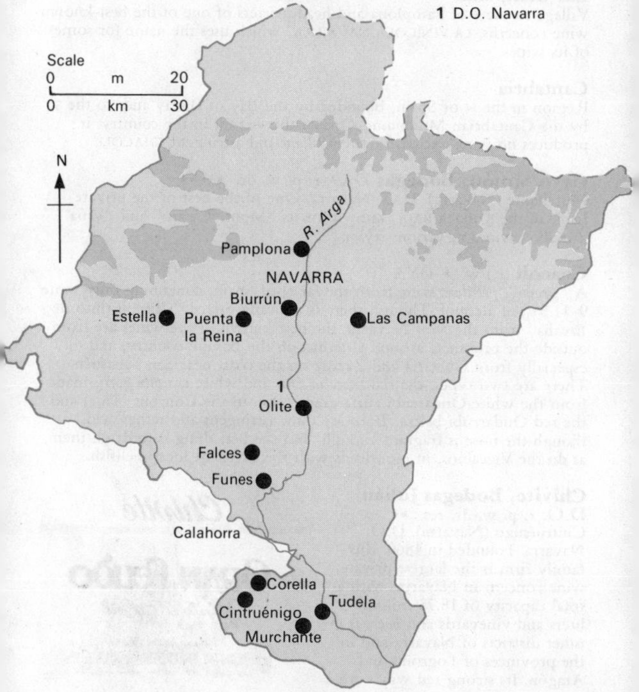

1 D.O. Navarra

Scale
0 m 20
0 km 30

N

R. Arga
Pamplona
NAVARRA
Biurrún
Estella
Puenta la Reina
Las Campanas
1
Olite
Falces
Funes
Calahorra
Corella
Cintruénigo
Tudela
Murchante

into the province of Navarra and including the town of San Adrián is separately described (see RIOJA).

The predominant grape is the black Garnacha tinta, but smaller amounts of the other grapes typical of the neighboring Rioja are also grown. These are the black Tempranillo, Graciano and Mazuelo, and the white Viura, Malvasía and Garnacha blanca.

Navarra has been a prolific producer of sturdy red wines since Roman times, and they are said to have been favorites of Catherine the Great of Russia in the early 18th century. In general, they resemble the stouter and fuller-bodied of the Garnacha wines from the Rioja Baja; those from the Ribera Baja in the S are even stronger and more robust and akin to those from Borja (see ARAGÓN). The wines from the best of the *bodegas* in the cooler N, while still containing some 13–14% of alcohol, can fairly be compared with good quality Rioja.

Like Aragón, the district may be visited en route to the Rioja from Barcelona via the A2 and A68 *autopistas*; and the A15 to Pamplona, branching off the road to Logroño beyond Tudela, will take you through the heart of the wine-growing areas.

Baja Montaña, Comarca p. ★→★★
Sub-division of the D.O. NAVARRA lying to the E of the province on the borders of Aragón. It is the highest and wettest of the wine-growing areas and produces some of the best rosés of 12–15% strength.

Beaumont y Cía S.A., H.
See SARRIA, SEÑORIO DE.

Las Campanas
Village to the S of Pamplona and headquarters of one of the best-known wine concerns, LA VINÍCOLA NAVARRA, which uses the name for some of its wines.

Cantabria
Region in the N of Spain, bounded by the Bay of Biscay and, to the S, by the Cantabrian Mountains. One of the wettest in the country, it produces no wine except for the *pétillant* and astringent CHACOLÍ.

Cayo Simón, Bodegas D.O. r. p. w. dr. ★→★★
Murchante (Navarra). D.O. Navarra. One of the best of the private firms in the RIBERA BAJA, known for its "Monte Cierzo" and "Viña Zarcillo" wines in various styles.

Chacolí (r.) w. ★ DYA
A "green", *pétillant* wine from the far N of Spain, containing only some 9–11.5% of alcohol. Though there is a locally prized "Chacolí tinto de Ezcaba" from the N of Navarra, the best known of the wines are from outside the province, around Guérnica in the Basque country, and especially from Guetaria and Zarauz on the coast near San Sebastián. There are two types, the red *txacoliñ zuri* and white *txacoliñ gorri*, made from the white Ondarrubi zuria grape (akin to the Courbut blanc) and the red Ondarrubi beltza. Both are thin, astringent and rather acid, though the nose is fragrant enough; and the best thing is to drink them, as do the Vizcaínos, in mouthfuls with the excellent local shellfish.

Chivite, Bodegas Julián
D.O. r. p. w. dr. res. ★★
Cintruénigo (Navarra). D.O. Navarra. Founded in 1860, this family firm is the largest private wine concern in Navarra, with a total capacity of 18.75 million liters and vineyards and *bodegas* in other districts of Navarra and in the provinces of Logroño and Aragón. Its strong red wines are

soft, full-bodied and fruity; and the white 2-year-old "Chivite" is well-balanced with a flowery nose. The older *reservas* include the 5-year-old "Cibonero" and 10-year-old "Parador".

Cintruénigo
Wine town just to the S of the Ebro in the RIBERA BAJA.

Corella w. sw. ★→★★
Corella makes small amounts of a luscious Moscatel near CINTRUÉNIGO.

Ebro, River
After crossing the Rioja, the Ebro skirts the far S of Navarra, flowing through the RIBERA BAJA. The other more northerly wine districts lie in the basins of its tributaries, the Ega, Arga, Zidacos and Aragón.

Ezcaba, Chacolí tinto de r. dr. pt. ★
One of the few wines to be made in the mountainous N of Navarra, astringent and *pétillant*, like the better-known CHACOLÍS from Cantabria.

Falces r. p. ★→★★
Wine-growing area in the S of the RIBERA ALTA making good red and rosé wines and of interest for possessing one of the few monasterial *bodegas* to survive in Europe, that of Nuestra Señora de la Oliva.

Funes
This village between FALCES and Calahorra is the site of a well-preserved Roman winery dating from the 1st century A.D. With cement paving and chambers for making and storing the wine, its capacity was of the order of 75,000 liters.

Irache, Bodegas D.O. r. p. w. dr. res. ★→★★ 64, 66, 70
Estella (Navarra). D.O. Navarra. Some of the 2-year-old red wine from this *bodega* in the *comarca* TIERRA DE ESTELLA has been shipped to the U.K. Plummy colored, full-bodied with a yeasty vinous nose, it is not much above *vino corriente* standards. There are also more mature *reservas* available only in Spain.

Ochoa, Bodegas D.O. r. p. w. dr. ★→★★ 75, 78, 80
Olite (Navarra). D.O. Navarra. Well-known private *bodegas* in the RIBERA ALTA making sound red and rosé wines.

Olite
Olite, S of Pamplona in one of the best of the wine-growing areas of the RIBERA ALTA, is the site of a fortified palace, once the favorite residence of the Kings of Navarra. Begun by Charles III ("The Noble") in 1403, in its finished form it was the largest in Spain. Much remains, and it has entered a new lease of life as the Parador Nacional Príncipe de Viana. Lying more or less centrally in the wine area, this is an ideal base for visiting vineyards and *bodegas*, and its restaurant offers a good selection of regional dishes and local wines.

Pamplona
Pamplona, too, capital of Navarra, dear to Hemingway and famous for the bull-running through its streets during the Festival of San Fermín in early July, is a good center for visiting the more northerly wine areas. An elegant city with a fine cathedral and a spacious central square, it possesses numerous good restaurants and an extremely comfortable 5-star hotel, Los Tres Reyes.

Perez Lahera, Bodegas D.O. r. p. w. dr. ★
Tudela (Navarra). D.O. Navarra. Situated in Tudela, the most sizeable town of the RIBERA BAJA, the firm produces a wide range of wines under labels including "Castillo de Barillas", "Viña Santi" and "Navin".

Puente la Reina
A small town SW of Pamplona and only a few kilometers from the most famous of Navarra's *bodegas*, that of the Señorio de SARRÍA, Puente la Reina was one of the staging posts on the medieval pilgrim route from France to Santiago de Compostela, its medieval bridge the

joining place of the two main roads over the Pyrenees. Well worth a visit are its great stone bridge across the River Arga, and honey-colored churches, especially those of the Crucifix (Crucifijo) and St James (Santiago), decorated with the scallop shells of the pilgrims.

Ribera Alta, Comarca r. p. (w. dr.) ★→★★
Lying centrally between VALDIZARBE and BAJA MONTAÑA to the N and RIBERA BAJA to the S, this is the largest of the sub-regions, with 30% of the province's vineyards. The best of its wines are the soft and fruity reds and rosés from around OLITE, containing some 11.5–15% of alcohol.

Ribera Baja, Comarca r. (w. dr.) ★
The Ribera Baja centers on the Ebro basin in the extreme S of the province. The climate is hotter and much drier than in the more northerly *comarcas* and the soils contain large amounts of alluvial silt, conditions producing large quantities of sugar in the grapes. Cascante and CINTRUÉNIGO are prolific producers of sturdy, full-bodied wines of up to 16% strength.

San Roque, Cooperativa D.O. r. p. w. dr. [★]
Murchante (Navarra). D.O. Navarra. Best of the cooperatives in the RIBERA BAJA, producing robust young wines, mostly red of full-bodied, sturdy character.

Sanguesa (r. w.) p.
Area in the hilly BAJA MONTAÑA centering on the basin of the River Aragón. Its soils are a mixture of gravels and chalk, and the best of its wines are the fresh and very drinkable rosés.

Sarría, Señorio de D.O. r. (p. w. dr.) res. [★★→★★★] 64, 70, 73, 75, 78
Puente la Reina (Navarra). D.O. Navarra. The Señorio has been making wines since medieval times, and today they are among the best from Navarra and up to good Rioja standards. The *bodega* was originally in PUENTE LA REINA, but the present vineyards and model winery were the brainchild of a Sr. Huarte, of the large Spanish construction company, who bought the abandoned estate in 1952. Its 1,200ha (2,890 acres) embrace a large French-style château, orchards, farms, a stock-raising establishment, 60km (41 miles) of cypress-lined private roads and 100ha (247 acres) of vineyards, planted with Tempranillo (60%), Garnacha (20%), Mazuelo (10%), and Graciano (10%), together with extra growths in small amounts of Cabernet Sauvignon for red wines, and Malvasía, Viura and Garnacha blanca for the white.

The wines are made in Rioja style and matured in the *bodega's* 6,000 *barricas*, 70% of Armagnac oak and the rest of American or Yugoslavian.

The wines include a white "Blanco seco"; a fresh young rosé; the sound 3-year-old red "Viña Ecoyen"; a more mature and very smooth and fruity "Viña del Perdon" of some 13% strength; and the excellent old "Gran Vino del Señorio de Sarría" red *reservas*, which continue to improve for a decade or more in good vintages.

Tierra de Estella, Comarca ★→★★
Sub-division of the D.O. Navarra, lying to the NE of the Rioja Alavesa and centered on the old town of Estella, a place of Romanesque churches and balconied houses overhanging the River Ega, and once the court of the Kings of Navarra. Its wines are very similar in character to those of VALDIZARBE, further E, some full-bodied and robust reds and finer *reservas*.

Valdizarbe, Comarca ★→★★★
This sub-division of the D.O. Navarra, immediately S of PAMPLONA in the basin of the River Arga, because of its chalky soils and more temperate climate, produces perhaps the best wines of the region as a whole, including those of the Señorio de SARRÍA and the VINÍCOLA NAVARRA.

Vinícola Navarra D.O. r. (p. w. dr.) res. ★→★★★

Las Campanas (Navarra). D.O. Navarra. The company was founded in 1880, but still matures some wine in the large oak vats brought from France and inherited from an earlier concern. It is the largest exporter of Navarra wines, and among its labels are the red "Las Campanas Extra", a hearty wine for everyday drinking; the more refined red and white "Castillo de Olite" (formerly labeled as "Las Campanas"); and the very superior full-bodied and fruity red "Castillo de Tiebas", available both as a 5-year-old and in older vintages, such as that of 1964.

Vinícola Navarra, Cooperativa r. p. w. dr. ★
Bïurrun (Navarra). Cooperative near Las Campanas bottling its wines under the label of "Castillo de Monjardín".

The cooking of Navarra has similarities both with that of Aragón, to the E, and the Basque country (of which the northern area is part). The mountain region in the N is famous for its lamb, served as *espárragos montañeses* ("mountain asparagus") – in fact, lamb's tails stewed in sauce – *cochifrito*, a fricassée (see EXTREMADURA), or in a spicy *chilindrón* sauce (see ARAGON). Another speciality is the trout, sometimes with ham.

The local wines are varied enough to accompany these dishes without looking further afield. The vegetable dishes and fish call for a white wine; try a rosé with the snails and choose a good red with the lamb.

Caracoles a la corellana
Snails cooked with garlic, parsley, cloves, bay leaves, thyme and lemon juice.

Caracolillas de Navarra
Small snails cooked in earthenware dishes with olive oil, tomatoes, green peppers, chillis, breadcrumbs and seasoning.

Cardón a la Navarra
Boiled cardoon (a vegetable like celery) with a white sauce with ham.

Menestra de habas de Tudela
Fresh broad beans cooked with garlic, mint, saffron, almonds, artichoke hearts, boiled eggs, white wine, thyme and seasoning.

Ternasco asado
Roast leg of lamb basted with lemon juice and white wine.

Tortilla de Tudela
Omelette made with the excellent local asparagus.

Truchas a la Navarra
The trout is first marinated and then cooked in an earthenware dish with onions, red wine, pepper, mint, thyme and bay leaves.

Truchas con jamón
Fried trout served on top of or stuffed with slices of fried ham.

Restaurants

Pamplona ★★ *Josetxo* (particularly recommended for its game and *foie gras* with grapes; good wine list); ★★ *Rodero* (sophisticated French and local cuisine); ★ *Shanti* (thoroughly traditional restaurant serving regional dishes).

Puente la Reina *Mesón del Peregrino* (pleasant country style).

Tudela ★ *El Choko* (good local dishes, pleasant red house wine).

New Castile-La Mancha

Between them, the two Castiles occupy the wide central plateau of Spain. Old Castile, so called because it was the first part of the area to be reconquered from the Moors, stretches N from Madrid. S of the capital the landscape becomes increasingly arid, and the central and southern parts of New Castile are known as La Mancha.

The climate is of the Mediterranean type, with long, very hot summers and low rainfall; for this reason the grapes contain large amounts of sugar and produce full-bodied wines with a high content of alcohol and little acid. Since the land, though lying between 500–800m. (1,650–2,650ft.), is in the main flat, the vineyards extend in unbroken expanses – in reality a patchwork of holdings belonging to small proprietors.

This is *par excellence* the land of the cooperatives, of which there are no less than 485 in the central region as a whole. Because of its huge size and despite a low yield of about 16–18hl/ha, the region supplies about 35% of the country's output of wine, much of it going to other less prolific areas for blending and the surplus being used for distillation.

The typical grape is the white Airén (or Lairén), its thick skin affording some protection against the beating sunshine, of which, on average, there are 200 days in the year. It is a favorite with the small proprietors because it produces proportionately 3 times as

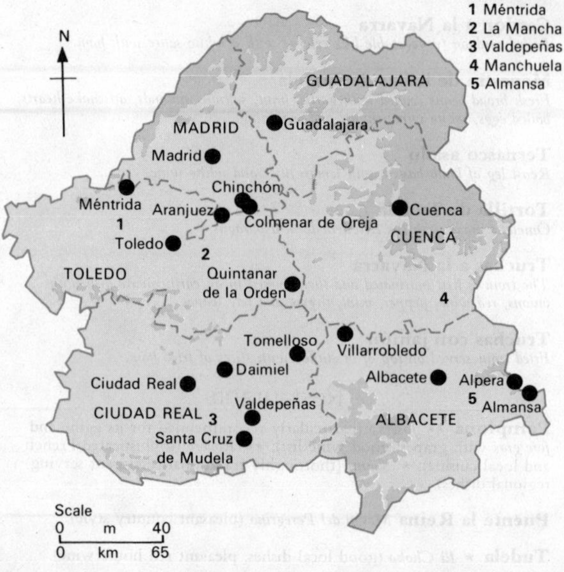

D.O. Zones
1 Méntrida
2 La Mancha
3 Valdepeñas
4 Manchuela
5 Almansa

N
GUADALAJARA
MADRID
Guadalajara
Madrid
Chinchón
Méntrida
Aranjuez
Colmenar de Oreja
Cuenca
CUENCA
Toledo
TOLEDO
Quintanar de la Orden
Tomelloso
Villarrobledo
Daimiel
Albacete
Alpera
Ciudad Real
Valdepeñas
Almansa
CIUDAD REAL
ALBACETE
Santa Cruz de Mudela
Scale
0 m 40
0 km 65

much must as the other most important grape of the region, the black Cencibel (known in the Rioja as the Tempranillo and in Catalonia as the Ull de Llebre or Ojo de Liebre).

Some 90% of the wines from the central area are white; but perhaps the best is the red Valdepeñas from the extreme S of La Mancha bordering Andalucía, made with a proportion of the black Cencibel and famous since the days of Philip II and of his son, the Emperor Charles V, who had them sent across Europe on muleback during his campaigns in the Low Countries in the 16th century.

Apart from Valdepeñas, the other demarcated regions of the area are Almansa, Mancha, Manchuela and Méntrida. The undemarcated district of Tierra de Madrid also makes worthwhile wines in much smaller amount.

Almansa D.O. r. w. ⋆
Bordering the Levante and just N of the D.O. zones of Yecla and Jumilla (see VALENCIAN AREA), the region centers on the town of Almansa with its story-book castle. The soils are chalky, and in its 10,640ha (26,500 acres) of vineyards the predominant grape variety is the black Monastrell (43.5%); the Garnacha tinta and Tintorera account for another 33.1% and there is also some white Forcallat, Airén and Bobal. Since the area was little affected by phylloxera, 83% of the vines are ungrafted and produce wines high in alcohol and extract.

The typical wines are deep in color, full-bodied with little acid and of 12–15% of alcohol. Their quality depends on the proportion of Monastrell, but most are sold in bulk for blending. Only 3 concerns in the region, of which the best is Bodegas Miguel CARRIÓN in Alpera, bottle the wines.

Aloque r. dr. ⋆⋆
The lightest style of VALDEPEÑAS, made with a blend of black and white grapes, usually Cencibel and Airén, dry, deep in color and of some 13–15%. Considering their strength, the wines are surprisingly light and fresh in taste, and much drunk in Madrid.

Arganda-Colmenar de Oreja r. w. dr. ⋆⋆→⋆⋆⋆
Undemarcated district to the N of the capital in the TIERRA DE MADRID. The principal grape varieties are the black Tinto Madrid and Tempranillo, and white Malvar and Jaén. When blended they produce smooth red wines, and the district also makes a pleasant straw-colored white of 12–13.5% strength.

The wines were at their most popular during the 17th century, when the Court transferred from Valladolid to Madrid. At that time the present airport of Barajas was a flourishing vineyard, producing white wines reputedly more fragrant and delicate than those of Rueda, while Carabanchel, now the site of the great prison, made a luscious Moscatel. Today, the best wines from the area are made by Bodegas HIJOS DE JESÚS DIAZ.

Ayuso D.O. r. w. dr. ⋆
Villarrobledo (Albacete). D.O. Mancha. Family firm selling its wines under the labels of "Ayuso", "Estola" and "Armiño".

Carrión, Bodegas Miguel D.O. r. ⋆→⋆⋆
Alpera (Almansa). D.O. Almansa. Small family firm making the best wine from ALMANSA, the smooth and fragrant red "Tinto Selecto", and ageing it for 3–4 years in large oak vats.

Calatrava, Campo de
Sub-division of the D.O. MANCHA, bordering the D.O. VALDEPEÑAS in the direction of CIUDAD REAL.

Campo La Daimielana, Cooperativa de D.O. (r. p.) w. dr. ★
Daimiel (Ciudad Real). D.O. Mancha. Large and well known cooperative selling its wines, mainly white, under the name of "Clavileño".

Ciudad Real
Important wine-making town and capital of the province of the same name in LA MANCHA.

Ecusa D.O. (r. p.) w. dr. ★
D.O. Mancha. Large family concern in La Mancha selling its wines as "Taray".

Hijos de Jesús Diaz, Bodegas r. ★★→★★★
Colmenar de Oreja (Madrid). The red wines from this *bodega* were "discovered" by CLUVE (Club de Selección de Vinos) and have since been rated with those of the Rioja and Catalonia.

La Invencible, Cooperativa D.O. r. p. w. cl. dr. ★→★★
Valdepeñas (Ciudad Real). D.O. Valdepeñas. Best of the cooperatives in VALDEPEÑAS. Its light red *clarete* is particularly attractive.

López Tello, Bodegas D.O. r. cl. w. dr. ★→★★
Valdepeñas (Ciudad Real). D.O. Valdepeñas. One of the oldest *bodegas* in VALDEPEÑAS making typical wines by thoroughly traditional methods in clay TINAJAS.

Madrid
Madrid lies at the center of the TIERRA DE MADRID, a wine-growing district of some interest; and in view of the dearth of accommodation in the wide plains of La Mancha, a stopover in the capital is in any case more or less obligatory for a visit to this region. Nevertheless, its main interest on a wine tour is that, between them, its hundreds of restaurants offer the widest possible spectrum of regional wines and cooking from the length and breadth of Spain. Apart from wines, if there for the first time one could hardly leave without, for a start, visiting the magnificent Prado gallery, the arcaded 16th-century Plaza Mayor or the Palacio Real. The Ritz Hotel is one of the most perfect in Europe; the best guide to Madrid's countless other hotels and to its restaurants is the *Guía del Viajero*, published by the Banco Exterior de España and available in an English edition as *The Traveller's Guide*, and, published in 1983, *The American Express Pocket Guide to Spain.*

Mancha D.O. (r.) w. dr. ★→★★
La Mancha, embracing the province of Ciudad Real and parts of those of Toledo, Albacete and Cuenca, comprises the larger part of the great central *meseta* of Spain and extends at an average height of some 700m. (2,300ft.) from the River Tagus in the N to the Sierra Morena, dividing it from Andalucía, in the S. This is Don Quixote country, an arid, treeless expanse, bitingly cold in winter and mercilessly hot in summer, clothed with unbroken expanses of wheat, olives or vines.

The D.O. Mancha, at the center of the area, is by far the largest in Spain, with 471,310ha (1.2 million acres) under vines and an output in 1979 of 1.6 billion liters of wine, most of it made in cooperatives. The subsoil is chalky with a layer of clay above, and by far the most predominant grape, amounting to some 90%, is the white Airén (or Lairén). The typical wines are light yellow in color, with a pleasant enough nose but without much fruit, containing very little acid and of 13–14% strength. Because of their somewhat neutral character, they are supplied in vast quantities to other regions for blending and further huge amounts are distiled.

Manchuela D.O. r. p. w. dr. ★
Lying to the E of the D.O. MANCHA and bordering the regions of Utiel-Requena (see VALENCIAN AREA) and ALMANSA, Manchuela has 74,142ha (185,000 acres) under vines and produced 150 million liters of wine in 1979. Its wines are not distinguished nor of marked character, resembling either the *claretes* and *vinos de doble pasta* of Utiel-Requena or the whites of LA MANCHA. None of them are bottled.

Megía S.A., Luis D.O. r. p. w. ★→★★
Valdepeñas (Ciudad Real). D.O. Valdepeñas. A *bodega* more notable for its size and the modernity of its equipment, including plant for continuous vinification and huge nitrogen-capped *depósitos* of 1.5 million liters capacity, than for the quality of the end product.

Méntrida D.O. r. ★→★★
Méntrida, with 32,820ha (82,000 acres) under vines and an output of 150 million liters in 1979, lies SW of Madrid in the N of the province of Toledo. 85% of the grapes are Garnacha tinta, producing robust red wines, deep in color and of 14–15% strength. The bulk go for blending, but one can sometimes find better wines, like those of Bodegas La Cerca, in the bars of Madrid.

Montiél, Campo de
Sub-division of the D.O. MANCHA bordering the D.O. VALDEPEÑAS.

Morenito, Bodegas D.O. r. p. w. dr. res. [★★]
Valdepeñas (Ciudad Real). D.O. Valdepeñas. Large and well-known family firm founded in 1896 with an annual production of some 12 million liters, 90% of it bottled. It is one of the 3 firms in Valdepeñas to mature its best wines in oak. "Especial" *blanco*, *rosado* and *tinto*; "Fino Tres Pistolas"; "Fino Morenito"; "Reserva 72".

Navalcarnero r. ★
A little to the S of the capital, this is a sub-division of the undemarcated TIERRA DE MADRID. Its dark red and slightly astringent wines have a following locally and in Madrid, but are apt to oxidize rapidly and lose their freshness because of the high content of Garnacha.

Nuestro Padre Jesús del Perdón, Cooperativa D.O. (r. p.) w. dr. [★→★★]
Manzanares (Ciudad Real). D.O. Mancha. A cooperative with a capacity of 40 million liters, bottling its wines under the name of "Yuntero". The dry white is particularly good.

San Roque, Bodegas D.O. w. dr. [★→★★]
Villanueva de Alcardete (Ciudad Real). D.O. Mancha. Maker of some of the best Manchegan white wine.

San Martín de Valdeiglesias r. ★
Small undemarcated area in the TIERRA DE MADRID lying between the D.O.s MÉNTRIDA and Cebreros (see OLD CASTILE-LEÓN). Its sturdy red wines, made from the Garnacha tinta, Tinto Navalcarnero and white Albillo, resemble those from Cebreros.

Sánchez Rustarazo, Bodegas D.O. r. [★★]
Valdepeñas (Ciudad Real). D.O. Valdepeñas. Founded in 1900, this family concern makes some of the most honest VALDEPEÑAS, fermenting the wine in the traditional clay TINAJAS and ageing some of them, like its "Solar de Hinojosa", in oak casks.

Tierra de Madrid r. ★
Small wine-growing area in the immediate vicinity of Madrid, long-

known for its sturdy red wines. It comprises the sub-districts of SAN MARTÍN DE VALDEIGLESIAS, NAVALCARNERO and ARGANDA-COLMENAR DE OREJA.

Tinajas
These large pear-shaped vessels, made of the local clay and derived from the Roman *orcae*, some 3m. (10ft.) high and of about 1,600 liters capacity, have traditionally been used in La Mancha, Málaga and Montilla-Moriles for fermenting the wines. In VALDEPEÑAS they are also used for maturing it. They are progressively being replaced by much larger cylindrical receptacles of cement reinforced with steel rods.

Toledo
Rising dramatically above the River Tagus, Toledo, with its superb medieval cathedral and collections of paintings by its adopted son, El Greco, is by far the most interesting place in LA MANCHA. It is also the only one with any choice of comfortable hotels: the 3-star Carlos V, Alfonso VI and Hostal del Cardenal, and the 4-star Parador Nacional Conde de Orgaz, poised above the city on a hill with fine views.

Valdepeñas
Town in the S of the province of Ciudad Real long famous for its red wines, and which has given its name to the local D.O. and is the headquarters of the Consejo Regulador. There are *bodegas* in almost every street, in the form of courtyards with a high, blank wall pierced by a high arch and double doors. Many are now disused, but the town still boasts some 80 of all sizes currently making wine. An unpretentious place of low houses and sunbaked streets, it does not now possess a single hotel, and the only place to stay is at the 3-star Meliá El Hidalgo outside the town on the NIV towards Madrid.

Valdepeñas D.O. r. (w. dr.) ★★
The demarcated region lies in the most southerly part of the province of Ciudad Real and possesses 35,101ha (87,750 acres) of vineyards, which produced some 1.5 billion liters of wine in 1979. The soil is a mixture of gravel, clay and chalk, and average annual rainfall is only 400mm. (16in.). Although the typical wines are red, some 93% of the grapes are white Airén, the balance consisting of the black Cencibel (or Tempranillo) and Garnacha Tintoreta. The wines are vinified with 90% Airén, but such is the amount of color and extract in the black grapes that they emerge a deep ruby color. The tradition has been to make and mature the wines in earthenware TINAJAS, from which they are usually sold young in their first or second year. Although one or two *bodegas* age their superior growths in oak, this is not normal practice because Airén musts oxidize easily and it would be too expensive to use a high proportion of Cencibel.

The Airén contributes a fragrant nose to the finished wine, but is also responsible for low acidity; and the color, body and fruity flavor derive from the Cencibel. Alcoholic degree lies between 12.5–14%. Valdepeñas also makes white wines similar to those of the D.O. MANCHA.

Of the 249 *bodegas* in the D.O. Valdepeñas, only 41 bottle their wine. Apart from those separately listed, other leading bodegas are those of Ramón Hidalgo Peñuelas, Guerola and Videva – but it must be said that some of the best and freshest Valdepeñas comes unnamed from the jugs of bars and restaurants in Madrid.

Villarrobledo
Villarrobledo, off the road from Madrid to Albacete, was the source of much of the clay for making TINAJAS.

Virgen de las Viñas, Cooperativa D.O. r. w. dr. res. ★→★★
Tomelloso (Ciudad Real). D.O. Mancha. This cooperative, with a capacity of 46 million liters, sells its wines under the label "Tomillar". Best is the red "Gran Reserva de Cencibel".

Visan S.A. D.O. r. (w. dr.) ★→★★
Santa Cruz de Mudela, Valdepeñas (Ciudad Real). D.O. Valdepeñas. Private firm making pleasant wines, especially the "Castillo de Mudela" and "Viña Tito".

With its roasts, its nourishing *potajes* (thick *potages*) and *cocidos* or *ollas* (stews), the cooking of New Castile is in many ways similar to that of Old, though, because of its more limited resources, more austere.

The only counsel can be to drink the strong reds with the more substantial meat dishes and *potages*, and the whites with lighter fare.

Atascaburras
Rabbit stewed with garlic.

Bizcochos borrachos
Sponge cakes in the shape of rings soaked in wine or liqueurs.

Caldereta de cordero
Ragout of lamb with tomatoes, peppers and seasoning.

Callos a la madrileña
Tripe Madrid style, highly spiced and a model to other countries' tripe dishes.

Ensalada manchega
Salad containing dried cod, tuna, hard-boiled egg, olives and onions.

Espárragos de Aranjuéz
Aranjuéz with its royal palace, S of Madrid, produces some of the most luscious fresh asparagus (and the best strawberries) in Spain.

Lágrimas de aldea
A stew of pork, potatoes, black pudding or chorizo.

Marmita de verduras
A vegetable hot-pot.

Miel con hojuelas
Pancakes with honey.

Mojete
A vegetable dish resembling ratatouille.

Morteruelo
Highly spiced regional version of liver pâté.

Perdices estofadas
Partridge stewed in white wine with chopped ham and seasoning.

Pisto manchego
A vegetable dish after the style of ratatouille *with scrambled eggs.*

Queso frito
Wedges of cheese, dredged in egg and breadcrumbs and fried

Queso manchego
Best known of Spanish cheeses, made in large rounds from ewe's milk.

Tortilla a la magra
An omelette made with strips of cooked fillet of pork.

Restaurants

Madrid A vast range. For the ultimate in sophisticated cooking and wines, ★★★★ *Zalacain* and ★★★★ *Jockey* are outstanding. Among the others, a few personal favorites are: ★★ *Valentín* (popular with actors, bullfighters and visitors, long wine list); ★★ *Bajamar* (for fresh seafood, flown in daily from Galicia); ★★ *Lhardy* (one of the oldest and most traditional); and ★ *Luarqués* (simple food well cooked, excellent value).

Manzanares *Parador Nacional de Manzanares* (a gastronomic oasis).

Toledo ★ *Hostal del Cardenal*; ★ *Venta de Aires.*

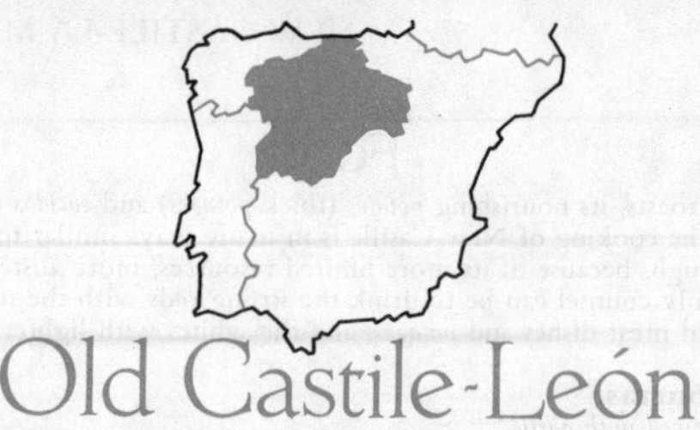

Old Castile-León

Old Castile and the ancient Kingdom of León, united in 1230, are the very heart of Catholic Spain. It was their monarchs who planned and carried through the counter-offensive against the Moors; and the very names of their cities – Ávila, Segovia, Salamanca, Burgos, Valladolid and León – seem to echo the "slow old tunes of Spain".

Apart from the enclave of Cebreros in the Sierra de Gredos near Ávila, it is only the northern area, especially around the basin of the River Duero, which produces wines in any quantity. The land is often bleak and arid, bitterly cold in winter and fierily hot in summer; and in areas such as Toro the annual rainfall amounts to only a meager 300mm. (12in.). In some districts, once famous for their wines, production has declined disastrously, either because of the difficulty of cultivating the vines in such cruel conditions or because heavyweights like Toro have fallen out of fashion.

Nevertheless, Old Castile produces worthwhile wines in great variety, notably the stylish reds from the Ribera del Duero, the refreshing whites from Rueda and the *claretes* of Cigales and El Bierzo; while the Leonese *bodegueros* have improved notably.

There is a profusion of vine varieties, described more fully in the A–Z listing, but among the best and most typical are the black

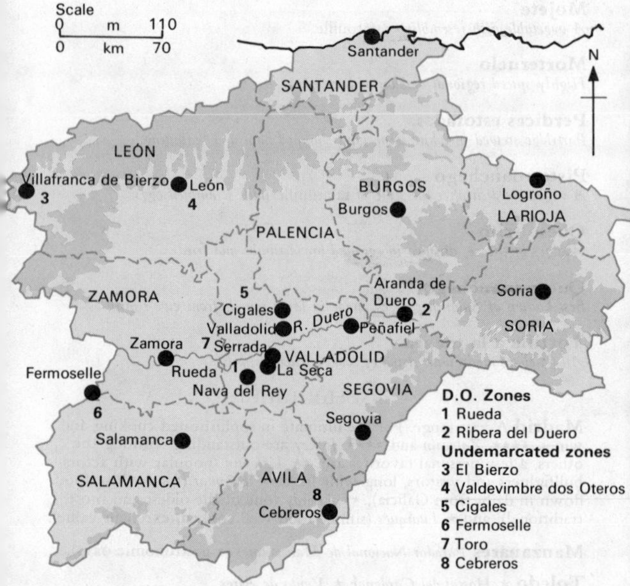

Scale
0 m 110
0 km 70
N
Santander
SANTANDER
LEÓN
Villafranca de Bierzo 3
León 4
BURGOS
Burgos
Logroño
LA RIOJA
PALENCIA
ZAMORA
5
Cigales
Valladolid
R. Duero
Aranda de Duero 2
Peñafiel
Soria
SORIA
Zamora
7 Serrada
VALLADOLID
Fermoselle
Rueda 1
La Seca
Nava del Rey
SEGOVIA
6
Segovia
Salamanca
SALAMANCA
AVILA
8
Cebreros

D.O. Zones
1 Rueda
2 Ribera del Duero
Undemarcated zones
3 El Bierzo
4 Valdevimbre dos Oteros
5 Cigales
6 Fermoselle
7 Toro
8 Cebreros

Tinto Fino or Tinto Aragonés, a variant of the Tempranillo, grown in the Ribera del Duero; the white Verdejo, native to Rueda; and the Prieto Picudo, a black grape with a white pulp, used for making rosés in León. The white "Jerez" or Palomino is also widely grown, but its musts are not of the same quality as in its native habitat in the S of Spain. In one remote district of León there are even hybrids resulting from the direct crossing of American and native vines, but they are frowned upon by the authorities as containing a toxic alkaloid, the ill-famed *malvina*, and wines of this type may not be exported.

As in most parts of Spain, a great deal of the wine is made in cooperatives; but perhaps nowhere have small proprietors making wine for consumption in the immediate vicinity survived in greater numbers. In districts such as Los Oteros and Valdevimbre near León, the serried peasant *bodegas*, dug deep into the ground with a mounded earth roof, look like prehistoric earthworks.

Though various of the regions, especially El Bierzo, well merit demarcation, their small size and difficulties of organization have postponed it, and there are only two Denominaciones de Origen, those of Rueda, instituted in 1980, and the even more recently demarcated Ribera del Duero.

Agrícola Castellana Sociedad Cooperativa D.O. w. dr. am. ★→★★

La Seca (Valladolid). D.O. Rueda. This large and well-run cooperative in the TIERRA DE MEDINA was founded in 1935 and now has a storage capacity of 8 million liters. It makes both the traditional *flor*-growing RUEDA from a blend of Verdejo and Palomino, ageing it either in *solera* or in loosely stoppered glass carboys in the open, and also fresh young wines made from 100% Verdejo. Typical of the first type are the "Campo Grande fino" and "Dorado 61", both sherry-like in flavor and of about 15% strength. The "Verdejo Palido", light greenish in color, dry, fragrant, fruity and pleasantly astringent, is of 12.5% strength and a good example of the fresh young wines now being made in the area.

La Bañeza cl. ★

An area to the W of the city of León and part of the undemarcated Comarca de León. It was formerly widely known for its *claretes de aguja* (light red wines with slight sparkle), but little wine is now made except in primitive subterranean cellars for local consumption.

Barrigón Tovar, Pablo (r.) cl. ★→★★

One of the only two private firms to make a genuine *clarete* from CIGALES, a wine with a long and honorable tradition. Apart from a 3-year-old red, "San Pablo", it bottles *claretes* in 4 other styles: 3-year-old "San Pablo"; 6-year-old "Barrigón"; 8-year-old "Viña Solana" and "1956 Viña Cigaleña". The older wines, matured in oak, are best.

Benavente cl. ★

Like LA BAÑEZA, Benavente once made good *claretes* with a slight sparkle, but many of its vineyards have now been abandoned. The Parador, housed in the 12th-century castle of Fernando II of León, is an attractive base from which to visit RUEDA, CIGALES and TORO.

El Bierzo r. w. p. ★→★★★ 72, 74, 76, 78, 79

El Bierzo, in the NW corner of the province of León bordering Galicia, is ideally suited for the production of quality wines. In its 9,299ha (23,240 acres) of vineyards the climate is halfway between the dry heat of Castile and the rain and humidity of Galicia. It would seem that this is one of the regions most likely to be demarcated in the near future.

Vines are thickest on the ground around Villafranca and Ponferrada, and the most predominant vine varieties are the black Mencía and Alicante, and the white Palomino.

The fragrant and fruity red wines age well in cask, developing a good ruby color, and are smooth and silky with not more than 12% of alcohol. The whites, averaging 10.5–11.5%, are fruity, flowery on the nose and better balanced than the somewhat acidic wines of Galicia. There are also excellent rosés, made mainly with the Mencía and with a refreshing residual acidity.

The temptation has always been to sell the wines to Galicia and Asturias, where they find a ready market. The cooperatives of Cacabelos and Villafranquina bottle worthwhile and representative wines under the names of "Fontousal" and "Padorñina"; but the most sophisticated from the region are those of the PALACIO DE ARGANZA and VALDEOBISPO.

Castilla la Vieja, Bodegas de Crianza D.O. r. w. p. ★→★★
Rueda (Valladolid). D.O. Rueda. Founded some dozen years ago by a group of local growers to elaborate their wines in the best possible fashion, it ages them in oak and makes a well-balanced white, fruity reds and traditional *solera* wines after the style of sherry.

Cebreros r. cl. ★
Situated in the province of Ávila in the Sierra de Gredos W of Madrid, Cebreros produces wines from the black Garnacha and Tinto Aragonés and the white Albillo.

Robust and heady *tintos* and *claretes* with a minimum of 13% of alcohol, they are much in demand for everyday drinking in Madrid and the surrounding area. A delightful place to stay is the Parador de Gredos, a former hunting lodge of King Alfonso XIII, set high in the mountains among pine forests.

Cigales r. cl. ★→★★
The 5,315ha (13,320 acres) of vineyards of Cigales are planted with the white Palomino, Verdejo and Albillo, and the black Garnacha, Tinto del País and Tinto Madrid. Its *claretes,* famous since medieval times, are made by mixing the black and white grapes, destalking them and fermenting them *en blanc.* It was light red wines of this type which from time immemorial were the most popular in the taverns of Valladolid, but what now passes for Cigales *clarete* is more likely to be a blend of red wine from Zamora with a white from La Mancha.

The fact that much of the wine is made in archaic subterranean *bodegas* for local consumption, and that production of good quality Cigales *clarete* is now more or less in the hands of only 2 sizeable private concerns, those of Pablo BARRIGÓN TOVAR and Hijos de FRUTOS VILLAR, has militated against the demarcation of this small region.

Conde Camazón, Vicente cl. res. ★★
Cigales (Valladolid). This small firm bottles excellent 3-year-old and *reserva clarete,* but in minuscule quantity.

Fermoselle r. ★
Fermoselle lies between the basins of the Rivers Duero and Tormes in the SE corner of the province of Zamora, almost within a stone's throw of the Portuguese border. Its granitic and schistous soils, and its blistering summers and low rainfall, resemble those of the Upper Douro; that its wines, though in some ways resembling the Portuguese, are not their equal, is probably because the predominant grape, the Juan García, is not of the same quality as the Portuguese varieties.

During the 18th century, Fermoselle produced an annual 1 million liters of wine, and the place is hollow with disused cellars hewn from the granite; but it is now difficult to find the authentic full-bodied red wine with its strange resinous but not unattractive nose and flavor, most of it being sold in bulk for blending.

Frutos Villar, Hijos de r. cl. w. dr. ★→★★
Cigales (Valladolid). One of the 2 major concerns in Cigales, making the white "Viña Calsina", which suffers from spending too long in oak, and the reliable "Calderona" *clarete.*

Grupo Sindical de Colonización No. 795 r. cl. (p. w. dr.) ★→★★
Cebreros (Ávila). Makers of "El Galayao", available in different styles and perhaps the best of these sturdy wines.

Gutierrez, Hijos de Alberto D.O. w. dr. and sw. am. ★→★★
Serrada (Valladolid). D.O. Rueda. The firm bottles a variety of fresh white RUEDA wines, "San Martín", "Viña Cascarela" and "Blanco Serrada", and also the traditional *solera*-made "Solera la Moya" and "Valdealino".

León
Situated high on the Castilian plateau, the old city of León, capital of the medieval kingdom, is the center of an increasingly important wine-producing area. The Gothic cathedral with its airy flying buttresses and magnificent stained glass windows is one of the finest in Spain; and you need stir no further than the memorable Hotel San Marcos, housed in a splendid 16th-century monastery, to sample a good range of wines from the *comarca* of LEÓN and EL BIERZO in its sophisticated restaurant.

León, Comarca de r. p. w. dr. ★→★★
The name used to describe the wine-growing area to the SE of the city of León. It comprises, in order of importance, the following sub-divisions: VALDEVIMBRE, LOS OTEROS, LA BAÑEZA, León, Tierra de Campos, VALDERAS, La Antigua, Payuelos and RIBERA ALTA DEL CEA.

Los Arcos, Bodegas r. p. w. dr. [★★]
León. Small private *bodega* making good BIERZO wines, of which one of the best is "Santos Rosado".

Los Curros, Grupo D.O. r. cl. w. dr. g. ★→★★
Rueda. D.O. Rueda. A typical old-style Castilian *bodega* with cellars 23m. (76ft.) below ground. Although it does not destalk the grapes or ferment them "cold", the *bodega* makes some pleasantly fruity wines and energetically promotes its white "Viña Cantosán".

Nava del Rey
Largest of the townships in the TIERRA DE MEDINA SW of Valladolid and now part of the D.O. RUEDA.

Los Oteros r. p. w. dr. ★→★★
With 3,077ha (8,685 acres) under vines, Los Oteros, to the E of the road from León to Benavente, is second in importance of the sub-divisions of the *comarca* of LEÓN. The most important of the grapes is the Prieto Picudo, grown in clay soils. Much of the wine is made in tiny peasant *bodegas*, constructed by digging deep into the ground, installing the simplest of beam presses, mounding up the soil on top and leaving a chimney for the escape of carbon dioxide. The typical wine made in these primitive cellars is a *clarete* of 10–13.5%, but methods are so archaic, and at times unhygienic, that on occasion the volatile acidity is so high the wine tastes of raspberry vinegar. See VALDEVIMBRE.

Palacio de Arganza, Bodegas r. p. w. dr. res. ★★→★★★
Villafranca del Bierzo (León). Installed in the 15th-century palace of the Dukes of Arganza, the *bodega* was founded in 1805 and has for long been the most famous in EL BIERZO. A disastrous fire in 1979 destroyed much of the *bodega*, but most of its oak casks and old *reservas* survived unharmed. Its wines are sometimes confused with the better known "Viña Ardanza" from Bodegas La Rioja Alta, but are, of course, entirely different in style. Two of the best are the white "Vega Burbia", clean and fragrant with a refreshing touch of acidity; and the well-balanced red "Almena del Bierzo" with its fruity nose and flavor and long finish.

Peñafiel
Township in LA RIBERA DEL DUERO surmounted by a magnificent 12th-century castle, beneath which the Cooperativa de RIBERA DEL DUERO maintains cellars for maturing its wines; another medieval survival is the extraordinary jousting ground and the houses surrounding it.

Peñalba López, Bodegas D.O. r. [★★]
Aranda de Duero (Burgos). D.O. Ribera del Duero. Small firm with its own vineyards making and ageing in oak a good fruity red wine from the Tinto Fino grape.

Ribera Alta del Cea r. cl.
Small wine-growing area between León and Palencia producing red wines from hybrids obtained by the direct crossing of European and American vines. Since the wines contain small amounts of a toxic alkaloid, the so-called *malvina*, they are blended with others from the area. The district also produces pleasant *claretes* made from a blend of Mencía, Prieto Picudo and Palomino.

Ribera de Burgos D.O. r. cl. ★→★★
The part of the D.O. RIBERA DEL DUERO lying within the province of Burgos and centering on Aranda del Duero. The predominant grape varieties are the Tinto del País, Tinto Madrid, Jaén, Valenciano, Albillo, Tinto Aragonés and Tempranillo. Its typical wines are the *claretes* or "*claros*", most of them being made by small proprietors or in cooperatives. Some of the best are produced by the Bodega Cooperativa Santa Eulalia de la Horra and bottled as "Conde de Siruela".

Ribera del Duero D.O. r. cl. ★★→★★★
This newly demarcated region, some of whose red wine is the best in Spain outside the Rioja and Catalonia, borders the River Duero for a distance of some 110km. (66 miles) with a maximum width of 30km. (21 miles) from Tudela de Duero near Valladolid to just E of El Burgo de Osma. The larger and central part of the region lies within the province of Burgos; there are small areas within the provinces of Soria to the E and Segovia to the S, but the best of the wines are made around Peñafiel and Valbuena in the province of Valladolid. Here the vines grow on chalky, pine-fringed slopes bordering the Duero, and the predominant grape is the Tinto Fino or Tinto Aragonés, a variant of the Riojan Tempranillo, whose musts are particularly suitable for maturation in oak. This area is famous for the legendary VEGA SICILIA but most of the wine is made in Peñafiel by the Cooperativa de RIBERA DEL DUERO, one of the first in Spain to age its wines in oak.

Ribera del Duero, Cooperativa de D.O. r. (p.) [★★]→★★★
Peñafiel (Valladolid). D.O. Ribera del Duero. The old-established cooperative numbers 230 members and its storage capacity runs to 1.2 million liters and 2,000 American oak casks for maturing the wines, which average 11.5–12.5% of alcohol. The youngest wine is the 2-year-old "Ribera Duero" aged in cement *depósitos*, a deep plummy color, fresh and tasting of blackberries. The 5-year-old "Peñafiel" spends 2 years in oak *barricas*; and there are also "Protos" *reservas*, aged for much longer in cask and bottle. The wines, which are now shipped to the U.K., have been much admired by connoisseurs for their clean fruity nose, deep flavor and long finish.

Riscal, Marqués de
See VINOS BLANCOS DE CASTILLA S.A.

Rueda D.O. w. dr. am. ★★
This small region to the SW of Valladolid, long known as the TIERRA DE MEDINA, takes its name from the village of Rueda, which, with Nava del Rey, La Seca and Serrada, is a main center for making the wines. The predominant grape varieties are the native Verdejo and more recently introduced Palomino, grown in calcareous clays. The district makes nothing but white wine, for which it has been famous since the 17th century. The traditional Rueda, amber-colored and of some 15% strength, is a *flor*-growing white matured either in loosely stoppered glass carboys or in *solera*, and tasting like a rough sherry. More recently, and following the lead of the Marqués de Riscal, which has built a large modern winery near Rueda, the region has been producing fresh and

attractive young white wines, made mainly with the Verdejo.

Sanz, Vinos D.O. r. p. w. dr. am. res. ★→★★
Rueda (Valladolid). D.O. Rueda. Large family *bodega* founded in 1900. It makes wines in various styles, including a "Solera 62" and red *reserva*, but the most attractive is the fresh young rosé.

Seca, La
Small village and wine-making center in the D.O. RUEDA.

Serrada
Another of the wine-making villages of the D.O. RUEDA; much of the house wine in the bars and restaurants of Valladolid is sold as "Serrada".

Tierra de Medina
Traditional name for what is now the D.O. RUEDA. Before the phylloxera epidemic of 1909 there were some 90,000ha (268,000 acres) under vines, but this is now reduced to 24,000ha (59,600 acres).

Tierra del Vino
Wine-growing area near Toro in the province of Zamora, once famous for its strong red wines, but now virtually abandoned.

Toro, Comarca de r. ★
This undemarcated region to the E of Zamora, with 15,290ha (45,000 acres) under vines, is one of the most parched in Spain with an annual rainfall of only 300mm. (12in.). In strength and body its red wines are rivaled only by those from Priorato (see CATALONIA), Yecla and Jumilla (see VALENCIAN AREA) and were formerly among the most prized in Spain, being much drunk by the students and academics of Salamanca University. The principal vine varieties are the Tinta de Toro and Tinto de Madrid, together with some Garnacha. A little of the wine is bottled by the Cooperativa de Morales de Toro, Bodegas Luis Mateos and Hijos de FRUTOS VILLAR, but the great bulk finds a ready market for blending.

A pleasant stopping place, especially if you are *en route* for Galicia, is the Parador de los Condes de Alba y Aliste, with its magnificent Renaissance courtyard, in the historic old town of Zamora.

Valdeobispo, Bodegas r. p. w. dr. ★★→★★★
Small private concern in EL BIERZO with its own vineyards. The wines are carefully made and bottled only in good years, but are apt to suffer from being aged overlong in oak without sufficient time in bottle.

Valderas r. cl. ★
As in the neighboring small area of RIBERA ALTA DE CEA, most of the vines are hybrids; the wines are similar in style.

Valdevimbre r. cl. ★→★★
With 4,861ha (12,145 acres) under vines, Valdevimbre is the largest of the sub-districts of the *comarca* of LEÓN. It borders LOS OTEROS and at their best its *claretes* are aromatic, light and fruity. They are traditionally made by adding whole bunches of Prieto Picudo to the must during secondary fermentation, so prolonging it and giving the wine a refreshing "prickle". In some of the more primitive *bodegas*, the proprietors try for the same result by adding fizzy lemonade!

Some of the best of the wine is bottled by the Cooperativa Vinícola Comarcal under the label of "San Tirso". See also VILE.

Valladolid
The home of a famous university and once the capital of Spain, Valladolid is the best base for visiting the wine areas of RIBERA DEL DUERO, RUEDA and CIGALES. When there, do not miss the 15th-century Colegio de San Gregorio, which houses the National Museum of Polychrome Sculpture, with its outstanding collections both of sculpture and painting. The best hotels are the 4-star Conde Ansúrez, Felipe IV and Olid Meliá; and for practical reasons the somewhat old-fashioned Felipe IV is to be preferred, because, in a city whose narrow one-way streets are jammed with traffic, it possesses an underground garage.

Vega Sicilia S.A., Bodegas D.O. r. ★★★→★★★★ 53, 64, 66, 67
Valbuena del Duero (Valladolid). D.O. Ribera del Duero. Vega Sicilia is a name to conjure with in Spain, where its wines, all of them red, are strictly rationed and supplied only for state functions and to the best hotels and restaurants. The estate of some 900ha (2,680 acres) borders the river in the Ribera del Duero, E of Valladolid, at a height of 765m. (2,650ft.). As long ago as 1864, select French vines were acquired from Bordeaux and acclimatized in its chalky, pine-fringed vineyards. They are currently being replanted with the same 3 varieties, Cabernet Sauvignon, Merlot and Malbec, whose musts are blended with those of the native Tinto Aragonés, Garnacha and white Albillo. Its director, Don Jesús Anadón, believes in vinifying and maturing his wines very slowly; only the must which separates naturally after light crushing is used, and after vinification in epoxy-lined cement vats the Vega Sicilia is matured for not less than 10 years in oak with a further 2 in bottle. The *bodega* also makes a 3-year-old and 5-year-old red "Valbuena".

The wines, of 13.5% alcohol or more, are full-bodied, deep in color, complex and intensely fruity, with a fragrant nose, compounded of oak and fruit, and long finish. It should be added that some experts criticize Vega Sicilia for the degree of volatile acidity, preferring the Valbuena with its shorter period in cask.

VILE r. p. w. dr. ★→★★★
León. The somewhat unfortunate abbreviation stands for Planta de Elaboración y Embotellado de Vinos S.A., a large private consortium owning a modern winery with a capacity of 12 million liters and 2,500 casks for maturing the wines. The group owns vineyards of its own, but buys most of the grapes, mainly Prieto Picudo, Tempranillo and Mencía for the red and rosé wines, and Verdejo and Palomino for the white, from independent proprietors in VALDEVIMBRE and LOS OTEROS.

Its crisp young red and white "Rey León" have proved very popular in the U.K., as has also the 2-year-old red and rosé "Castillo de Coyanza". Among its more select and older wines are the "Palacio de Guzmán" in various styles and the full-bodied red "Don Suero" *reservas*.

Vinos Blancos de Castilla S.A. D.O. w. dr. ★★
Rueda. D.O. Rueda. The *bodega* was constructed some years ago, with advice from Professor Peynaud of Bordeaux University, by the Rioja firm of the Marqués de Riscal, which did not at the time market a white wine. It has a capacity of 2 million liters, and the wines are "cold fermented" in stainless steel tanks. They are made with some 90% Verdejo, but Professor Peynaud considered that they were improved by blending a little Viura and also by maturing them for a few months in oak casks. The tendency has subsequently been to cut down or eliminate the period in oak. Fresh and fruity, they are sold under the label of the Marqués de Riscal, most of the output going for export.

WINE & Food

If one had to name a single type of dish most typical of Old Castile, it would be the roasts, of lamb, sucking pig and kid; and the baby milk-fed lamb or *lechazo* is at its best around Valladolid. However, the region has much else to offer: partridge from the mountains, trout from the cold streams, and the rib-warming *cocidos* made from the ubiquitous chick-peas and local varieties of cured pork sausage.

Arroz con cordero

Rice with tomato sauce and stewed lamb, finished in the oven to crisp the top.
A light *clarete* with a little residual acidity, such as ★ "Castillo de Coyanza" or ★★ "Calderona" from Cigales.

Besugo al ajoarriero

Sea bream in a sauce made with olive oil, garlic, onions, parsley and vinegar.
A fresh young Rueda, e.g. ★★ "Verdejo Palido"

Cachelada leonesa

Potatoes boiled with seasoning and chorizo, *from which they take the cheerful orange color and spicy flavor.*

Cochinillo asado
Roast milk-fed sucking pig of a tenderness and succulence rarely found in Britain or the U.S.A., where the piglets are killed older.
This calls for a good red *reserva* such as ★★★ "Valbuena" or ★★★★ "Vega Sicilia" if you can find it.

Cocido castellano
A substantial potage *of chick-peas, brisket, marrow bones, ham bones, black pudding, porkmeat, potatoes and green vegetables.*
Go the whole hog and wash it down with a sturdy Cebreros!

Cordero asado/Lechazo
Roast lamb/milk-fed baby lamb, often cooked in a baker's oven.
A good red, e.g. ★★ "Peñafiel" or ★★★ "Protos"

Judías blancas a la castellana
Stew of haricot beans, fresh tomatoes, onions, garlic and seasoning.
Try the local red house wine.

Leche frita
Squares of a stiff custard, dredged in beaten egg and breadcrumbs and fried crisp in hot olive oil.

Lentejas zamoranas
Lentils stewed with black pudding, onions, paprika, garlic, parsley and seasoning.

Liebre en su salsa
Hare, marinated in white wine and garlic, then cooked in an earthenware dish with onions, carrots, turnip, nutmeg and red wine. The sauce is thickened with the liver.
A good red, such as ★★ "Almena del Bierzo" from the Palacio de Arganza.

Mantecadas
Small cakes made with butter, flour and eggs and baked in paper cups.

Olla podrida
See COCIDO.

Pantortillas de Reinosa
Fluffy pancakes made from puff pastry flavored with anís *and eaten cold.*

Pisto castellano
A vegetable dish resembling ratatouille.

Rebozos zamoranos
Small cakes made with flour, eggs and lemon.

Ropa vieja
Meat from a cocido *served with a sauce made with fresh peppers, eggplants and tomatoes.*

Truchas a la montañesa
Trout cooked in white wine with bay leaves and onions.
A white wine with a hint of oak, such as ★★ Marqués de Riscal.

Restaurants

León ★★ *Novelty*; ★ *Rey Don Sancho* (in the Hotel San Marcos); *Regia* (local fare and Bierzo wines in a 13th-century house near the Cathedral).

Palencia ★★ *Lorenzo*; ★ *Casa Damián* (both restaurants, run by the same family, are worth the stop when approaching Valladolid from Burgos or Santander).

Peñafiel *Asador Mauro* (roast sucking pig and baby lamb, regional wines).

Valladolid ★★ *Mesón Panero*; ★ *Asón*; ★ *Mesón La Fragua* (all offer well-cooked Castilian dishes and regional wines).

Rioja

Apart from sherry, Rioja is the best known of Spanish wines, and thanks to good quality and reasonable prices, foreign sales have leapfrogged in recent years: in Britain alone, they have increased from 180,000 liters in 1970 to the current figure of some 2.2 million liters, about the same level as the U.S.A. consumption. Canada and West Germany are other important markets. The bulk of its wines are red and have traditionally been characterized by the long periods which they spend in cask and their oaky nose and flavor, but in recent years the Rioja has also been making a new style of white wine, light, fresh and fruity, without age in wood.

The Rioja was the first of the Spanish regions to be demarcated, when a Consejo Regulador was set up in 1926 to control production and quality. It now comprises some 45,000ha (111,500 acres) of vineyards lying within the provinces of La Rioja

(formerly known as Logroño), Alava and Navarra, with an average production of 110 million liters of wine. The vineyards extend for some 120km (79 miles) on both sides of the River Ebro, which flows from the rocky Conchas de Haro in the hilly W of the region to Alfaro in the E. The valley is bounded by mountains on either side and is of a maximum width of 40km (24 miles). The soils are a mixture of calcareous clay, ferruginous clay and alluvial silt, with a predominance of calcareous clay in the Rioja Alavesa to the N of the river.

In the W of the area the climate is temperate and fairly predictable, with mild, wet springs, short, hot summers, long, warm autumns and a little snow and frost in winter. The hotter and more Mediterranean-like Rioja Baja in the E is classified as semi-arid.

The D.O. Rioja is divided into the 3 sub-regions of La Rioja Alta, La Rioja Alavesa and La Rioja Baja, of which the first 2 produce the more delicate wines. In this chapter the sub-region, not the province or D.O. zone, is given in brackets.

Wine was being made in the Rioja long before the Roman occupation of the area; and the traditional method, still practised in the *bodegas* of smallholders, was to tip the bunches of grapes, stalks and all, into open stone troughs or *lagos*. Fermentation then proceeded in stages, with progressively firmer crushing of the grapes. Production of Rioja in its present style began after the

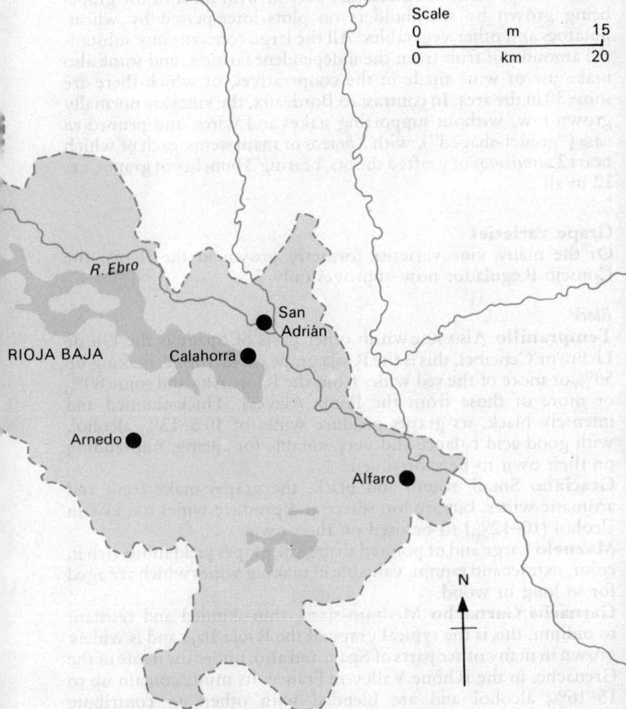

double disasters of oidium and phylloxera in France in the late 1900s, when *négociants* moved into the district and introduced the methods currently employed in Bordeaux, notably the destalking of the grapes and the ageing of the wines in 225-liter oak casks. Long after the French reduced the period in wood, the Riojans continued to age the wines, both red and white, for long years in oak (see OAK in A–Z) – hence the characteristically vanilla-like bouquet and flavor – and it is only recently that more attention has been given to bottle age. With the production of "cold-fermented" white wines without maturation in cask, matters have recently turned full circle, and it is to be hoped that innovations do not proceed too fast and furiously, since the traditional white Riojas are wines with a style and character all their own.

The first great Rioja boom took place during the latter decades of the 19th century; and the *bodegas* constructed at that period – Riscal, Murrieta, López de Heredia, CVNE, La Rioja Alta and the rest – are still among those producing the best wines. There was another phase of expansion, financed by banks, sherry firms, Spanish industrialists and foreign wine concerns, during the 1970s. The new *bodegas* are characterized by their size and the modernity of their equipment, but all of them, in conformity with the regulations of the Consejo Regulador, mature their better red wines in the traditional 225-liter oak *barricas.*

Although most of the old-established *bodegas* own sizeable vineyards of their own, and some of the newer, such as Berberana and Sogeviñas, have embarked on extensive new plantations, traditional patterns of agriculture persist, with most of the grapes being grown by smallholders on plots interspersed by wheat, potatoes and other vegetables. All the large concerns buy substantial amounts of fruit from the independent farmers, and some also make use of wine made in the cooperatives, of which there are some 30 in the area. In contrast to Bordeaux, the vines are normally grown low, without supporting stakes and wires, and pruned *en vaso* ("goblet-shaped"), with 3 *brazos* or main stems, each of which bears 2 *sarmientos* or grafted shoots, bearing 2 bunches of grapes, i.e. 12 in all.

Grape varieties

Of the many vine varieties formerly grown in the Rioja, the Consejo Regulador now approves only 7:

Black

Tempranillo Also known in other parts of Spain as the Ull de Llebre or Cencibel, this is the Rioja grape *par excellence,* making up 50% or more of the red wines from the Rioja Alta and some 80% or more of those from the Rioja Alavesa. Thick-skinned and intensely black, its grapes produce wines of 10.5–13% alcohol, with good acid balance and very suitable for ageing, but tending on their own to be short-lived.

Graciano Small, round and black, the grapes make fresh and aromatic wines, but are too scarce and produce wines too low in alcohol (10–12%) to be used on their own.

Mazuelo Large and of pointed shape, the grapes yield musts rich in color, extract and tannin, valuable in making wines which are aged for so long in wood.

Garnacha/Garnacho Medium-sized, thin-skinned and resistant to oidium, this is the typical grape of the Rioja Baja and is widely grown in many other parts of Spain and also, under the name of the Grenache, in the Rhône Valley in France. Its musts contain up to 15–16% alcohol and are blended with others to contribute alcoholic degree and body. On their own, however, Garnacha wines oxidize very easily and it is difficult to judge their age from the color, since they soon turn a brick red.

White

Viura Also known as the Macabeo in other parts of Spain, the Viura yields musts with about 11% of alcohol and plenty of tartaric acid. Being resistant to oxidation, they are particularly suitable for making light and fruity white wines by "cold fermentation".

Malvasía Vigorous and large-leaved, these vines are somewhat prone to attack by mildew. The grapes, white tinted with red when fully mature, produce fresh wines of about 11%, often made in admixture with Viura.

Garnacha blanca Not so much used in the Rioja as the other two white varieties, the Garnacha blanca produces pleasant white wines, but higher in alcohol and with less acid than the others.

There is a popular superstition that red Riojas are made in *solera* (see SHERRY). This is entirely untrue, but they *are* made by blending wines from different grape varieties, often grown in separate areas of the region, and there is sometimes a limited admixture of wines of different vintage, the date on the label referring to the predominant vintage. It was usual in the past – and the custom persists in Spain itself – to label them with a description such as 3° año or 5° año, meaning that the wine had been bottled during the third or fifth calendar year after the harvest. Without knowing how long the wine had been in bottle, it was impossible to say how old it was or in what year it had been made; and all wines exported to EEC countries are now labeled with a vintage.

Vintages

Because of the more predictable climate and the practice of blending a proportion of better wine with the poorer growths, vintage years are not as variable as in Bordeaux, but are still important, and increasingly so as the Consejo Regulador tightens the regulations. Outstanding among earlier years were:

1915	1925	1947	1955
1920	1931	1948	1958
1922	1934	1949	1964
1924	1942	1952	1968

Ratings for more recent years follow, though it must be said that in some generally disastrous years, when the crop, because of hailstorms or excessive rain, was affected by mildew or oidium, the only two pests in the Rioja, individual *bodegas* still made good wines – such as the 1971 red Riscal or 1977 "Cune".

Year	Yield (millions of liters)	Rating
1970	114	excellent
1971	55	poor
1972	99	very bad
1973	128	good
1974	131	average
1975	84	fair
1976	93	good
1977	65	very bad
1978	81	excellent
1979	140	average
1980	125	good
1981	130	very good

As when visiting most wine areas, it is a great advantage to have a car, though, once in Logroño, there is a charming local train which wends its leisurely way by Fuenmayor, Cenicero and Briones to Haro, depositing you on the doorstep of many of the *bodegas* and affording better views of the Ebro and the vineyards than those from the main road.

The quickest approach to the region is to fly to Bilbao, hire a car and drive to Haro or Logroño, 1½–2 hours away off the A68 *autopista*. An alternative is to take the car ferry to Santander and join the A68 at Bilbao, or, again, drive from Barcelona by way of Zaragoza and the A2. This route will take you through the heart of the Rioja Baja. It is easy enough to make a leisurely circuit of the Rioja Alta and Rioja Alavesa in a day by driving from Logroño to Haro on the N232 by way of Fuenmayor, Cenicero and Briones, and returning by the road N of the Ebro, also labeled the N232, through Labastida, Abalos and Laguardia. It is especially worthwhile to visit Briones and Laguardia, just off the road, 2 of the most picturesque hilltop towns of the Rioja.

Stay either in Logroño or Santo Domingo de la Calzada for the Rioja Alta and Rioja Alavesa, or in Calahorra for the Rioja Baja (see individual entries for hotels). There are numerous restaurants serving good regional food and wines in towns and villages up and down the region (see WINE AND FOOD).

A list in English of *bodegas* which receive visitors may be obtained from: Rioja Wine Information Centre, 140 Cromwell Road, London SW7 4HA, U.K.

Abalos
Picturesque village E of Haro in a small enclave of the RIOJA ALTA N of the Ebro. Dominated by the mountains of the Sierra Cantabrica and surrounded by vineyards, it possesses an old palace and impressive 15th-century church, and is the headquarters of Bodegas REAL DIVISA.

AGE, Bodegas Unidas S.A. D.O. r. (p.) w. dr. res. ★→★★
Fuenmayor (Rioja Alta). This large *bodega* was formed in 1964 by the union of 3 much older concerns, Azpilicueta, Cruz García and Entrena, and is now jointly owned by the American firm of Schenley and the Banco Español de Crédito. Its wines are vinified in Navarrete and bottled in the main *bodega* in Fuenmayor. The best of them are the red "Marqués de Romeral", "Fuenmayor" and "Siglo" *reservas*, the latter presented in a distinctive sack. Older vintages of "Romeral" were very fine. The bodega also makes dry white "Romeral" and "Siglo" and a semi-sweet "Blanco Parral".

Ageing
Riojas, both red and white, have traditionally been aged in cask for much longer than Bordeaux or Burgundy wines, and have sometimes been criticized for a pronounced oaky nose and flavor (see OAK). The present trend is to cut down on the period in cask and to give the better red wines at least a year or two in bottle.
See also CRIANZA.

Alambrado
A fine wire mesh often used around bottles of *reservas*, now decorative but originally designed to prevent the fraudulent replacement of the contents.

Alavesas S.A., Bodegas D.O. r. (p.) w. dr. res. ★★→★★★ 68, 70, 73, 74, 75
Laguardia (Rioja Alavesa). A fairly new concern with 400ha (995 acres) of vineyards, and a modern *bodega* with a capacity of 18 million liters and 10,000 oak BARRICAS, which has rapidly made a name for the quality of its wines. Made entirely from grapes grown in the near vicinity, its red wines (containing 90% Tempranillo and 10% Viura) are light in color and body, fragrant, soft, quick to mature and thoroughly

typical of the RIOJA ALAVESA. The whites, also labeled as "Solar de Samaniego" (after a local poet), are pleasantly acidic and refreshing.

Alfaro
Town at the E extreme of the RIOJA BAJA. The home of two *bodegas*, it takes its name from El Faro ("the lighthouse"), the furthest point on the Ebro reached by the Phoenicians in their shallow-draught boats. It is an attractive little place with some fine baronial houses and a beautiful 17th-century church.

Arnedo
Picturesquely situated in the gorge of the River Cidacos with its red sandstone cliffs, Arnedo is one of the pleasantest of the towns of the RIOJA BAJA and possesses 2 hotels, the 3-star Victoria and 2-star Virrey, and a most individual restaurant, Sopitas (see WINE AND FOOD).

"Banda Azul" D.O. r. [★★]
Made by Federico PATERNINA, this is one of the biggest-selling of 3° año red Riojas. It went through a bad period after the transfer to the large modern *bodega* in Haro, but thanks to a massive investment in new oak casks, it is now a pleasant and reliable young wine.

Barrica
The 225-liter oak cask, a legacy of the *vignerons* from Bordeaux who settled in the Rioja during the phylloxera epidemic of the late 19th century, in which all the CRIANZA wines must statutorily be matured.

Berberana S.A., Bodegas D.O. r. (w. dr.) res ★→[★★★] 66, 70, 74, 75, 76, 78
Cenicero (Rioja Alta). The company, now one of the largest in the Rioja, was founded in 1877 by the Berberana family in Ollauri, where it still maintains cellars for ageing the wines in bottle. It underwent a major expansion in 1972 and has very recently been taken over by RUMASA. The new vinification plant in Cenicero incorporates modern stainless steel fermentation tanks and a huge ageing floor accommodating 40,000 oak BARRICAS. Apart from vineyard holdings in the RIOJA ALTA, Berberana has embarked on ambitious new plantations of some 900ha (2,220 acres) at Monte Yerga near Aldeanueva del Ebro in the RIOJA BAJA, where it is growing a high proportion of Tempranillo and Viura in addition to the Garnacha typical of the area. The red "Carta de Plata" is one of the biggest-selling 3° año wines; it also makes an inexpensive "Preferido" *sin crianza* (see CRIANZA); and full-bodied and velvety older wines, including the 5° año "Carta de Oro", together with a *reserva* and "Gran Reserva". It has recently introduced a fragrant, fresh and fruity new-style white Rioja without age in wood.

Beronia, Bodegas D.O. r. res. [★★→★★★]
Ollauri (Rioja Alta). This small firm, with 10ha (25 acres) of vineyards in one of the best areas of the RIOJA ALTA, began operations in 1970, working from a small *bodega* in the village of Ollauri. It has recently completed sizeable and elegant premises in its vineyards with a capacity of 2 million liters and some 4,000 oak casks. The wines, made with some 85% of locally grown Tempranillo and a little white Viura, are fermented in temperature-controled stainless steel tanks at temperatures as near as possible to 21°C, so as to conserve the full flavor of the fruit. They are subsequently aged for up to 2 years in BARRICA and a minimum of 2 years in bottle. Don Javier Bilbao Iturbe, whose wines are now marketed by Gonzalez Byass, is scrupulous in his methods, employing,

for example, egg whites for clarification, and paying the strictest attention to hygiene – the walls of the *bodega* are coated with an anticryptogrammic paint obtained specially from England.

Beronia produces only 2 wines, a 5° año red and a *reserva*, both of them a deep ruby-orange in color with good fruity nose and flavor, excellent balance and long finish. They are among the best of those from the newer *bodegas*.

Bilbainas S.A., Bodegas D.O. r. (p.) w. dr. or sw. sp. res. [★★] →★★★ 66, 70, 73, 74, 75, 76, 78
Haro (Rioja Alta). Bilbainas, founded in 1901, was one of the first firms to build a *bodega* adjacent to the newly opened railhead from Bilbao, and its wines have long been known in the U.K., where at one time it maintained its own cellars and sales office. It owns 275ha (685 acres) of vineyards, mostly around Haro, with a smaller holding at Leza in the Rioja Alavesa. Its wines include the dry white and red "Viña Paceta" and sweeter "Cepa de Oro"; a light and first-rate "Viña Zaco"; the more fully bodied red "Viña Pomal", made basically with grapes from Leza; and good "Vendimia Especial" *reservas*. The firm also makes wines by the champagne method (see SPARKLING WINES).

Bordelesa
Alternative name, reflecting its Bordeaux origins, for the 225-liter oak BARRICA.

Briones
A little E of Haro, the small hilltop town of Briones, with its stone-built baronial houses, statuesque church and long views over the Ebro, is one of the most attractive in the RIOJA ALTA.

Calahorra
The largest town in the RIOJA BAJA, the birthplace of Quintillian and famous for its protracted siege by Pompey, Calahorra is a convenient stopping place *en route* to Logroño from Zaragoza and as a base for visiting the sub-region. There is a comfortable Parador, the Marco Fabio Quintillano.

Campo Viejo S.A., Bodegas D.O. r. (p. w. dr.) res. ★→ [★★★] 61, 63, 64, 66, 70, 71, 78
Logroño (Rioja Alta). Owned by the ubiquitous firm of SAVIN and situated in Logroño itself, Campo Viejo is one of the largest firms in the Rioja with a total capacity of 50 million liters. Its widely advertised "San Asensio" is among the biggest selling of 2° año red Riojas *sin crianza* (see CRIANZA), and the *bodega* also produces some big, fruity red *reservas*, including the first-rate 1970.

Carlos Serres S.A., Bodegas D.O. r. (p. w. sw.) res. ★→★★★
Haro (Rioja Alta). Well-known Haro firm, whose younger wines include the "Rioja Fino Clarete" and semi-sweet "Rioja Fino Blanco Topacio". Its best wines are the red "Carlomagno" *reservas*.

"Carta de Oro" r. [★★]
Soft and velvety 5° año red wine from BERBERANA.

"Carta de Plata" r. ★
A younger 3° año red from BERBERANA. It has been criticized in Spain for lack of consistency, but the quality of the wine shipped abroad is always reliable.

Casa del Vino
See LAGUARDIA.

Castillo de Cuzcurrita D.O. r. res. dr. ★★→★★★
Rio Tirón (Rioja Alta). The old 14th-century castle houses its own small *bodega* making good but somewhat astringent red wines from grapes grown in its own vineyards. They are labeled as "Señorio de Cuzcurrita", "Castillo Cuzcurrita" and "Reserva Conde de Alacha".

"Castillo de Ygay" r. 1934 ★★★★ 60 ★★★
Gran reserva from the MARQUÉS DE MURRIETA, made only at long intervals and in exceptional years. The 1934 was one of the most

complete and beautiful Riojas which I have ever tasted. The 1960, recently available, is a deep, oaky and very fruity wine, albeit with a trace of volatile acidity, but should be drunk now, as in all probability it will not repay further ageing in bottle.

Cenicero
Town on the Ebro W of Logroño in the RIOJA ALTA, and the headquarters of 5 important *bodegas.* It was the burial place of the Roman legions stationed in the area, hence the name, which in Spanish means "ashtray". Cenicero stages an interesting wine festival in September, held in its large, covered *pelota* court.

Compañía Vinícola del Norte de España (CVNE) D.O. r. (p.) w. dr. or sw. res. ★★→★★★ 66, 68, 70, 73, 74, 75, 76, 78
Haro (Rioja Alta). CVNE was founded in 1879 in the full flush of the 19th-century Rioja boom, and has been making excellent wines ever since – at one time they included sparkling wine made by the champagne method and a brandy. The 3° año "Cune" is one of the most reliable of young red Riojas; and the "Imperial" and "Viña Real" *reservas,* the latter a full-bodied and aromatic Alavesa made in Elciego, are outstanding. CVNE is now making a new-style white Rioja without maturation in wood, but its "Monopole", so popular in Spain itself with its restrained hint of oak, remains one of the best of traditional white Riojas.

Corral S.A., Bodegas D.O. r. (p. w. dr.) ★→★★ 71, 73, 75, 78
Navarrete (Rioja Alta). One of the newest *bodegas* located in Navarrete. Its wines, of which the best is the "Don Jacobo" red *reserva,* do not as yet live up to the modernity of the equipment and tend, on occasion, to be excessively oaky and somewhat astringent.

Crianza
Literally "nursing", and in terms of wines the word refers to their maturation in oak cask. The regulations of the Consejo Regulador are strict; and to be labeled "*con crianza*", a Rioja, red or white, must be matured for 2 years with a minimum of 1 in a 225-liter oak BARRICA. *Reservas* usually spend 6 years between cask and bottle, and *gran reservas* 8 (but see GLOSSARY). Riojas need not, however, be aged in oak to qualify for *denominación de origen*; and there are no rules as regards the ageing of wines *sin crianza* ("without ageing"). A 2° año wine may, indeed, have seen no oak at all and be less than a year old, as the description means that it has been bottled during the calendar year after the harvest.

"Cumbrero" D.O. r. w. dr. ★★
Label used by Bodegas MONTECILLO for its excellent 3° año red and white Rioja.

CVNE
Abbreviation of COMPAÑÍA VINÍCOLA DEL NORTE DE ESPAÑA, whose wines are also known colloquially in Spain as "Cune".

De la Torre y Lapuerta S.A., Bodegas D.O. r. res. ★
San Adrián (Rioja Baja). Its wines, labeled as "Campo Burgo", are intriguingly made in a single large vat located in a sugar refinery and are typical of the stout, honest-to-goodness Garnacha growths from the far SE of the Rioja, more akin to sturdy wines produced in the Ribera Baja (see NAVARRA) than the delicate wines from the N of the region.

"Domecq Domain" D.O. r. w. dr. ★★→★★★ 75, 76
Label used abroad for the well-made wines from the SOCIEDAD GENERAL DE VINOS S.A., sold in Spain as "Privilegio del Rey Sancho".

Ebro, River
The Ebro flows through the Rioja from W to E, entering it through the rocky gorge of the Conchas de Haro and leaving it near Alfaro in the Rioja Baja. The vineyards extend upwards from both sides of the river or are located in the valleys of its 7 tributaries, the Tirón, Oja, Najerilla, Iregua, Leza, Cidacos and Alama.

El Coto, Bodegas D.O. r. w. dr. ★★→★★★ 73, 76, 78, 79
Oyón (Rioja Alavesa). Large new *bodega* founded in 1973 with a capacity of 6.5 million liters and 7,000 oak BARRICAS. Its red wines, made with some 85% of Tempranillo from the RIOJA ALAVESA and labeled as "Coto de Imaz", are light and very soft with a fragrant nose. Among the best is the well-balanced 1978, with deep raspberry flavor.

Elciego
Hill village in the RIOJA ALAVESA over the Ebro from Cenicero, a place of steep, narrow streets, with a church at the top dominating the surrounding vineyards, and famous as the home of the *bodegas* of the MARQUÉS DE RISCAL.

Estación de Viticultura y Enología
Government laboratory in HARO, working in conjunction with the Consejo Regulador. Its main work is the analysis of wines to ensure that they conform to the standards of the *Reglamento*, but it also conducts wider research into the production and properties of Rioja wines.

Faustino Martínez, Bodegas D.O. r. (p.) w. dr. res.
[★★] →★★★ 64, 68, 70, 73, 78
Oyón (Rioja Alta). The Martínez family has been making good wines in Oyón, just N of Haro, since before 1860, and began bottling them in 1931. It is still a family firm, and owns 250ha (620 acres) of vineyards in one of the best areas of the RIOJA ALAVESA. There are some 10,000 BARRICAS in its cellars; but the *bodega* does not believe in ageing its wines overlong in oak, and its *gran reserva*, the "Faustino I", outstanding in the 1964, 1968 and 1970 vintages, spends only 2 years there, followed by more in bottle. The other red wines are the "Faustino V" and "Faustino VII"; and the *bodega* was one of the first in the field with a new-style white Rioja, "Faustino VII", not aged in oak, light and fresh with an intriguing lemony finish.

Franco Españolas S.A., Bodegas D.O. r. (p.) w. dr. or sw. res. ★→★★★ 64, 73
Logroño (Rioja Alta). Large and old-established firm with *bodegas* in the heart of Logroño just across the bridge over the Ebro, taken over by RUMASA in 1973. The semi-sweet white "Diamante" has long been a favorite in Spain and goes well with desserts. The *bodega* also makes a dry and oaky "Viña Sole", and a big-selling young red, "Sin Rival". Its "Rioja Bordon" is a full-bodied red, but perhaps the most stylish of the wines are the lighter "Royal" *reservas* and "Royal Tete de Cuvée" *gran reservas*. First-rate in the older vintages, the wines have more recently tended to be somewhat acidic and lacking in depth.

Fuenmayor
On the main road from Logroño to Haro and close to the Ebro, Fuenmayor, together with CENICERO, is next in importance to HARO among the Riojan wine towns.

Gomez Cruzado S.A., Bodegas D.O. r. (p.) w. dr. or sw. 64, 76, 78 ★→★★
Haro (Rioja Alta). One of the old *bodegas* in Haro, at one time belonging to Carbonell, the well known producers of olive oil and Montilla. Makers of the inexpensive "Predelicto" wines, the red "Viña

Dorana" and "Regio Honorable" *gran reserva,* and white "Viña Dorana" and "Viña Motulleri" *reserva.*

Gurpegui, Bodegas D.O. r. (p. w. dr.) res. ★→★★ 70, 73
San Adrián (Rioja Baja). Small family firm, founded in 1921 and owning 100ha (247 acres) of vineyards in the vicinity of San Adrián. Its wines include the red, white and rosé "Viña Berceo", the light red "Cancerbero" and red "Berceo" *reservas.*

Haro
Near the W tip of the region, Haro, a busy little town with a population of some 9,000, is the wine capital of the RIOJA ALTA and the home of no less than a dozen *bodegas.* Built uphill and downhill above the Ebro, it is a place of narrow streets and stylish old houses, with a wide central square, one of whose points of interest is the wine shop of Juan Gonzalez Muga specializing in old and rare vintages and special offers on Riojas from the local *bodegas.* Haro is the headquarters of a government wine laboratory, the ESTACIÓN DE VITICULTURA Y ENOLOGÍA. It has no hotel, but there are a couple of good restaurants (see WINE AND FOOD). At Briñas, on the road N to Vitoria facing the rocky Conchas de Haro, there is a wine museum displaying bottles from most of the *bodegas* in the Rioja.

Hormilleja
Village near Nájera in the center of vineyards producing most of the Garnacha grown in the RIOJA ALTA.

Labastida
Village in the RIOJA ALAVESA NE of Haro, and home of one of the best cooperatives in the region.

Labastida, Cooperativa Vinícola de D.O. r. (p.) w. dr. res. ★→★★★ 66, 70, 75, 78
Labastida (Rioja Alavesa). The cooperative, founded in 1956 and enlarged in 1965, has 158 *socios* (members) growing grapes in 3 of the best areas of the region (Labastida, Samaniego and Villalba). With a total capacity of 3 million liters, it is the only cooperative in the Rioja to possess oak BARRICAS and to bottle its wines.

The quality of the fruit is reflected in that of its wines. The fresh young white, unaged in oak and made almost entirely from Viura with a small amount of Blanquirroja, is the best of its type in the Rioja. A pale straw color, round and intensely fruity both in nose and flavor, it is made not by "cold fermentation", as one would suppose, but by leaving the grapes overnight in a cement *depósito,* running off the must which separates under the weight of the load and transferring it to a separate vat for fermentation. The reds, too, are first-rate – higher in strength than most Alavesas, and containing up to 13.5–14% alcohol, they include a pleasant young "Manuel Quintano"; a well-balanced "Montebuena"; and excellent "Gastrijo" and "Castillo Labastida" *reservas* and *gran reservas* with a fruity Tempranillo nose, raspberry flavor and long finish.

Laguardia
Old walled town crowning a hill in the heart of the RIOJA ALAVESA, and a landmark for miles around. Its narrow streets and old, dark houses are honeycombed with small peasant *bodegas,* now mostly disused, and there are 3 large modern wineries on the outskirts. Quiet enough on weekdays, at weekends and on holidays it is a target for visitors from Bilbao and San Sebastián, who come to picnic and to fill their carafes with local wine.

The old baronial house of the Fabulista Samaniego, the 18th-century author of some rather pointless fables, formerly housed a pleasant hotel, but has recently been converted into a center for the study of Alavesa wines, the Casa del Vino. Apart from its interesting exhibits on local history as well as viticulture and oenology, it possesses modern laboratories and advises the smaller producers or *cosecheros.*

Lagunilla S.A., Bodegas D.O. r. (p.) w. dr. res. ★→★★
Fuenmayor (Rioja Alta). Founded in 1885, the firm was one of the

pioneers in introducing American grafts after the phylloxera epidemic of the early 1900s. It now occupies a large modern *bodega* outside Fuenmayor, and has been bought by Crofts, part of the I.D.V. group. The best of its wines are the red "Viña Herminia" *reservas*.

Lan S.A., Bodegas D.O. r. (p.) w. dr. res. ★★ 70, 73, 75
Fuenmayor (Rioja Alta). Large modern *bodega* founded in 1969 and recently taken over by RUMASA. Equipped with the most modern and sophisticated plant, it possesses 25,000 BARRICAS for ageing its wines, which include a fresh white "Lambros" not matured in oak; a brisk and fruity, though somewhat acidic, "Landa"; and "Viña Lanciano" *reservas*, with good nose, cherry flavor and slightly acidic finish.

Logroño
Capital of the province of La Rioja, Logroño, with a population of 108,000, is the only large town in the Rioja and the commercial center of the wine industry. It is a handsome city, built by the Ebro with a spacious tree-lined square, the Espolón, the focus of the Fiesta de San Mateo, held from September 21st to mark the beginning of the grape-picking season. It is the headquarters of the Consejo Regulador and of the Grupo de Exportadores and also of 3 of the largest Rioja *bodegas*, FRANCO ESPAÑOLAS, CAMPO VIEJO and OLARRA. It possesses numerous good restaurants (see WINE AND FOOD), and its hotels are the 4-star Bracos and Carlton Rioja and 3-star Gran Hotel; but the favorite with the wine community is the 3-star Murrieta, which has the advantage of a good cafetería and restaurant.

López Agos y Cía S.A. Bodegas D.O. r. w. dr. res. ★→★★
Fuenmayor (Rioja Alta). A new *bodega*, founded in 1973, with a capacity of 2.25 million liters and 2,000 oak BARRICAS. It makes a young red "Agos" and "López Agos" *sin crianza* (see CRIANZA), a light red "Señorio Agos" and a dry white "Agos Oro", both aged in oak.

López de Heredia Viña Tondonia S.A., Bodegas R. D.O. r. (p.) w. dr. or sw. res. ★★→★★★★ 68, 70, 73, 76, 78
Haro (Rioja Alta). López de Heredia was founded in 1877 at the height of the phylloxera epidemic in France, and is one of the most traditional of the *bodegas*; all its buildings are of quarried stone, the vessels for making and maturing the wine of American oak, and the cellars, like the famous El Calado, are tunneled out of the sandstone 17m. (54ft.) below ground, so that the temperature remains at even 12°C with a relative humidity of 80% all the year round. The wines, made with no concessions to modernity, start rather tannic, but age gloriously after long periods in oak. They include a beautiful white 1971 "Tondonia" with a subtle blend of oak and fruit and the legendary 1953, a revelation to people who think that white wines of this age must necessarily be flat and oxidized. The youngest of the red wines is the stylish young "Cubillo", and the older reds include 5° año and 6° año "Tondonia" and "Bosconia", the "Bosconia" being rather softer and fuller-bodied. Some of the *reservas*, such as the 1942 "Bosconia", can only be described as classics.

Marqués de Cáceres, Bodegas D.O. r. (p.) w. dr. res. ★★→★★★ 70, 71, 73, 78
Cenicero (Rioja Alta). The *bodega* was founded in 1972 by Don Enrique Forner, who, with his brother, owns a château in the Haut-Médoc, and its methods are more similar to those of Bordeaux than most of the concerns in the Rioja, since it was planned with advice from Professor Peynaud of Bordeaux University. It describes itself as a "Unión Vinivitícola", the red wine being made by a group of substantial local producers or in the neighboring cooperative in Cenicero, and later

blended and matured in the *bodega* itself. The inexpensive red wines are labeled as "Rivarey" and the others as "Marqués de Cáceres"; the *reservas* are fruity, well balanced and less oaky than the typical red Riojas, with a blackberry flavor and long finish. The firm was the first to introduce a new-style white Rioja, the "Marqués de Cáceres", made by "cold fermentation" and unaged in cask. Exceptionally light, fresh and fruity, it is still perhaps the best wine of its type.

Marqués de Murrieta S.A., Bodegas D.O. r. (p.) w. dr.
★★→★★★★ 60, 68, 70, 74, 76, 78
Ygay (Rioja Alta). Second only in seniority to the MARQUÉS DE RISCAL, the *bodega* was founded by the Marqués de Murrieta in Ygay, a village just E of Logroño, in 1870. With Riscal, it has traditionally been regarded as the aristocrat of Riojas, and the *bodega* is strictly traditional in its methods. 40% of the grapes are grown in the surrounding vineyards belonging to the *bodega* and the rest by regular suppliers under careful supervision. The wines are fermented in cement vats and aged for long periods in oak, the transfer of wine from one container to another being effected by gravity and not by pumping. Until recently, at any rate, they were kept in BARRICA and bottled only immediately prior to shipment.

The youngest of the reds is the soft and fruity 4° año "Etiqueta Blanca", and there is also a very round and fruity white wine of similar age. Pride of the *reservas* is the superb "CASTILLO DE YGAY", one of the most sought-after and expensive of Spanish wines. It is made only at very rare intervals, and the next in line after the glorious 1934 is the 1960. For connoisseurs of old and rare wines, the *bodega* rates the best vintages of earlier years as 1920, 1925, 1931, 1934, 1935, 1942, 1948 and 1949.

Marqués de Riscal S.A., Herederos de D.O. r. (p.) res.
★★→★★★★ 64, 65, 68, 70, 71, 73, 76, 78, 80, 81
Elciego (Rioja Alavesa). Founded in 1860 by a trio of aristocrats including the Marqués de Riscal, the *bodega* was designed by a *vigneron* from Bordeaux and was the first in the Rioja to use French methods for making its wines. Then, as now, a proportion of Cabernet Sauvignon was used, though as elsewhere in the RIOJA ALAVESA the preponderant grape is the Tempranillo.

Riscal now has 20ha (49 acres) of vineyards under Cabernet, half of the vines old and the rest young, and uses some 5% in all its red wines. These have always been light, stylish and elegant, and more in the style of claret than most Riojas. At times they have tended to be a little hard when young, but given time in bottle they age graciously, gaining both in fragrance and intensity of flavor. Even in years like 1971 and the notorious 1972, when Riscal rejected some 40% of the crop, the *bodega* has made good wines; and it is difficult to describe vintages such as 1952 and 1938 as anything but perfect. The remarkable 1922, deep in color, gloriously fragrant and fruity and long in finish, reminds one of nothing so much as one of the best old *crus* from St Emilion.

As at MARQUÉS DE MURRIETA, none of the wine is sold younger than in its fourth year. The *bodega* possesses a library of all the vintages from its inception, and its director Don Francisco Salamero Arrazubi considers that the best of the older vintages of the present century were: 1910, 1920, 1922, 1925, 1938, 1942, 1943, 1947, 1950, 1964, 1965 and 1968.

Riscal makes a little rosé in the Rioja, but its white wine is from Rueda, near Valladolid (see OLD CASTILE-LEÓN).

Martínez Lacuesta Hnos. Ltda. D.O. r. (p.) w. dr. or sw. ★→★★★ 70, 73, 76
Haro (Rioja Alta). This old-established *bodega* in the center of Haro was founded in 1895 and remains in the family under its present head, Don Luis Martínez Lacuesta. The *bodega* has a sizeable capacity of some 4 million liters with 7,000 oak BARRICAS for maturing the wines. At one time it owned vineyards and made its wine, but this is now bought from local cooperatives for maturation and bottling. Its red wines, familiar to travelers on Iberia Airlines, are of two types "Rioja clarete" and the fuller-bodied "Campeador". Both contain a fairly high proportion of Garnacha (80% in the case of the 1981 "Rioja clarete") and tend to be orange-ruby in color, fairly astringent and markedly

oaky in nose. Don Luis considers the best of the older vintages to be the 1958 and 1964 "Reserva Especial". The 1928 was outstanding.

"Monte Real" D.O. r. ★★★
Among the best of the red wines from Bodegas RIOJANAS, this is made with a high proportion of Tempranillo, both from CENICERO in the Rioja Alta and from the RIOJA ALAVESA.

Montecillo S.A., Bodegas D.O. r. (p.) w. dr. ★★ →★★★ 70, 75, 76, 78
Navarrete (Rioja Alta). Founded in 1874, the company now belongs to the sherry firm of Osborne (see SHERRY). It owns 77ha (190 acres) of vineyards and a new vinification plant near NAVARRETE, and *bodegas* for maturing its wines in CENICERO. Its 3° año red and white "Montecillo" are excellent wines and first-rate value; and the firm also produces good red "Viña Monry" *reservas,* of which one of the best was the 1970.

Muga S.A., Bodegas D.O. r. w. dr. res. 70, 73, 75, 76
★★→★★★★
Haro (Rioja Alta). This small family firm was founded in 1926, but moved to a new *bodega* near the station in Haro in 1971. It is entirely unlike the other great new *bodegas* constructed during the Rioja boom of the seventies in that it possesses only 500 BARRICAS – the minimum entitling it to export its wines – and everything is done in traditional style by a tiny and dedicated workforce, headed by the Muga brothers themselves. Its wines reflect the care that goes to their making and are currently among the best from the Rioja. Those labeled as "Muga", made with grapes grown in the firm's own vineyards and others bought from farmers in Abalos, are exceptionally light and fragrant *claretes,* while the "Prado Enea" is a deeper-colored, velvety and more fully bodied wine, sold in bottles with wax capsules. The 1970 was exceptional. The firm also produces small quantities of a dry white wine and of a pleasant and very light sparkling wine made by the champagne method (see SPARKLING WINES).

Nájera
On the hilly southern fringes of the RIOJA ALTA, W of Logroño, this picturesque little township is the site of a former residence of the Kings of Navarra; and the 11th-century Monastery of Santa María contains the tombs of many of the kings and queens of Navarra, Castile and León.

Navarrete
Hill town and wine-making center SW of Logroño. It was the site of the battle in 1367 in which the Black Prince and Peter the Cruel defeated the forces of Henry of Trastamara, and possesses a beautiful 16th-century church and baronial houses.

Oak
The pioneer of the oak barrel for maturing wines, now the "trademark" of the Rioja, was Manuel Quintano, who in 1787 encouraged a group of producers in LABASTIDA to make their wines along French lines. The experiments were short-sightedly discontinued; and it was not until the phylloxera epidemic of the late 19th century and an influx of *négociants* from Bordeaux that ageing in oak became standard practice.

Because of its dense and even texture, permitting slow transpiration of oxygen, the favorite type of oak is American, though Limousin oak is also employed. Maturation is much faster in new barrels, and although the casks are systematically scoured, washed and disinfected after each racking of the wines (decantation from the lees), the pores of the wood gradually become clogged. This is a factor which is not sufficiently recognized when visitors to the *bodegas* exclaim at the time their *reservas* spend in wood. Owing to the high cost of replacing them, some of the barrels in the older *bodegas* are 50 years old.

It is perhaps because the casks in the newer *bodegas* are so much richer in essential oils and resins, conferring an excessively oaky bouquet on the wines, that the *canard* about oak essence has arisen. Such artificial extracts exist, but no self-respecting *bodega* uses them – and would in fact be heavily penalized if caught *in flagrante delicto,* and the fact that the new concerns have invested millions of pounds in oak BARRICAS hardly supports stories of its widespread employment.

Although maturation in oak, in combination with adequate bottle age, is essential in making good red wines, its use in making white Riojas has declined, since the producers are finding that it is a great deal less expensive to make the fresh young white wines, now so popular abroad, without maturing them in oak.

Oja, River
Tributary of the Ebro, flowing into it at Haro, which has given its name to the region.

Olarra S.A., Bodegas D.O. r. (p.) w. dr. or sw. res. ★★→★★★ 70, 73, 75, 76, 78
Logroño (Rioja Alta). The firm was founded in 1972 by a group of Spanish industrialists, and its *bodegas*, on the outskirts of Logroño, in the shape of a three-pointed star symbolizing the 3 sub-regions, are among the largest in the region, equipped with stainless steel fermentation tanks and highly sophisticated computerized systems for controlling the flow of the must and other operations. Maturation is, however, carried out by traditional methods in its 25,000 oak BARRICAS. Its wines are well-made and of high standard, and include a dry, refreshing and well balanced "Blanco Seco Olarra" and excellent red "Cerro Añón" *reservas*, typically full and fruity, of which the 1970 was outstanding.

Oyón
Industrial town in the RIOJA ALAVESA, just across the river from Logroño and the home of the Bodegas EL COTO and FAUSTINO MARTINEZ.

Ollauri
Small village in the RIOJA ALTA just S of Haro and the birthplace of Bodegas PATERNINA and BERBERANA, both of which still maintain their original cellars there for ageing their wines in bottle.

Palacio S.A., Bodegas D.O. r. (p.) w. dr. or sw. ★→★★
Laguardia (Rioja Alavesa). The old *bodegas*, on the road to Elciego, produced a most enjoyable red "Glorioso", round, full and fruity; but since the firm was bought by Seagrams and moved to a modern *bodega* just outside LAGUARDIA, "Glorioso" has not been up to its old standards. The rare 1923 "Bodas de Oro" *reserva especial* is very fine, if you can find it. The firm also makes a fresh young dry white "Semillón" and a sweet white "Regio".

Palacios, Bodegas José D.O. r. (p.) w. ★
Alfaro (Rioja Baja). Makers of somewhat run-of-the-mill RIOJA BAJA wines.

Paternina S.A., Federico r. (p.) w. dr. res. ★→★★★
Haro (Rioja Alta). Founded in 1896 by Don Federico Paternina Josué, Paternina was already one of the largest and most successful of the firms in the Rioja before its purchase by the RUMASA group. Since its inception it has moved successively from the original cellars in Ollauri to a larger *bodega* bought from a Haro cooperative and to the present great modern plant with its 53,000 BARRICAS capable of maturing 12 million liters of wine. "BANDA AZUL", with a brief lapse from popularity during teething troubles at the new plant, has always been a household word among the younger red Riojas; and the more mature "Viña Vial" is a big, fruity, well-balanced wine. There is also a pleasant "Gran Reserva", though in recent years it has never quite matched the gloriously complete 1928. The traditional dry white "Banda Dorada" was a round and fairly oaky wine, but, like other big shippers, Paternina is now making it (under the name of "Rinsol" in Spain) by cold fermentation in stainless steel vats; and the style is now light and fruity, more along the lines of a Loire or dry Alsatian wine.

The crowning glory of Paternina is the rare old vintages kept in the deep cellars of the old *bodega* at OLLAURI. No system of stars could do justice to such beautiful old wines as the 1902, 1910, 1920, 1935, 1947 and 1959.

"Principe Pio" r. w. dr. ★★
Wines made for Emilio Lustau S.A. (see SHERRY) by the UNIÓN VINIVITÍCOLA in their *bodegas* at Cenicero, of which the best is the fresh young white.

Ramón Bilbao, Bodegas D.O. r. (p.) w. dr. res. ★
Haro (Rioja Alta). I have frankly not been fortunate in my tastings of these wines, but they have their following in Spain. They include the young red "Monte Llano"; the more mature "Monte Seco" and "Monte Rojo"; and the "Turzaballa" and "Ramón Bilbao" *reservas*. There are also rosés and a white "Monte Llano".

Real Divisa, Bodegas D.O. r. (p.) w. dr. ★★
Abalos (Rioja Alta). *Bodegas* of some note in a small enclave of the RIOJA ALTA to the N of the Ebro, producing worthwhile red wines made mainly from the Tempranillo.

Rioja Alavesa D.O. r. (w. dr.) ★★→★★★
The smallest of the 3 sub-regions of the D.O. Rioja with an area of 7,000ha (17,460 acres) under vines, the Rioja Alavesa is located in the province of Alava and extends N of the River Ebro from near the Conchas de Haro to a line a little E of Logroño. Because of the temperate climate, the southerly exposure of the vineyards and the composition of the soil, which is almost entirely calcareous clay, the Rioja Alavesa produces some of the best wines from the whole region – in the opinion of many experts, *the* best. Another factor is the very high proportion of Tempranillo used in making the red wines.

There are some dozen large *bodegas* which export their wines and others own vineyards in the area, blending the musts with those from the RIOJA ALTA. The main production centers are at LABASTIDA in the W, and Elciego, LAGUARDIA and Oyón towards the E.

In general, the red Alavesa wines are big, fruity and soft (though one or two are very light) with a pronounced and characteristic Tempranillo nose, somewhat resembling that of Cabernet Sauvignon, but mature more rapidly than those from the Rioja Alta and do not last as long. In poor years the Consejo Regulador authorizes the addition of a little Garnacha tinta from the RIOJA BAJA, so as to obtain the necessary body and alcoholic degree, of which the minimum requirement is 11–11.5%.

The sub-region also produces smaller amounts of white wine with good acid balance, mainly made from the Viura and Malvasía.

Rioja Alta D.O. r. (p.) w. dr. or sw. ★★→★★★★
Together with the RIOJA ALAVESA, the sub-region of the Rioja Alta produces the best Rioja wines. It lies within the province of La Rioja, extending (apart from a small northern alcove around Abalos) S of the Ebro from the Conchas de Haro in the W to just beyond Logroño in the E. The soils are more mixed than those of the Rioja Alavesa, comprising calcareous clay, ferruginous clay and alluvial silt. On the basis of this and of the micro-climate, oenologists have sub-divided the area, from W to E, into the zones of Cuzcurrita, Haro, San Asensio and Cenicero-Fuenmayor. The wines from the wetter and hillier area of the W tend to be more acidic and lower in alcohol than those from Cenicero, where there is a transition in climate from humid to semi-arid and a change to predominantly calcareous soils, particularly suitable for growing the Tempranillo grape.

There are some 30 large *bodegas* in the Rioja Alta; and the main production centers are HARO in the W, CENICERO and FUENMAYOR in the center, and LOGROÑO and NAVARRETE in the E.

Although the Tempranillo is the basic grape of the Rioja Alta, as of the Rioja Alavesa, its red wines contain a higher proportion of Mazuelo, Graciano and Garnacha, and tend to be brisker and fresher in nose, a little more acidic and longer lasting. As in the Rioja Alavesa, the whites are made mainly from the Viura and Malvasía, with smaller amounts of the Garnacha blanca. It is difficult to be more specific, since the large *bodegas* sometimes use a blend of wines made from grapes grown both in the Rioja Alta and Rioja Alavesa.

La Rioja Alta S.A., Bodegas D.O. r. (p.) w. dr. res.
★★→★★★★ 64, 68, 70, 73, 76, 78
Haro (Rioja Alta). A medium-sized family concern founded in 1890 and

one of the first to build a *bodega* in the hallowed area near the railway station in Haro, La Rioja Alta has consistently maintained the quality and prestige of its wines. It owns some 250ha (620 acres) of vineyards, both in the RIOJA ALTA and RIOJA BAJA, and possesses 23,000 BARRICAS for ageing its wines, made by strictly traditional methods. These include a pleasant young 3° año "Viña Alberdi" (sold in the U.K. as Sainsbury's Rioja); the fruity, full-bodied and velvety red "Viña Ardanza" (named after one of the 5 families which founded the *bodega*); a lighter and very stylish "Viña Arana"; and the excellent "904" *reserva*. It also makes a traditional white Rioja aged in cask, the "Metropol Extra", and the fresh young "Leonora", only briefly matured in oak.

Rioja Baja D.O. r. (w. dr.) ★→★★
The largest of the sub-regions of the D.O. Rioja, the Rioja Baja extends from just E of LOGROÑO along the Ebro to Alfaro in the SE. The larger part of the area lies in the province of La Rioja, S of the river, but there is also a narrow strip in Navarra to the N. The soils of the Rioja Baja are almost entirely composed of alluvial silt and ferruginous clay; the climate is semi-arid, of the Mediterranean type and the predominant grape is the red Garnacha tinta, which yields musts high in alcohol and extract, but quick to oxidize. For these reasons the typical wines are coarser than those of the cooler and hillier RIOJA ALAVESA and RIOJA ALTA, and are often used for blending to confer alcoholic degree and body. Nevertheless, the bold departure of Bodegas BERBERANA in planting the Tempranillo and Viura in calcareous soils in the higher part of the area, at Monte Yerga near Adeanueva del Ebro, has proved very successful.

There are 6 major *bodegas* in the Rioja Baja, and the main centers of production are San Adrián, Alfaro, Arnedo and Aldeanueva del Ebro, a sunbaked town which produces better asparagus and peppers than wine and is curiously named, because it is not, as the name implies, either a hamlet, new, or near the Ebro.

The typical wines are full-bodied reds, high in alcohol and more akin to those of the Ribero Baja (see NAVARRA) than the delicate growths of the Rioja Alta or Rioja Alavesa.

Rioja Santiago S.A., Bodegas D.O. r. (p.) w. res. ★→★★★
Haro (Rioja Alta). Old-established firm with *bodegas* in HARO, just across the bridge over the Ebro, and extensive vineyards near Labastida in the RIOJA ALAVESA. Long before its takeover by Pepsi-Cola, the firm hit on the ingenious idea of marketing its wines, sold under the name of "Yago" (or St. James, the patron saint of Spain), in a square bottle – hence making them immediately identifiable and saving a great deal of space in casing them. The younger red wines have suffered from pasteurization, a process which puts a summary end to their development in bottle, but the older vintages of the "Condal" *reservas* are very fine. Above all, Santiago specializes in bottled *sangría*, made by adding citrous essence to red wine and marketed by Pepsi-Cola in the U.S.A. as "Monsieur Henri".

Riojanas S.A., Bodegas D.O. r. (p.) w. dr. or sw.
res. ★★→★★★ 64, 66, 68, 70, 73, 78
Cenicero (Rioja Alta). This large and old-established *bodega*, founded in 1890, was built in flamboyant style with a castellated keep and with advice from Bordeaux; and there were French technicians working there until the early years of World War II. It is of interest in that part of the wine is still made in the old-fashioned Riojan style by fermenting the grapes in open stone *lagos*. It draws its grapes both from the RIOJA ALTA and RIOJA ALAVESA from some 200ha (494 acres) of vineyards owned either by the company or its shareholders and also from private farmers. Small amounts of selected Garnacha grapes from the RIOJA BAJA are also used.

Its wines include a dry white "Medieval", a semi-sweet white "Albina", and an inexpensive red 2° año "Canchales". It also makes good "Viña Albina" *reservas*; but perhaps the most interesting wines are the red "Monte Real" *reservas* made with a sizeable proportion of Tempranillo from the Rioja Alavesa.

Among the best of the older vintages were 1890, 1915, 1922, 1934, 1942, 1950 and 1956.

RUMASA
This great Spanish conglomerate, with extensive interests in banking, hotels and property as well as wines of all types, sometime ago took over the important Rioja firms of PATERNINA and FRANCO ESPAÑOLAS. It has recently bought Bodegas LAN and acquired a majority shareholding in BERBERANA. See also SHERRY.

Salceda S.A., Viña D.O. r. res. ★★→★★★ 70, 73, 76
Elciego (Rioja Alavesa). The present *bodega*, just beyond the bridge over the Ebro on the road from Cenicero to Elciego, is of modern construction, dating from 1974, and is equipped with stainless steel fermentation tanks together with the traditional oak BARRICAS for ageing the wines. Of medium size, it makes only red wine. Its first vintage was the excellent 1970; and its 1973 was a particularly pleasant wine, fruity and well balanced.

San Mateo, Festival of
One of many such festivals in the wine-growing districts, the Fiesta de San Mateo begins in LOGROÑO on September 21st, rather before the official start of grape-picking on October 10th, and lasts for a week, with a uniformed band parading the streets, bullfights and firework displays in the Plaza del Espolón at midnight.

Savin S.A.
Savin is one of the largest Spanish wine companies, specializing in inexpensive branded wine made to good standards. It possesses wineries up and down Spain (see also CATALONIA and VALENCIAN AREA); in the Rioja it operates a *bodega* at Aldeanueva del Ebro in the RIOJA BAJA and also controls CAMPO VIEJO in Logroño.

Santo Domingo de la Calzada
Just outside the demarcated region, Santo Domingo, S of Haro, is on the old pilgrim route from France to Santiago de Compostela, and is one of the pleasantest places to stay when visiting the Rioja. Its 12th-century cathedral incorporates an unusual feature, a live cock and hen housed behind a grille high on one wall in commemoration of a miracle wrought by St. Dominic, patron saint of the pilgrims. The Parador, facing the church and built in medieval times as a hospice for the pilgrims, offers comfortable accommodation and regional cooking and wines.

S.M.S., Bodegas D.O. r. res. ★★
Villabuena (Rioja Alavesa). S.M.S. are the initials of the family which owns the firm – Samaniego Milans del Bosch Solano. Founded before 1900, the *bodega* now has a capacity of some 300,000 liters and 600 oak BARRICAS. The wines, all red, are made entirely with grapes grown in vineyards belonging to the family. They are fermented in wooden *tinos* before spending a year in cement vats and being further matured in cask and in bottle. Until 1981 the grapes were not destalked, so that the wines are dark in color, and mature more slowly than most from the ALAVESA. Those currently available include a 3° año "Valserrano"; a fruity 5° año with a hint of cedar in the nose; and an excellent 1970 Gran Reserva, fragrant, full-bodied, with a lot of fruit and a long, somewhat tannic finish.

San Vicente de la Sonsierra
Picturesque village near LABASTIDA dominated by a ruined castle with magnificent views over the Ebro and across the Rioja.

Sociedad General de Vinos S.A. D.O. r. (p.) w. dr. ★★→★★★ 73, 76, 78
Elciego (Rioja Alavesa). The origins of the company date from the early 1970s, when the sherry concern of Pedro Domecq and the Canadian firm of Seagram joined forces to take over Bodegas PALACIO. The partners later parted ways, and Pedro Domecq constructed its own *bodega* with modern stainless steel fermentation tanks and a capacity of some 13,000 oak BARRICAS for maturing the wines. It has also planted 571ha (1,365 acres) of new vineyards in one of the best parts of the RIOJA ALAVESA, a venture notable among other aspects for training the

vines in Bordeaux style, rather than pruning them low in the traditional Riojan fashion.

Apart from a pleasant and inexpensive young "Viña Eguia", the best known of its wines are the dry white and red "Domecq Domain" (sold in Spain as "Privilegio del Rey Sancho"). After a promising start with the red 1973, the 1976 is a first-rate Alavesa wine, well balanced, deep and fruity.

Sogeviñas
See SOCIEDAD GENERAL DE VINOS, S.A.

Vega Delicia S.A. D.O. r. res. ★→★★ 71, 73
Ollauri (Rioja Alta). Small company making wines of some interest, the 3° año "Vega Andia" and "Vega Delicia" *reservas.*

Unión Vitivinícola S.A.
See MARQUÉS DE CÁCERES, BODEGAS

Velázquez S.A., Bodegas D.O. r. res. ★→★★
Cenicero (Rioja Alta). One of the smaller *bodegas*, labeling its wines as "Monte Velaz", "Campo Blanco", "Garoa" and "Savory"

"Viña Albina" D.O. r. ★★★
Well known red wine from Bodegas RIOJANAS.

"Viña Ardamza" D.O. r. ★★★
One of the most consistently satisfying of red Riojas, smooth, fruity and full-bodied, from Bodegas La RIOJA ALTA.

"Viña Bosconia" D.O. r. ★★★
An excellent red Rioja from the traditional Bodegas LÓPEZ DE HEREDIA made mainly with grapes grown in its Bosconia vineyards on the S bank of the Ebro.

"Viña Pomal" D.O. r. ★★→★★★
Full-bodied red Rioja from Bodegas BILBAINAS made with grapes from its vineyards in Leza in the RIOJA ALAVESA.

"Viña Real" D.O. r. ★★★
Excellent red ALAVESA *reserva* from the COMPAÑÍA VINÍCOLA DEL NORTE DE ESPAÑA (CVNE), made in an outlying *bodega* in Elciego.

"Viña Tondonia" D.O. r. w. dr. ★★★→★★★★
First-rate and long-lasting red and white Riojas from Bodegas LÓPEZ DE HEREDIA.

Ygay
Hamlet in the Rioja Alta a little E of Logroño with the *bodegas* of the MARQUÉS DE MURRIETA on its outskirts.

WINE & Food

It is perhaps a little pretentious to talk of the cuisine of the Rioja. What the area offers is a range of genuinely regional dishes based on the excellent lamb, pork, kid and spicy *chorizo* sausage, and fresh vegetables in season. When André Simon first wrote about the Rioja, he was, in fact, more enthusiastic about the vegetables than the wines and it is still an experience to visit the great open market in Logroño.

The meals served to guests in the *bodegas* themselves, often in a great cellar lined with casks, are simple and well-designed to show off the wines, and usually begin with fresh local asparagus or a *menestra* of vegetables, followed by small lamb chops cooked over glowing vine shoots and ending with the ubiquitous *flan* (cream caramel) or the luscious peaches preserved in syrup. Such simple delights are not to be despised; and when Paul Bocuse was engaged by the Compañía del Norte de España to cook its centenary banquet, the story goes that, having sampled the *patatas riojanas* prepared by the *bodega*'s regular cook, he asked why he had been sent for.

Alubias con chorizo
A rib-warming stew made with haricot or butter beans, chopped onions, garlic, olive oil and highly cured chorizo *sausage, further seasoned with sweet paprika powder and parsley.*
This calls for a full-bodied 2- or 3-year-old red, or a *jarra* of the local house wine.

Bacalao a la riojana
Dried cod cooked with olive oil, onions, garlic, strips of canned red pepper and sweet paprika powder.
Drink one of the traditional oaky white Riojas with sufficient character to stand up to the rich assortment of flavors, e.g. a white "Tondonia" from López de Heredia, or the rather less oaky but complex "Monopole" from CVNE.

Cabrito asado
Roast kid Rioja style.
A good chance to show off the qualities of one of the many red *reservas.*

Callos a la riojana
Highly spiced tripe Riojan style.

Cardo
Cardoon, a celery-like vegetable, served braised as a starter.
Choose from among the numerous white Riojas, perhaps one with a hint of oak, such as Olarra, or the white "Samaniego" from Bodegas Alavesas.

Chuletas de cordero
Small lamb chops grilled over glowing vine shoots and served in the bodegas *to set off the better reds and* reservas.

Cordero lechal asado
Milk-fed baby lamb roasted in a baker's oven.
Choose the best red *reserva* you can run to, e.g. a 1970 from Riscal, La Rioja Alta, López de Heredia, Muga, Riojanas, CVNE, etc.

Chorizo a la brasa
Chorizo, *the spicy cured pepper sausage, often home made, and roasted whole.*
Since this is extremely hot, a chilled glass of one of the new-style light white Riojas, such as the Marqués de Cáceres or Faustino VII, is a refreshing accompaniment.

Espárragos
The Rioja Baja grows some of the best Spanish asparagus, which is served as a starter either with sauce vinaigrette *or mayonnaise.*
Take your choice of the dry white wines.

Malvices
Tiny birds (red-wings) fried crisp and eaten whole.
Clarete or other light red wine.

Melocotones en almíbar
Particularly large and luscious local peaches preserved in syrup.
Try a sweet or semi-sweet wine, such as the "Diamante" from Franco Españolas.

Menestra de verduras a la riojana
A mixed vegetable dish made from whatever is in season, such as broad beans and peas, together with chopped onions, tomatoes, bacon or ham, seasoning and sometimes hard-boiled eggs. It is cooked in olive oil and light red wine.
A *clarete* or light 3-year-old red wine goes well with it.

Morcilla Dulce
Morcilla *is a blood sausage akin to black pudding, usually made with onions and savory rice, but in this version it is prepared with cinnamon, other sweet spices and a little sugar.*
Although it is usually eaten as a starter, anything but a sweet or semi-sweet white wine would seem tart.

Patatas a la riojana
Potatoes in a clear orange sauce with chorizo.

Picadillo
A variant on CHORIZO A LA BRASA, *the filling of the sausage being ground, cooked and served hot.*
This definitely calls for a chilled and cooling dry white wine. As an alternative to those already mentioned, try "Rinsol" from Paternina or the dry "Lambros" from Lan.

Pimientos rellenos a la riojana
Regional variant on stuffed peppers, filled with a mixture of ground pork, beaten egg, nutmeg, garlic, parsley and a little pepper and salt, fried in hot olive oil and served in a piquant sauce.
Order a full-bodied and robust red.

Pochas riojanas
Substantial stew made from a local variety of haricot bean, allowed to fatten in the pod but not dried, and taking its dark red color from the chorizo *with which it is cooked.*
Best eaten with a *jarra* of the local red house wine or a robust bottle of Rioja Baja.

Revuelto de ajos
Eggs scrambled with tender young garlic shoots.
The traditional white Riojas, oaky or slightly oaky, balance this very well.

Sopa de ajo con huevos
Traditional Castilian garlic soup, seasoned with sweet paprika powder and thickened with bread and beaten egg.
Better to leave the table wine for later and ask for a glass of *fino* sherry.

Restaurants

Arnedo *Sopitas* (tunneled into the cliff with individual dining alcoves; try the excellent *revuelto de ajos*).

Cenicero *Bar-Restaurant Conchita* (tiny and typical of the region; Loly's *pochas* are a triumph).

Fuenmayor *El Porrón* (much patronized by the *bodegueros*).

Haro ⋆ *Beethoven II* (good regional cooking); ⋆ *Terete* (the classical Haro restaurant, simple surroundings, marvelous roast baby lamb and long list of *reservas*).

Logroño ⋆ *Mesón de la Merced* (sophisticated and comfortable in converted wine cellar, excellent roast baby lamb); *Machado* (regional cooking and Rioja wines); *San Remo* (regional cooking and wines); *El Cachetero* (small, popular, good selection of wines); *Robinson's English Pub* (for dancing and a late nightcap).

Oyón *Mesón de la Cueva* (good regional food in atmospheric surroundings).

Santo Domingo de la Calzada *El Rincón* (inexpensive and vastly popular; its specialty is *callos a la riojana*).

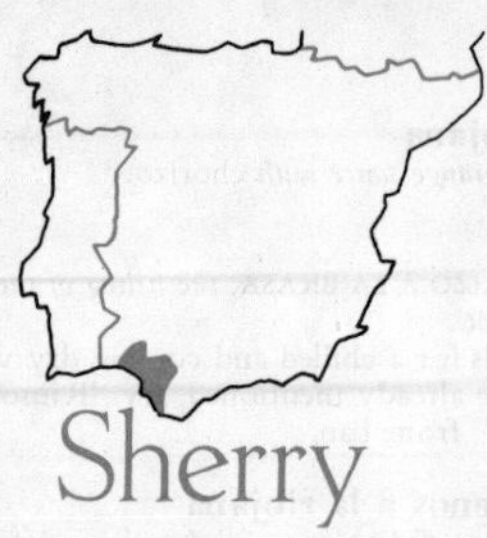

Sherry

Sherry is, of course, the classical Spanish wine and one with particularly close associations with Britain, since the great sherry boom took place with the active participation of British merchants, many of whom settled in Jerez. Further than this, the U.K. consumes more sherry than Spain and, followed by the Netherlands, is still the largest foreign market. During the current depression, sherry, in common with most other fortified wines and spirits, has suffered something of a set-back; but this is not the first in its long history. A glass of chilled *fino* remains the most satisfactory preliminary to a meal and the least likely to interfere with what follows, and, for a wine of such character and one so expensive to make, sherry of all types remains most reasonably priced. The producers are actively fighting back with, for example, a campaign for drinking it "on the rocks"; and in the long run quality and value must surely tell.

The wines were well known even in Roman times, but it was Sir Francis Drake's raid on Cádiz in 1587 and seizure of some 2,900 pipes (110-gallon barrels) which firmly established them in England. The British presence had begun to be felt after the

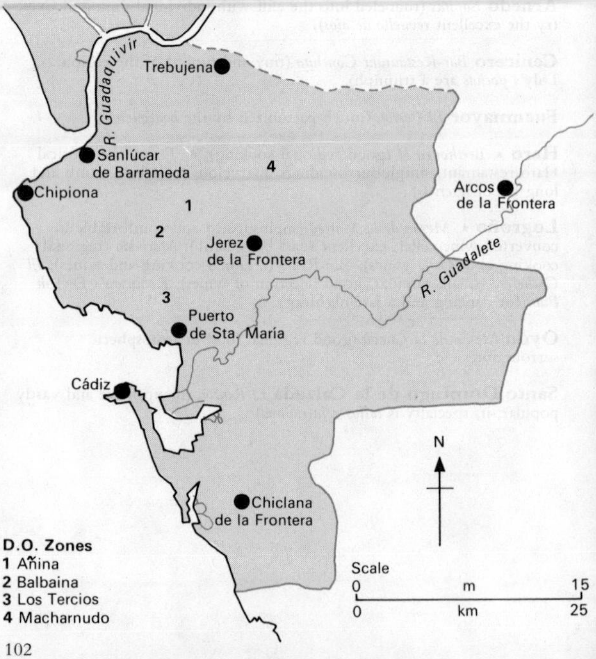

R. Guadaquivir
Trebujena
Sanlúcar de Barrameda
Chipiona
4
1
2
3
Arcos de la Frontera
Jerez de la Frontera
R. Guadalete
Puerto de Sta. María
Cádiz
N
Chiclana de la Frontera

D.O. Zones
1 Añina
2 Balbaina
3 Los Tercios
4 Macharnudo

Scale
0 m 15
0 km 25

expulsion of the Jews from Spain by the Catholic Monarchs in 1492; and during the late 18th and early 19th centuries English, Scottish and Irish merchants arrived in force. Their names survive in those of such famous sherry houses as Duff Gordon, Osborne, Garvey, Terry, Sandeman, and Williams & Humbert.

The sherry district occupies a triangle with its apex near Cádiz, bounded by the Guadalquivir and Guadalete rivers and embracing the main centers of Jerez de la Frontera, Puerto de Santa María and Sanlúcar de Barrameda. The whole area is in the province of Cádiz. The best vineyards lie within a 32km (20 mile) radius N and W of Jerez, and the soils are of three classes. The most highly rated is the dazzlingly white *albariza*, containing some 40% of chalk, together with sand and clay, which enables it to retain moisture throughout the year in a region where average rainfall amounts to only 550mm. (22in.) and temperatures rise to 40°C during the long, cloudless summers. Other types are the darker *barro* and a sandy *arena*, used mainly for Moscatel grapes.

The sherry grape *par excellence* is the white Palomino, which grows best in the chalky *albariza* and is used for all the different types of sherry and almost exclusively for the *finos*. Next in importance is the Pedro Ximénez, which can, as in Montilla (see MONTILLA-MORILES), produce excellent dry wines, but is principally used in Jerez for sweet dessert wines. Smaller amounts of Moscatel are also grown for blending with sweet sherries.

Sherry owes its entirely individual character to the method used in making it. Unlike table wines, it is matured with free access to the atmosphere, in a loosely stoppered cask with an air space above the liquid. This would ordinarily result in fairly rapid oxidation, were it not that the new wine spontaneously grows a *flor* (or "flower") on the surface of the liquid. This layer of yeasts both regulates the access of air to the must and eliminates harmful vinegar-producing bacteria. The growth varies according to the type of wine and is thickest with *finos* (and even more so with the *manzanillas* from Sanlúcar de Barrameda) and less vigorous with the fuller-bodied *olorosos*, which are soon fortified to kill it and to protect the wine during physico-chemical maturation.

The other difference between the making of table wines and sherry is that it is aged by the *solera* system, providing for the progressive blending of older and younger wines. The *solera* with its accompanying *criadera* consists of long rows of oak butts arranged in the *bodega* in tiers. Each row of butts or "scale" contains wine of the same type but of different age. When wine is required for shipment or bottling, it is drawn off from the butts at the bottom containing the oldest wine. The contents are then made good from the "scale" immediately preceding it in age, and so on through the whole system of casks. In this fashion there is regular "refreshment" of older wine with younger, and as Richard Ford said in 1846, "houses are enabled to supply for any number of years exactly that particular color, flavor, body, etc., which particular customers demand." There are therefore no vintages in sherry, and a description such as "Solera 1847" refers to the year in which the *solera* was first laid down.

The basic styles of sherry are the dry and light *finos*, such as "Tio Pepe" or "La Ina", drunk chilled as an apéritif; the rather fuller *amontillados*, either dry or semi-dry; and the dark, fully bodied *olorosos*, the most maderized and fragrant of the wines. In their natural state, *olorosos*, such as "Rio Viejo", are completely dry and are best drunk before a meal; but they are often blended with sweet wine to make a dessert sherry or cream, of which one of the best known is "Bristol Cream". This does not exhaust the possibilities, however, and other varieties such as *manzanilla*, *palo cortado* and pale cream are described in the A–Z listing.

In the past it was very much a question of making the wine and then waiting to see how it would develop before deciding for which of the different styles it was most suitable. Modern methods have enabled the *bodegas* to make these decisions at a much earlier stage; and in the latest of the continuous vinification plants, wine destined as a *fino* is drawn off after the lightest crushing of the grapes, which are then more firmly pressed to obtain the must for the *olorosos*.

In all essentials, sherry continues to be made along strictly traditional lines, but there have been many other innovations in recent years. Gonzalez Byass has instituted an imaginative program for eliminating plant diseases by the cloning (vegetative reproduction) of virus-free vines; the bacchanalian rite of treading the grapes with nail-studded cowhide boots has given way to modern horizontal or continuous presses. The wine is increasingly (but not always) fermented in temperature-controled stainless steel tanks rather than in butts, and the bulk of the wine is no longer shipped in cask, but bottled in the *bodega*, although some of the large *bodegas* have found that their big-selling sherries reach the customer fresher if they are shipped in containers topped up with inert gas and bottled abroad.

Apart from visits to the *bodegas*, the sherry region is a delightful one in which to spend a holiday. There are the Atlantic beaches of places like Puerto de Sta. María, Rota and Chipiona; the great nature reserve of the Coto de Doñana across the Guadalquivir; the rugged mountains and hunting of the Sierra de Cádiz; the historic buildings of Cádiz and Sevilla; and by no means least the superb seafood from the Bay of Cádiz. Jerez is at its best in the late spring, when the blue of the jacaranda blossom rivals that of the sky, or in the early autumn at harvest time.

The quickest way to reach the area is to fly to Madrid and then on to Jerez by an internal flight or by the fast and luxurious TALGO train; alternatively, one may fly to Sevilla, 84km (52 miles) to the N by the A4 *autopista*, and hire a car. Once there, a car is not a necessity, as there is a local electric train to Puerto de Sta. María and bus services to other places.

The larger *bodegas*, such as Pedro Domecq, Gonzalez Byass and Williams & Humbert, are well organized for visits, which always end with a generous tasting, with *fino* served as it should be, from chilled half-bottles. Visiting hours are normally from 9.30–13.00, but it is always advisable to check by letter or telephone beforehand. A letter of introduction from a wine merchant or shipper smooths the way in the case of smaller establishments.

As to the vineyards, you can get good views of the famous areas of Macharnudo and Carrascal to the N of Jerez by branching off the A4 from Sevilla at Las Cabezas and following the hilly by-road, through this almost lunar landscape of whitish sunbaked clay, by way of Lebrija and Trebujana and into Jerez.

Serving sherry

Sherry is often ruined by improper serving and storage, especially fresh and delicate *finos* which are easily spoilt by oxidation. *All* sherries should be served in a glass tapering towards the top and large enough to be filled only a third or half full to allow for the development of the bouquet (see COPITA). *Fino* begins to deteriorate after about 3 months in bottle; and once the bottle is opened, the contents should either be drunk within 3 days or poured into a tightly corked half-bottle. Many of the complaints about popular *finos* arise from the habit of keeping half-empty bottles for weeks on the shelves of a warm bar.

Much the same applies to the lighter *amontillados*, though they deteriorate more slowly. *Olorosos*, especially the sweeter styles, last much longer in bottle, and the rich dessert sherries sometimes improve because of the slow consumption of sugar, which gives them a dryish finish.

Fino and light *amontillado* should be served chilled, but not iced. The best thing is to leave it for a few hours in the door of a refrigerator before serving it; and the wine will also keep longer if stored in the refrigerator. Rather than suffer a lukewarm *fino* in a bar, it is better to ask for it to be poured into a larger glass and drink it "on the rocks"– though chilling is preferable. *Olorosos*, the fuller-bodied *amontillados* and cream sherries should be drunk at room temperature.

Albariza
The best of the soils, white in color and containing some 40% of chalk, the residue consisting of sand and clay.

Amontillado
Style of sherry, amber yellow in color, with a dry nutty flavor and of about 16.5–18% strength. It takes its name from wines formerly prepared in Montilla (see MONTILLA-MORILES), and the genuine article is made by allowing a *fino* to age for a further period after the FLOR has died or been eliminated by addition of alcohol.

Amoroso
Traditional name, in Spanish "loving", not now much used, for a smooth, sweet *oloroso* made by adding Pedro Ximénez wine and VINO DE COLOR.

Añada
A young vintage wine as yet unblended in a CRIADERA.

Añina
District between Jerez de la Frontera and Sanlúcar de Barrameda, rated 4th in order of merit of those with ALBARIZA soil.

Arcos de la Frontera
Picturesque town E of Jerez, perched on a rocky crag above the River Guadalete. With its narrow alleys and white houses, and mosques masquerading as churches, it is one of the pleasantest places to stay when visiting the region. There is a comfortable Parador housed in the old Casa del Corregidor, with splendid views over the gorge of the Guadalete.

Arena
Reddish, sandy soil containing some 10% of chalk and the least favored in the region, except for the Moscatel vine.

Arrope
A non-alcoholic syrup, prepared by evaporating down must to 20% of its original volume and used in making the VINO DE COLOR for sweet *oloroso* and cream sherries.

Balbaina
District to the W of Jerez, adjoining ANINA and LOS TERCIOS, and rated 3rd in order of merit of those with ALBARIZA soil.

Barbadillo S.A., Antonio
Sanlúcar de Barrameda. Founded in 1821, Barbadillo is the largest of the firms in Sanlúcar, with offices in the former bishop's palace and a complex of *bodegas* facing the church of Santa María de la O in the center of the town; even its Bodega Nueva ("new cellar") dates from 1850. It possesses vineyards in the areas of BALBAINA, CARRASCAL, Campiz and San Julián, and has gone into partnership with HARVEY'S in the development of 1,000ha (2,470 acres) of new vineyards and the most modern of vinification plants in Gibalbin, E of the A4 to Sevilla. Although Harvey's has a 10% holding in the company, it remains very much a family concern. The patriarchal Don Manuel Barbadillo, a noted Andalucian poet, is the doyen of *manzanilla* wines and has written the most authoritative book on the subject.

Barbadillo makes a superb range of *manzanillas*, including a fresh and aromatic "Sanlúcar" *fina*; the "Solear" *manzanilla pasada*, resembling a *fino amontillado* from Jerez; an entirely beautiful dry *oloroso*; and an exceptionally round and satisfying "Eva Cream". It is also producing a fresh and fragrant young table wine from Palomino grapes, labeled as "Castillo de San Diego".

Barro
A mud clay containing up to 10% of chalk, dark in color because of the presence of iron oxide, and 2nd in quality of the soils.

Bertola S.A.
Jerez de la Frontera. The firm was founded in 1911 in partnership with the old-established port concern of C.N. Kopke & Co. Ltd., as Kopke Bertola y Cía. Lda. It was subsequently taken over by Diez Hermanos and is now part of the RUMASA combine. Best known of its sherries is the "Bertola Cream".

Bienteveo
These rough shelters, made of poles thatched with esparto grass, are still occasionally to be seen in the vineyards and were formerly manned by armed guards to prevent the depredations of thieves helping themselves to the ripe grapes. The literal translation is "I see you well".

Blázquez S.A., Hijos de Agustín
Jerez de la Frontera. Old-established firm known particularly for its "Carta Blanca" *fino*; it also markets *finos*, *amontillados* and cream sherries under the labels of "Don Paco", "Don Agustín" and "Balfour", and makes the reliable and inexpensive "Felipe II" brandy.

See also SPIRITS, AROMATIC WINES & LIQUEURS.

"Bristol Cream"
A proprietary name belonging to John HARVEY and Sons of Bristol, who decided during the 19th century to produce an even richer dessert sherry than the popular "Bristol Milk" by blending it with older *olorosos*. It is now the biggest-selling sherry in the world, with very large sales in the U.S.A.

"Bristol Milk"
Bristol has for centuries been one of the most important ports in the U.K. for the shipping of wines, and has imported dessert sherries under the name of "Bristol Milk" since the 17th century. The best known labels are those of HARVEY'S and Avery's of Bristol.

Butt (bota)
The standard butt used for maturing sherry in the SOLERA is of 500 liters capacity, and is made of American oak. There are also larger butts, less pointed in shape, such as the *bocoy* of 600 liters. Butts have become increasingly expensive and represent an appreciable proportion of the cost of a wine which is more expensive than most to produce. Since sherry butts are used for maturing Scotch whisky, some of the firms have arranged for them to be bought by the distilleries in Scotland and to pass them on after a couple of years' use in the *bodega*.

Brown Sherry
English name for a dark dessert sherry, usually only of very moderate quality.

Burdon, John William
John William Burdon, who began by working for DUFF GORDON, became one of the most successful of 19th-century sherry shippers. The firm was eventually taken over in 1932 by Luis CABALLERO S.A., which still markets a well known range of sherries under the Burdon label. They include "Burdon Fino", "Bristol Milk", Golden Oloroso", "Pale Medium" and *amontillado*.

Caballero S.A., Luis
Puerto de Sta. María. The Caballero family were making wines in CHIPIONA as long ago as 1795 and shipping them from 1830. In 1932,

by way of another takeover, the firm became the successors to John William BURDON, whose firm was one of the most successful of the English enterprises in Jerez during the 19th century. Apart from the Burdon sherries and its own well known "Don Guiso Fino" and "Gran Señor Choice Old Cream", the firm also markets a "Benito" *fino*, *amontillado*, cream and pale cream, and makes one of the most popular *ponches* (see SPIRITS, AROMATIC WINES & LIQUEURS).

Cádiz
Capital of the province embracing the sherry region, Cádiz, S of Jerez de la Frontera on a peninsula connected by a stone causeway, is one of the most stylish of Spanish cities. The only city uncaptured by Napoleon during the Peninsular War, it is a place of glittering white houses, narrow streets and handsome squares, bounded by shaded gardens and a wide promenade with views out to the Atlantic. Its large port is now the main center for shipping sherry.

Cádiz also has claims to being the gastronomic capital of Andalucía; the waters of its bay and the surrounding coast supply fish and shellfish in extraordinary variety, and its *freidurías*, where you may buy them freshly fried to take away, were the forerunners to the British fish-and-chip shop.

The quietest and most pleasantly situated hotel is the Atlántico, in a garden at the far tip of the peninsula overlooking the ocean. It belongs to the Parador chain and is thus very reasonably priced, its disadvantage being that it is a long walk through the narrow streets to the center – and it would be an adventurous driver who took his car. If you prefer something closer, try the 3-star Iscotel or 2-star Francia y Paris.

Camera
A wooden box containing a candle for judging the clarity of the wine.

Canoa
A wedge-shaped funnel traditionally used for transferring wine from one butt to another.

Capataz
The cellarman at a *bodega*, all-important in operating the SOLERA.

Carrascal
District to the immediate N of Jerez, whose ALBARIZA soils are rated 2nd in order of merit.

C.A.Y.D., S.A.
Sanlúcar de Barrameda. Founded some 100 years ago by the Bozzano family, of Italian descent, the *bodega* was sold in 1969 to the local Cooperativa de Campo Virgen de la Caridad, which was by then supplying most of its wine. This embraces some 1,000 members with vineyards in the locality; and the combined capacity of the cooperative and the original *bodega* is some 30,000 butts. The musts are fermented in cement *tinajas* (see MONTILLA-MORILES), the first of which were in fact constructed by craftsmen from Montilla, some of them developing as typical *manzanillas* and others as Jerez-type wines. The *manzanillas* include the "Bajo de Guia" and "Sanluqueña" *finas*, and the others the "Cayd" *fino*, *amontillado*, medium and cream.

Chiclana
Village on the border of the sherry district S of Cádiz, producing wine in large quantity, but not of the highest quality. Its *finos* are sometimes blended with the less expensive sherries.

Chipiona
Seaside town on the coast road from Sanlúcar de Barrameda to Puerto de Sta. María. Its ARENA vineyards are noted for their Moscatel, used in some of the sweet dessert wines.

Copita
The tall glass, narrowing towards the top, used for testing sherry. It should be filled only a third to a half full, so that the full aroma of the wine may be appreciated. The small Elgin glasses habitually used in

bars, pubs and restaurants, and filled to the brim, are entirely unsuitable for sherry, since the wine needs space and air for the nose and flavor to develop properly. When on vacation in the sherry area, it is well worth bringing back a set of *copitas* or the larger *catavinos.* If you are served sherry in an Elgin or small thistle glass, ask for it to be poured into a tulip-shaped brandy or wine glass.

Cream sherries
These sweet dessert wines are of two types. The dark, full-bodied mahogany-colored variety is made by sweetening an *oloroso* with a sugary must prepared from Pedro Ximénez and other grapes left to dry in the sun. The base wine for pale creams is a *fino*, sweetened with *dulce apagado*, a wine made by arresting the final stages of fermentation with brandy, so leaving some of the sugar.

See also AMOROSO, "BRISTOL CREAM" and "BRISTOL MILK".

Criadera
The literal meaning of the word is "nursery", and it is used to describe the series of butts from which wine is drawn off to "refresh" or replenish a SOLERA.

Croft Jerez S.A.
Jerez de la Frontera. Croft is one of the oldest names in the port trade, but has been associated with sherry only since 1970, when I.D.V. (International Distillers and Vintners), which had fallen heir to the company by way of W.A. Gilbey Ltd., decided to set up Croft Jerez S.A. to supply its large requirements of sherry. Starting from scratch, the company planted more than 500ha (1,240 acres) of vineyards, and in 1975 opened the Rancho Croft on the outskirts of Jerez, whose handsome, traditionally styled buildings with an eventual capacity of some 40,000 butts house one of the most modern of sherry establishments. Thanks to a new vinification plant and well organized handling procedures, the firm operates with only 35 workers, and at a time when other firms find themselves in difficulties, is one of the most flourishing in Jerez.

Its largest-selling sherry is the "Croft Original" pale cream; the other labels are "Croft Classic" (medium dry), "Croft Delicado" *fino*, "Croft Particular" pale *amontillado*, and a first-rate *palo cortado.*

Crushing
See ZAPATOS DE PISAR.

Cuvillo y Cía. S.A.
Puerto de Sta. María. The Cuvillo family has been making sherry in Puerto de Sta. María since 1783. Its principal market has always been in England, though the wines have often been sold under the labels of the shippers – at one time it was a major supplier of wine for Harvey's "BRISTOL CREAM". Among the best of its wines are the cream; the dry "Sangre" and "Trabajadero" *olorosos*; "Fino C"; and an excellent and very aromatic *palo cortado.*

Diestro S.A., Jaime F.
Jerez de la Frontera. A firm now within the RUMASA group particularly known for its *ponche* (see SPIRITS, AROMATIC WINES & LIQUEURS).

Diez-Merito S.A.
Jerez de la Frontera. Diez Hermanos, a company of French origin, was founded in 1976 and has always specialized in selling wines for sale as "own brands". More recently it has absorbed the old established firm of the Marqués de Merito and has been one of the fastest-growing of the private sherry concerns of recent times. Among its many labels are the "Lolita", "Palma" and "Imperial" *finos*; "Primo Paco" *amontillado*; "Oloroso Solera Victoria Regina", and various cream sherries.

"Don Zoilo"
Superior range of sherries made by ZOILO RUIZ MATEOS, of which the best known is the round and aromatic *fino*, one of the best in its class.

"Double Century"
The best known of PEDRO DOMECQ'S cream dessert sherries.

"Dry Don"
Popular *amontillado* from SANDEMAN.

"Dry Fly"
Proprietary name belonging to the English shippers Findlater Mackie Todd & Co. Ltd. It was first used before World War II to describe its superior "Findlater's Fino", which could not be protected by registration. More recently Findlater's has been marketing a very popular but somewhat sweeter apéritif sherry, under the same name.

"Dry Sack"
A medium *amontillado*, the most popular of the wines from WILLIAMS & HUMBERT, sold in a distinctive sack, though the name, of course, is derived from the old-fashioned English name for sherry (see SACK).

Duff Gordon y Cía. S.A.
Puerto de Sta. María. The company was founded in 1768 by a Scot, Sir James Duff, who was British Consul in Cádiz at the time. The firm flourished, and in 1833 his son, Cosmo Duff Gordon, entered into partnership with Thomas Osborne of the sherry firm of the same name. OSBORFE finally bought out the interest of the Duff Gordon family in 1872, but, in addition to its own sherries, has continued to market the Duff Gordon wines under that name, though they are sold only abroad and not in Spain itself.

Made in the original *bodegas*, they embrace a wide range, including the "Fino Feria", "Club Dry" amontillado, the popular "El Cid" medium-dry *amontillado* and "Santa Maria Cream". The firm also makes a brandy and a "Special Spanish Brandy".

"Duke of Wellington"
A good *fino* made by BODEGAS INTERNACIONALES in their vast new *bodega*.

"El Cid"
Big-selling *amontillado* from DUFF GORDON.

Fiesta de la Vendimia
The famous wine festival held in Jerez de la Frontera in mid-September to celebrate the beginning of the vintage. Dedicated each year to a different country or city where sherry is popular, it embraces flamenco, bullfighting and horse shows, and culminates in the pressing of the first fruits on the steps of the Collegiate Church, a ceremony presided over by the Queen of the Vintage and her attendants in traditional costume, chosen from the prettiest girls in Jerez.

Fina
A light, dry MANZANILLA from Sanlúcar.

Fino
The lightest, driest and most delicate style of sherry, a pale straw color and of 15–18% strength. It develops beneath the FLOR until final fortification and is at its fragrant best when freshly bottled. Once opened, it should be served chilled and drunk within a few days.

Flor
A film of yeasts of the genus *saccharomyces* growing spontaneously on the surface of certain types of sherry, especially finos, during maturation in SOLERA. It protects the wine from undue oxidation or conversion to vinegar and develops most thickly on wines aged in old butts.

Fortification
The addition to a wine of alcohol or brandy. When deficient in alcohol, *fino* sherries are lightly fortified at an early stage, and *olorosos* more strongly to kill the FLOR. *Finos* destined for export are further fortified before shipment or bottling with a 50% mixture of alcohol and mature sherry to prevent the reappearance of the *flor*.

Garvey S.A.
Jerez de la Frontera. Famous sherry house founded by William Garvey,

who emigrated from Ireland in 1780 and set up business in Sanlúcar de Barrameda about 1797. His *bodegas* were for long among the biggest in Jerez and are impressive even by modern standards, with an *oloroso solera* ranged along the side of an arcaded patio some quarter of a mile long. The firm was taken over in 1979 by RUMASA, which has fastidiously restored the old family mansion and also constructed a new vinification plant and further large *bodegas* for maturing the wine on the outskirts of Jerez.

Most of the wine is now fermented in cement *tinajas* (see MONTILLA-MORILES) rather than in butts or stainless steel. Of its excellent sherries, the best known is the "San Patricio" *fino*, named by William Garvey after the patron saint of his native Ireland. Others include the aromatic and fully flavored "Tio Guillermo" *amontillado*, the dry "Ochavico" and medium-dry "Long Life" *olorosos*, and the "Bicentenary Pale Cream".

Gonzalez Byass & Co. Ltd.
Jerez de la Frontera. One of the largest and most important sherry firms, still family controled, Gonzalez Byass was founded in 1835 by Don Antonio Gonzalez y Rodriguez, who later took into partnership the firm's London agent, Robert Blake Byass. The head of the firm until his death some years ago, Don Manuel Gonzalez Gordon, Marqués de Bonanza, was one of the most distinguished figures in Jerez, and wrote one of the best books on its wines: *Sherry, The Noble Wine* (1972).

The old *bodegas* in the center of the town, alongside those of PEDRO DOMECQ, are vast in size: the famous "La Concha", designed by Gustave Eiffel, houses 12,400 butts, and the more modern "Tio Pepe" *bodega*, on 3 floors, a further 30,000; but even these are dwarfed by the modern vinification plant of "Las Copas" on the road to Cádiz with its capacity of 60,000 butts. A quaint and human touch about one of the older *bodegas* is the small mice, carefully protected and fed – on sherry, of course.

"Tio Pepe" is the biggest-selling *fino* in the world, and deservedly so, since it remains one of the driest and most elegant. Other popular wines are the "Elegante" dry *fino*, "La Concha" medium *amontillado*, "Alfonso" dry *oloroso*, "San Domingo" pale cream and "Nectar" cream. Gonzalez Byass also makes some superb old *olorosos* in limited quantity, such as the dry "Apostoles Oloroso Muy Viejo" and two very old dessert sherries, the "Matusalem" and "Solera 1847" *oloroso dulce*, both almost black in color with deep maderized nose and dryish bitter-sweet finish, since most of the sugar has been consumed over the years.

See also SPIRITS, AROMATIC WINES & LIQUEURS.

Guadalete, River
The Guadalete, flowing into the Bay of Cádiz, fairly closely follows the E boundary of the fan-shaped sherry region.

Guadalquivir, River
Flowing into the Atlantic at Sanlúcar de Barrameda, the Guadalquivir forms the W boundary of the sherry region, dividing it from the salt marshes of the famous wildlife reserve of the Coto Doñana.

Harvey & Sons (España) Ltd., John
Jerez de la Frontera. The old Bristol company of John Harvey & Sons had its origins in an earlier company founded in 1796, with which the Harvey family became associated in the early 19th century. Long famous as sherry shippers and particularly for its "BRISTOL MILK" and "BRISTOL CREAM" it is now a subsidiary of Allied Brewers, and it was not until 1970 that it established its own vineyards and *bodegas* in Jerez by buying the old-established firm of Mackenzie & Co. It later acquired the adjoining large *bodegas* of the Marqués de Misa and in 1973 began

developing much larger vineyards in association with GARVEY and BARBADILLO. The continuous vinification plant which it operates at the Gibalbin vineyards with Barbadillo is the most modern in the region.

The old Misa *bodega* is one of the most impressive in Jerez, and a perennial attraction for visitors in the beautiful gardens of the old Mackenzie *bodegas* is the pool with its 65-year-old Mississippi alligator.

Apart from the world-famous "Bristol Cream", Harvey's markets an extensive range of sherries, including the inexpensive "Luncheon Dry" *fino* and *amontillado*; "Isabelita" *fino*; some half-dozen styles of *amontillado*; and "Bristol Milk" and the brown "Copper Beech" for those with a very sweet tooth. Its latest introduction is "Harveys Eleven", specially blended for drinking with ice and mixers as a counterblast to the vermouths increasingly popular with younger people.

Internacionales S.A., Bodegas

Jerez de la Frontera. Bodegas Internacionales is of the new generation of sherry firms. Belonging to RUMASA, it occupies the single largest building in Jerez, designed in modern style and completed in 1977, and adjoining Gonzalez Byass' new vinification plant on the road for Cádiz just outside Jerez. Besides producing a good *fino* and range of other sherries sold under the label of "The Duke of Wellington", the *bodega*, with its 63,000 butts, also houses the wines and *soleras* of the Marqués de MISA, VARELA S.L. and BERTOLA S.A., three of the companies acquired by the RUMASA group.

Jerez de la Frontera

Jerez (or Xeres) de la Frontera is the capital of the sherry region and, in corrupted English form, has given its name to the wine. The town was probably founded by the Phoenicians and was much fought over during the period of the Moorish occupation, hence the suffix of *de la Frontera* granted by King John I in 1380 (there is another Jerez de los Caballeros on the borders of Portugal). Its wines were well known in Roman times; but the trade greatly increased with the settlement of foreign traders, mostly English, after the expulsion of the Jews in 1492 and the massive participation of English, Scottish and Irish shippers, many of whom remained in the area, during the late 18th and 19th centuries.

With its old castle and walls, narrow streets and white Andalucian houses, its great roofed market and numberless *bodegas*, often set in decorative gardens, it is a most attractive place to stay, especially in late spring or autumn. The best hotel is the modern 4-star Hotel Jerez, whose amenities include a shaded garden, swimming pool and a spacious lounge, a crossroads for Jerez society before dinner.

Many of its *bodegas* are described separately; the others on the official list of shippers are:

Tomás Abad S.A.
Manuel de Argüeso S.A.
B.M. Lagos S.A.
José Bustamente S.L.
Díez Export S.L.
Manuel Fernández S.A.
Fernando García-Delgado S.A.
M. Gil Galán S.A.
Luis G. Gordon Sucr.
Emilio M. Hidalgo S.A.
José Ma. Guerrero Ortega
Lacave y Cía. S.A.
Maco S.A.
Antonio Nuñez
Luis Páez S.A.
Antonio Parra Guerrero
Cayetano del Pino y Cía. S.L.
J. Ruiz S.A.
Félix Ruiz y Ruiz S.A.
Bodegas Sánchez de Alva S.A.
Sánchez Romate Hnos. S.A.
Tabajete S.A.
Bodegas Valderrama S.A.
Juan Vicente Vergara S.A.
Vergara Gordon S.A.
Viñas S.A.

"La Ina"

PEDRO DOMECQ's big-selling and excellent *fino*, ı!shade less dry than some.

La Riva S.A.

Jerez de la Frontera. This well known Spanish house was founded in the latter part of the 18th century. It is now a subsidiary of PEDRO DOMECQ and continues to make and sell wines under its own label. "Tres Palmas" has always been one of the best *finos*.

Los Tercios
Reputed vineyard area with ALBARIZA soil, to the SW of JEREZ and adjoining that of BALBAINA.

Lustau S.A., Emilio
Jerez de la Frontera. One of the leading independent, family-owned firms, Lustau occupies *bodegas* incorporating part of the old city wall. It has recently built a large new *bodega* on the outskirts of Jerez and is one of the concerns which has best weathered the current recession through its policy of selling well-made "own brand" sherries. Its "Dry Lustau" in various styles are first-rate wines, especially the *oloroso* and *palo cortado*. In very limited amounts, Lustau also sells some remarkable "Almacenista" sherries from small, individual stockholders.

Macharnudo
Rated the best of the ALBARIZA areas, Macharnudo lies on high ground N of Jerez. At its center is Macharnudo Castle, familiar to enthusiasts of DOMECQ sherries for its picture on their labels. Built in the 17th century, the firm still uses it on occasion for receptions.

Manzanilla
A pale, crisp and very dry *fina* with a salty tang from SANLÚCAR DE BARRAMEDA made in a SOLERA sometimes containing as many as fourteen SCALES. The word is also used in Spain for camomile tea, from which it is probably derived because of a certain similarity in flavor. MANZANILLAS owe their special characteristics to the atmospheric conditions and the special methods of operating the SOLERAS in Sanlúcar. Not all the wines matured in Sanlúcar emerge as *manzanillas*, and *manzanilla* musts aged in Jerez develop as normal *finos*.

Manzanilla pasada
An old and mature *manzanilla*, resembling a light and very dry *amontillado*.

Marqués de Misa
Founded in the late 18th century, Misa became one of the largest shippers during the 19th. The firm was bought out by RUMASA, which still markets sherries under the name, while its impressive *bodega* was acquired by John HARVEY & Sons. The wines, now made at BODEGAS INTERNACIONALES, are sold under the labels of "Fino Chiquilla", "Amontillado Abolengo", "Oloroso La Novia" and "Brandy Royal".

Marqués del Real Tesoro S.A., Hnos.
Jerez de la Frontera. The first Marquis gained the title ("Royal Treasure") by using his own silver to forge cannonballs while in command of a fleet for the Royal Treasury. The *bodega* was founded by a descendant in the late 19th century. One of the smaller family firms, it is particularly noted for an excellent *manzanilla* and a good, natural unsweetened, nutty *amontillado*.

Medium sherry
An increasingly popular term used to describe an *amontillado* slightly sweetened with Pedro Ximénez wine (in my own opinion to its detriment) for foreign markets.

Mitad y mitad
A 50–50 mixture of alcohol and mature sherry used for fortification.

Oloroso
The darkest, softest, fullest-bodied and most fragrant of the styles of sherry, containing up to 24% alcohol. It is matured without FLOR and in its natural state is completely dry, but is often blended with Pedro Ximénez wine and VINO DE COLOR for making sweet dessert sherries.

O'Neale S.A., Rafael
Jerez de la Frontera. The oldest-established of the *bodegas* founded by British emigrants and also one of the first in Jerez to make brandy, it was begun by an Irishman, Timothy O'Neale, in 1724, and its *bodegas* incorporate part of the Moorish city wall. It remains a small family firm making fine wines in various styles under the labels of "El Cuadrado", "Spanish Arch" and "Festin".

Osborne y Cía S.A.
Puerto de Sta. María. Founded in 1772, Osborne is the largest of the firms in Puerto de Sta. María. As early as 1872 it bought the important firm of DUFF GORDON and has since launched sister concerns in Portugal, Mexico and the Rioja (see RIOJA/MONTECILLO). Its old *bodega* in Puerto de Sta. María, built in 1837, is one of the most beautiful in the region; and the modern vinification plant, where the wine is fermented in horizontal rather than vertical tanks to approximate more closely to the traditional butt, is among the most advanced.

The wines include "Fino Quinta", "Coquinero" and "Jauna" *amontillados*, the dry "Bailen" oloroso and "Osborne Cream". The firm is also one of the largest makers of Spanish brandy.

See also SPIRITS, AROMATIC WINES & LIQUEURS.

Palo cortado
A style of sherry between an *amontillado* and *oloroso*. Between 17.5–23%, it is classified as *dos* (the weakest), *tres* or *cuatro cortados* according to body and age. Genuine *palo cortado* is a beautiful wine with great depth and fragrance, but always expensive.

Palomino & Vergara S.A.
Jerez de la Frontera. This family firm, founded in 1765, was acquired by RUMASA in 1963 and occupies *bodegas* in the middle of Jerez, of which the centerpiece is the great glass-domed offices with the original mahogany and gilt counter and fitments. With its capacity of 40,000 butts, it is the largest of the many RUMASA sherry concerns after WILLIAMS & HUMBERT and BODEGAS INTERNACIONALES. Its strength has always been in the domestic market, and it does not at the moment export to Britain or the U.S.A., though it possesses flourishing export markets in Holland and Germany.

Its wines include a light, dry "Tio Mateo" *fino*; the "John Peter" *amontillado*; a dry aromatic "Los Flamencos" *oloroso*; and a round, full-bodied "Solera 1865" cream with more than a hint of Moscatel. The firm also makes a range of brandies, of which the oldest is the "Gran Canciller", and a really first-rate *ponche* (see SPIRITS, AROMATIC WINES & LIQUEURS) subtly flavored with cinnamon, vanilla and orange, and sold under the label of "J. Ruiz y Cía" as "Ponche Español".

Pajerete paxerete
A sweet Pedro Ximénez wine used for sweetening certain styles of sherry.

Pedro Domecq S.A.
Jerez de la Frontera. Pedro Domecq is the oldest of the large *bodegas* and the biggest single firm in the region, with extensive vineyards in MACHARNUDO and elsewhere, and 73 *bodegas* between Jerez, Puerto de Sta. María and Sanlúcar de Barrameda. In the oldest, "El Molino", built in 1730, there are butts laid down centuries ago and dedicated to historical figures such as Pitt, Nelson and Wellington. The firm was founded by an Irish emigrant in 1730, but greatly expanded by the Domecq family from the Basses Pyrenées in association with its English agent, father of the writer John Ruskin. Its present head, Don José Ignacio Domecq, is one of the great sherry authorities of his generation; and the family maintains ties with Britain, among other things mounting one of the world's crack polo teams from among its members.

The firm has extensive interests in Mexico and has begun production of an excellent Rioja (see RIOJA/SOGEVIÑAS). It is also one of the biggest makers of Spanish brandy, and has built a huge new *bodega* in Jerez, modeled on the Great Mosque in Córdoba, to house the *soleras* for ageing it.

Apart from the famous *fino* "La Ina", other sherries include one of the best dry *olorosos,* "Rio Viejo", the popular "Double Century" and an older and richer "Celebration Cream".

See also SPIRITS, AROMATIC WINES & LIQUEURS.

Pérez Marín, Hijos de Rainera
Sanlúcar de Barrameda. This small firm, founded in 1850, has long been known for making some of the best *manzanilla.* Its Bodegas la Guita took the name from the habit of a former member of the family, Domingo Pérez Marín, of refusing to sell his wine except for cash – *guita* in local slang. Its most famous wine is the delicious "La Guita" *manzanilla pasada,* an old and very fragrant *fina* on the point of conversion to *amontillado.* The other labels are the younger "Hermosilla" *manzanilla fina* and "Fino Bandera".

Pemartín y Cía S.A., José
Jerez de la Frontera. The business was founded in 1819 by a French emigré, but thanks to the extravagances of Julian Pemartín, whose house in Jerez was constructed along the lines of the Paris Opéra, went bankrupt in 1857. It was for a time taken over by Sandeman, but is now part of the RUMASA group. Its wines include the "Fino Viña Pemartín" and "Pemartín" dry, medium and cream.

See also SPIRITS, AROMATIC WINES & LIQUEURS.

"Plastering"
The light dusting of the grapes with gypsum (calcium sulphate) before vinification, a process strongly attacked in Victorian times, but beneficial in its effects and leading to improved acidity in the musts.

Puerto de Sta. María
Next in importance of the sherry towns to JEREZ, Puerto de Sta. María is particularly noted for its *finos, amontillados* and brandy, and was the main port for shipping sherry until it was supplanted in the 1920s by its larger neighbor Cádiz. It is a pleasant, open place with wide streets and houses with grilles and *miradors.* There are good beaches in the vicinity, served by resort hotels such as the 4-star Meliá Caballo Blanco and Fuentebravia; and on the outskirts is the lush Casino Bahía de Cádiz.

Officially listed shippers in Puerto de Sta. María without separate entries are:

Colosía Molleda, Ma. Loreto	Jesús Ferris Marhanda
Miguel M. Gómez S.A.	Portalto S.A.
González y Cía.	Carlos y Javier de Terry S.A.
José Luis González Obregón	Ximénez y Cía.
F. Javier Jiménez S.A.	

PX
Abbreviation for the Pedro Ximénez grape, used mainly for sweet wines in Jerez, but for dry in Montilla (see MONTILLA-MORILES). There is a legend that it originated in the Canaries, was thence taken to the Rhine and brought to Jerez by one Pieter Siemens, a soldier of the Emperor Charles V, in the 17th century. Unfortunately, this seems more picturesque than true.

Raya
A term employed in classifying musts and also used to describe less delicate styles of *oloroso.*

"Refreshment"
The replenishment of the butts of a SOLERA with younger wine as the most mature is drawn off for shipment or bottling.

Rota
Village on the coast W of Jerez, formerly known for its red Rota tent wine, but now the site of a great U.S. naval base.

Ruiz Mateos S.A., Zoilo
Jerez de la Frontera. Founded as a small wine company in Rota in 1857, Ruiz Mateos was the springboard for the now vast RUMASA empire, to which, in abbreviated form, it has given its name. The company moved

to Jerez in 1930 and in 1964 signed a contract with John HARVEY & Sons of Bristol for supplying all its large requirements of wine. This was later rescinded, but set Ruiz Mateos squarely on its feet.

The company now owns various vineyards in the best ALBARIZA areas and a number of *bodegas* in Jerez itself. Its administrative offices, and those of the RUMASA sherry group, now comprising 16 different companies, are housed in the handsome mansion of La Atalaya, set in decorative gardens and formerly belonging to the Vergara family of Palomino & Vergara. A point of interest for visitors is the superb Museum of Clocks and Watches, founded by José María Ruiz Mateos, President of RUMASA, and containing some 300 rare examples from Spain, Britain, France and elsewhere.

Pride of the company's sherries – and justifiably so, as they are among the best to be made in Jerez and correspondingly expensive – is the "Don Zoilo" range, including a *fino*, *amontillado* and cream. Zoilo Ruiz Mateos also makes one of the most prestigious of the Jerez brandies, the "Gran Duque de Alba".

RUMASA

The first steps in the formation of RUMASA have been described above (RUIZ MATEOS S.A., ZOILO). After the break with Harveys, the younger son of Don Zoilo Ruis Mateos, José María, moved to Madrid and set about the formation of what is now one of the largest groupings in Spain, embracing banks, insurance, shipping, chemicals, hotels and property.

RUMASA lost none of its early interest in wines and now owns some 35% of the *bodegas* in Jerez: Zoilo RUIZ MATEOS S.A., Unión de Exportadores de Jerez, WILLIAMS & HUMBERT Ltd., PALOMINO & Vergara S.A., MISA, PEMARTÍN, VARELA, BERTOLA, Otaolaurruche, Diestro, Lacave, Diez Morales, Valderrama, Vergara and Gordon, BODEGAS INTERNACIONALES and GARVEY. In the RIOJA, it has taken over Paternina, Bodegas Franco Españolas, Lan and Berberana; in Montilla, Monte Cristo and Pérez Barquero; and in the Penedès (see SPARKLING WINES), the sparkling wine firms of Castellblanch, René Barbier, Conde de Caralt and Segura Viudas. Its foreign acquisitions include the Augustus Barnett chain of off-licences in England.

RUMASA's emblem is an industrious bee; but the empire has recently been expropriated by the Spanish government and, in the words of one Spanish newspaper, "the bee has lost its sting". The future control of its constituent firms is as yet uncertain.

Sack

Old name for sherry (and also for Málaga and Canary), probably originating in the 15th century and derived from the Spanish *sacar* (to draw out).

"San Patricio"

One of the best-known *finos*, made by GARVEY S.A.

Sanlúcar de Barrameda

Sherry town W of Jerez at the mouth of the Guadalquivir estuary, famous for its dry *manzanillas*. A picturesque place with a wide beach opposite the wildlife reserve of Las Marismas, it possesses good seafood restaurants (see WINE AND FOOD) and a 3-star hotel, the Guadalquivir.

Apart from *bodegas* with separate entries, the other firms in Sanlúcar are:

Hros. de Argüeso S.A.
Manuel de Argüeso S.A.
Hros. de M. Barón S.A.
Delgado Zuleta S.A.
Ana Ma. Escobar Suárez
Gaspar Florido Cano
Manuel García Monge S.A.
Francisco García de Velasco
Infantes de Orleans Borbon S.A., Bodegas
José Medina y Cía S.A.
Carlos de Otaolaurruchi S.A.
Hijos de A. Pérez Megía S.A.
Rafael Reig y Cía S.A.
Pedro Romero S.A.
Miguel Sánchez Ayala S.A.
Vinícola Hidalgo y Cía S.A.

Sandeman Hnos. y Cía.

Jerez de la Frontera. The firm was founded by a Scot, George Sandeman, who started business as a shipper in London about 1790, acting as agent for DUFF GORDON and later setting up his own establishments in Oporto and Jerez. Until its recent takeover by Seagrams it remained a family firm. One of the largest concerns in Jerez, it makes its wines scrupulously and by the most traditional means, still vinifying the wine in cask and not in the stainless steel tanks now used by so many of the sherry firms.

The biggest-selling of its wines is the "Dry Don" *amontillado*; "Apitiv" is one of the best of *finos* and "Armada Cream" a first-rate dessert wine. In limited amount it also makes some quite exceptional wines, such as the "Imperial Corregidor" *oloroso* and a magnificent *palo cortado*.

"Scale"
Term used of a SOLERA to denote a row of butts containing wine of similar type and age.

Sobre tabla
Young wine which has been racked free of the lees and is ready for use in a CRIADERA.

Solera
Derived from the Latin *solum*, or Spanish *suelo* (meaning a floor), the word in its narrower sense applies to the butts at floor level from which sherry is withdrawn for bottling or shipment. More loosely it is used for the whole assembly of butts in which sherry is matured, including those of the CRIADERA from which the *solera* proper is replenished. The butts are arranged in tiers or SCALES containing wine of identical type, but progressively younger in age. As wine in limited amounts is from time to time taken from the last row of butts, or *solera* proper, these are topped up with rather older wine, and each scale is in turn "refreshed" or replenished from that immediately preceding it in age. This procedure is known as "working the scales", and is feasible because the younger wine rapidly takes on the characteristics of the older.

Soleras for producing *fino* require more scales, perhaps 7, than those used for the fuller-bodied *oloroso*: and the most complicated are those used in SANLÚCAR DE BARRAMEDA for making MANZANILLA, with up to 14.

Soto S.A., José de
Jerez de la Frontera. Apart from its sherries, which include "Fino Campero", "Fino Soto", "Amontillado la Uvita", "Oloroso la Espuela" and cream, the firm was the first to make a *ponche* (see SPIRITS, AROMATIC WINES & LIQUEURS), and its brand remains one of the best.

Sunning
In the past it was standard practice to lay out the grapes on esparto grass mats and to sun them briefly. Thanks to improved methods of judging the optimum time for picking, sunning is now mainly used for grapes intended for sweet wines and the effect is to concentrate the amount of sugar in the must.

Terry S.A., Fernando A. de
Puerto de Sta. María. This large firm, also brandy makers on a big scale, was founded in 1883 by the descendants of an Irish family which had settled in Spain as long ago as 1500. In 1981 the family sold both the *bodegas* and their famous establishment for raising the white Cartujano horses to ASEPEYO Catalana de Occidente, one of the largest Spanish finance houses. Under the new management, most of the wine is now being made in a huge complex outside Puerto de Sta. María, equipped with the latest in handling and pressing machinery, a modern vinification plant and some 40,000 butts. There are further large *soleras* in the atmospheric old *bodegas* in Puerto de Sta. María itself.

In Spain, the sherries are labeled as "Camborio" *fino*, medium, *oloroso* and cream. Some 90% of shipments to the U.K., amounting to a hefty 200,000–300,000 cases a year, go to Marks & Spencer, and are labeled as "St. Michael".

See SPIRITS, AROMATIC WINES & LIQUEURS.

"Tio Pepe"
The world's largest-selling *fino*, made by GONZALEZ BYASS, and one of

the driest and of consistently high standard. The wine sold in England is shipped in container and bottled at Dartford, and is all the fresher for this.

"Tres Palmas"
Excellent *fino* from LA RIVA.

Valdespino S.A., A.R.
Jerez de la Frontera. Old established Spanish sherry house, whose *bodegas*, gardens and patios are among the most beautiful in Jerez – the older *bodegas* were once part of an ancient monastery. The less expensive wines are sold under the label of "Matador"; Valdespino also makes a good *fino* and a delicious dry "Tio Diego" *amontillado*.

Varela S.L., Bodegas
Puerto de Sta. María. A company now within the RUMASA group, known particularly for its "Varela Medium" and "Varela Cream".

Venencia
An instrument used for withdrawing samples of sherry from the butt. In JEREZ, it consists of a small silver cup on a long whalebone handle; in SANLÚCAR DE BARRAMEDA, where it is even more important not to disturb the FLOR, the cup is smaller and the *venencia* is made in one piece out of bamboo.

Vino de color
A dark-colored wine used for blending with certain brown and dessert sherries and made by fermenting a sugary boiled-down must (see ARROPE) with a proportion of new must.

Williams & Humbert Ltd.
Jerez de la Frontera. The firm was founded in 1877 by Alexander Williams, until then working as a clerk for Wisdom & Warter. It subsequently became one of the most important in Jerez and is now part of the RUMASA group.

Its *bodegas* are among the most picturesque in Jerez; and points of interest for visitors are the splendid coaches and harnesses and the carefully preserved office of the British Vice-Consul, located within the *bodega* until the consulate was discontinued in 1979.

Its most popular wine is the "Dry Sack" medium *amontillado*; it also makes the well known "Canasta Cream" and "Walnut Brown", while "Pando" (sometimes, but wrongly, thought to have been named after the P. & O. shipping line) is a good *fino*.

Wisdom & Warter Ltd.
Jerez de la Frontera. The company was founded in 1854 by two Englishmen, Messrs. Wisdom and Warter, of whom *Punch* once wrote "Wisdom sells the wine, Warter makes it". The firm markets a wide range of sherries, including "Fino Oliva", "Manzanilla la Guapa", "Amontillado Royal Palace", "Oloroso Merecedos", "Wisdom's Choice Cream" and "Pedro Ximénez Wisdom".

Zapatos de pisar
The old-fashioned cowhide boots, studded with flat tacks and formerly used in crushing the grapes. Crushing is now carried out in horizontal

presses, either of the mechanical or pneumatic type, or in yet more modern vinification plants by a continuous process, in which a first light crushing produces musts for *finos* and later, heavier pressing, for the fuller-bodied *olorosos*.

On gastronomic maps of Spain, Andalucía is often labeled the *Zona de los Fritos* or "region of fried food"; and high on the list of such dishes must come the fries of mixed fish, sometimes called *parejas* in Cádiz – this being the name of the dish cooked by the fishermen while at sea in their boats.

Cooking in the sherry region is very much oriented towards fish and seafood, available in great variety from the Bay of Cádiz and the nearby Atlantic coastline. In places such as Sanlúcar de Barrameda, the shellfish is magnificently fresh and the lobsters, for example, are large enough to serve a party of 6. Another great speciality are the *gazpachos* or cold soups.

Sherry is, not surprisingly, often used in cooking, and more than this it is usual to drink a chilled *fino* throughout the meal rather than a table wine. Apart from the delicious iced cakes and fruit tarts from the sweet trolley, by far the most popular sweet is *tocino de cielo* (see MONTILLA-MORILES).

Acedías fritas
Fried baby soles.

Barbujitos
Small fresh anchovies, fried.

Bistec salteado al Jerez
Steak sautéed with sherry.

Boquerones de la Isla
Fried fresh anchovies, locally caught.

Cañaíllas de la Isla
A sea-snail typical of the coast. It is lightly boiled and eaten cold, the sharp tail of one snail being used to extract the meat from the others.

Cazón
Baby shark, marinated with paprika and vinegar.

Coquinas al ajillo
Cockles in garlic sauce.

Consomé al Jerez
Consommé with sherry, usually "fortified" with an extra dose at the table!

Dorada a la sal
Gilthead baked in a thick paste of sea salt, which is removed by the waiter at the table.

Fritura gaditana
A mixed fry of small fish.

Gazpacho andaluz
Cold, uncooked soup containing chopped tomatoes, cucumber and green peppers, together with olive oil, vinegar and garlic. Breadcrumbs may either be used in making it or served on the side.

Jamón de Jabugo
The best and most fully flavored type of the highly cured jamón serrano, *from a village near Huelva. Like Bayonne or Parma ham, it is eaten either on its own or with melon.*

Macedonia de frutas naturales
Fruit salad with sherry.

Naranjas acaramelizadas
Fresh oranges, cut up and served in a syrup containing caramel.

Paire
Scabbard fish, cut into steaks and grilled.

Pijotas
A tiny fish fried like whitebait.

Pipirrana con gambas
Prawns cooked with tomatoes and peppers.

Puntillitas
Minute inkfish, dipped in a light batter and fried in olive oil.

Riñones al Jerez
Calf's or pig's kidneys, sliced and sautéed in olive oil and served in a tomato sauce containing sherry.

Salchichas al Jerez
Fried sausages, flavored with sherry and served with squares of fried bread.

Sopa de pescado gaditana
A rich fish soup akin to bouillabaisse.

Tortilla suflé
A sweet soufflé omelette.

Urta a la roteña
Urta *is a fish for which there is no translation. It feeds on shellfish, acquiring great flavor, and is a speciality of Rota, on the coast W of Jerez, where it is cooked with a rich sauce of tomatoes and red peppers.*

Restaurants

Arcos de la Frontera *Mesón del Brigadier* (near the Lake of Arcos with terrace and views; well known for its meat and *charcuterie*).

Cádiz ⋆ *El Faro* (best in Cádiz, splendid range of locally caught fish and sophisticated cooking); *Ventorrillo del Chato* (period charm and well cooked Andalucian dishes).

Jerez de la Frontera ⋆⋆ *Gaitán* (small restaurant with first-rate Andalucian and Basque cuisine, moderate prices); ⋆ *El Bosque* (charming surroundings, international cuisine and some well cooked Andalucian dishes, good wine list); ⋆ *Venta los Naranjos* (on road to Sanlúcar, excellent fish and shellfish and wide variety of sherries); *Tendido* (opposite the bullring, local fish dishes and good wine list).

Puerto de Sta. María ⋆ *Don Peppone* (tiny place specializing in grills of meat and fish, well stocked cellar); *La Terraza* (luxurious restaurant of the Casino Bahía de Cádiz, international cooking).

Sanlúcar de Barrameda *Casa Juan* (beach restaurant serving the excellent local seafood); *Bigote* (the fishermen who supply the splendidly fresh seafood are paid in kind by eating here).

Sparkling Wines

Manufacture in Spain of sparkling wines by the champagne method was first begun by Don José Raventós, whose family firm of Codorníu is now the largest concern in the world to make wines of this type. To begin with, the wines were known as *champaña*, but the producers in Reims rightly objected that the name should be applied only to wines produced in the Champagne district of France; and they are now referred to as *cava*, a word also used, rather than *bodega*, to describe the establishments in which they are made.

90% of these wines are still produced in the Penedès region of Catalonia, also well known for its still wines (see CATALONIA), the balance coming from Ampurdán-Costa Brava and Lérida, further N in Catalonia, and the RIOJA.

The grapes used for the wines in the Penedès are mainly the white Xarel-lo, imparting alcoholic strength and color; the Macabeo (or Viura), contributing finesse and elegance; and the Parellada, grown up the hill slopes, conferring softness and aroma. Pink wines (never referred to as rosé when talking of sparkling wines) are made with a proportion of the black Cariñena or Garnacha tinta.

In modern installations, the must is extracted in horizontal presses and vinified in temperature-controled stainless steel tanks, and elaboration then follows the classical methods of Champagne. The young wine is dosed with a solution of sugar and with cultured yeasts, filled into stout champagne-type bottles, temporarily corked and left for a period of years in deep underground cellars until such time as the sugar has been converted into carbon dioxide and alcohol. The bottles are then, over a period of months, gradually upended, so that the fine sediment falls towards the neck of the bottle, which is finally frozen and uncorked, and the plug containing the sediment is forcibly expeled by the pressure of gas inside. A *licor de expedición* containing a little sugar is added; and the bottles are then re-corked and allowed to rest before labeling and despatch.

The large *cavas* have rationalized the process by using *girasols* to promote the descent of the sediment, forklift trucks and pallets for stacking the bottles in the cellars, and ingenious electronic systems for locating batches of bottles and bringing them to the bottling line for *dégorgement* (or removal of the temporary corks) and labeling; but none of these handling processes affects the elaboration or quality of the wine – as romantics would sometimes have one believe. Such differences as do emerge between champagne and *cava* result from the character of the grapes and soil and not from the method of manufacture.

Not all *espumosos* (or sparkling wines) are made by the champagne method. There are also sparkling wines whose second fermentation takes place, not in individual bottles, but in large pressurized tanks known as *cuves closes* or, in Spain, *gran-vas*. This process produces acceptable wines, albeit with a larger and shorter-lasting bubble, but still a great deal better than the *gaseosos*, made simply by pumping carbon dioxide into still wine. The *vinos de aguja* or "green wines", which develop a more subdued bubble or *pétillance* as the result of a naturally occurring secondary fermentation, are described under GALICIA.

There has been endless discussion about the relative merits of *cava* and champagne. In my own experience, *cava* tends to be a little softer, fuller in flavor and fruitier in nose; and champagne to possess more edge and finesse. Conventional wisdom is that nobody of any experience can fail to tell the difference, but that most discriminating of Spanish wine-makers, Miguel Torres, writes of a systematic series of comparative tastings that "the *cava* wines of San Sadurní de Noya have frequently been judged superior to their French homologues". They are certainly about half the price; and the only sensible thing is to drink and enjoy Spanish *cava* as a sparkling wine in its own right.

In 1981, no less than 12 million bottles of *cava* were exported to all 5 continents, so that its production is now a most important facet of the Spanish wine industry.

Styles of sparkling wine

In increasing order of sweetness, Spanish sparkling wines are labeled as:

Brut Natur or Nature	Extra dry
Brut	Dry
Seco	Fairly dry
Semiseco	Semi-dry
Semidulce	Semi-sweet
Dulce	Sweet

Rosado or Rose indicates a pink wine.

Ampurdán S.A., Cavas del

Perelada (Gerona). This is under the same management as the Castillo de PERELADA, well known for its *cava* wines, but since it produces still wines (see CATALONIA) and sparklers made by the *cuve close* method, Spanish regulations require that it be housed in a separate building across a public highway. Its "Perelada" is one of the biggest selling of Spanish *cuve close* wines.

Ampurdán-Costa Brava

Demarcated only for still wines, the area nevertheless produces the largest amount of sparkling wine outside the PENEDÈS, most of it made by the Castillo de PERELADA and CAVAS DEL AMPURDÁN.

Bilbainas, Bodegas

Haro (Logroño). One of the leading producers of RIOJA, Bodegas Bilbainas also makes limited amounts of "Lumen", "Royal Carlton Cuvée Especial" and "Royal Carlton Brut Nature" by the champagne method, using Viura and Malvasía grapes. The wines are made in deep cellars beneath the *bodega* by the most traditional methods, clearance after second fermentation taking place in PUPITRES and *dégorgement* being effected manually. The wines are dry and of good quality, but rather fuller in flavor than those from the PENEDÈS.

Caralt, Conde de 69, 71, 73, 76, 78, 80

San Sadurní de Noya (Barcelona). The Conde de Caralt was making *cava* wines long before it embarked on the production of still wine (see CATALONIA). The concern is now part of the RUMASA group and shares premises with SEGURA VIUDAS. Its dry and light sparkling wine is bottled under the label "Conde de Caralt".

Castellblanch S.A.

San Sadurní de Noya (Barcelona). When Castellblanch was founded by Don Jerónimo Parera Figueras in 1908, it was a family concern with only 3 employees and an annual turnover of 100,000 bottles of sparkling wine. Expansion took place rapidly under Don Jerónimo's son, and since RUMASA acquired the company in 1974, output has been boosted to 10 million bottles, made both by the champagne method and in *cuves closes*. In order of quality, its wines are sold as "Extra Cristal", "Brut Zero", "Extra", "Gran Crema" and "Carta Blanca".

Cava
Meaning "cellar", the word is used both to describe an establishment in which sparkling wines are made by the champagne method, and also such wines themselves.

Codorníu S.A. NV, 73, 75
San Sadurní de Noya (Barcelona). It was Don José Raventós of the family firm of Codorníu, engaged in wine-making since 1551, who in 1872 began the manufacture of sparkling wine by the champagne method in Spain, after studying practices in Reims. Today, Codorníu is the largest concern in the world to make wines of this type, with reserves of 75 million liters and sales of 35 million bottles a year, of which 4 million go for export.

The *cavas* and family mansion are situated in decorative gardens above 17km (11 miles) of underground cellars. The original buildings, designed in *fin de siècle* style with echoes of Gaudí and including an old press house converted into an impressive wine museum, have been declared a National Monument; and the former labeling hall is now used as a reception area for the 160,000 visitors who descend on the *cavas* each year.

Codorníu has no vineyards of its own and obtains the grapes from some 350 regular suppliers in the area. They are pressed in batteries of modern horizontal presses and vinified in cooled stainless steel tanks, of which there are 97, each of 20,000 liters capacity. Subsequent elaboration of the wine is by the traditional champagne method.

The best of its wines are the "Gran Codorníu Brut" and "Non Plus Ultra". Others are the "Rosé Brut", "Extra Dry", "Semi Dry", "Sweet", "Grand Cremant" dry and semi-dry, and "Delapierre", named in honor of a former French oenologist at the *cavas*.

Champaña
Name long used for Spanish wines made by the champagne method until, in deference to the French protests, the Spanish government forbade it.

Espumoso
Spanish name for sparkling wine.

Freixedas, Bodegas J.
Vilafranca del Penedès (Barcelona). Apart from its still wines (see CATALONIA), this large-scale producer and exporter also markets an "Extra" sparkling wine made by the champagne process.

Freixenet S.A. NV, 69, 71, 73, 75, 78
San Sadurní de Noya (Barcelona). Freixenet, founded in 1915, is second in size only to CODORNÍU, and between them the 2 concerns make 70% of all the *cava* wine from the PENEDÈS. Until recently it has made sparkling wine only by the champagne method, but has now, with SAVIN, acquired a 50% interest in L'Aixertell, a company making large amounts of *cuve close* wine.

The plant at San Sadurní is one of the most modern in the Penedès, and the wine is vinified at low temperature in ten huge stainless steel tanks of 600,000 liters capacity. Freixenet was also the first of the *cavas* to introduce GIRASOLS holding some 500 bottles in place of the traditional PUPITRES. Thanks to these innovations and most advanced handling and bottling equipment, it has been able to hold down the price of its *cava* wines without detriment to quality. Freixenet is currently the largest exporter of Spanish sparkling wines to the U.S.A., where it sold 250,000 cases in 1981.

Apart from splendid vintage wines, such as the "Cuvée D.S. 1969", named in honor of Dna. Dolores Sala, widow of the company's founder Don Pedro Ferrer Bosch, the best of the wines are the "Brut Nature" and popular "Cordon Negro". It also markets the less expensive "Carta

Nevada" and "Cremant Rosé", and has recently introduced a light, dry and fresh non-vintage "La Sirena".

See also CATALONIA.

Gaseoso

The cheapest (and nastiest) form of sparkler made by pumping pressurized carbon dioxide into still wines.

Girasol

A large octagonal metal frame on a faceted base holding 504 bottles, increasingly used in place of the traditional PUPITRE to effect the descent of sediment after completion of the second fermentation. The frame, with its complement of bottles, may be swung round in a few seconds by a couple of men; and Freixenet, which was the first of the *cavas* to introduce it on a large scale, claims that it gives more consistent results than the *pupitre*. Most of the *cavas* in the Penedès have begun to use the device, and it has also been tried out in Reims by the French champagne-makers.

Gonzalez y Dubosc S.A. NV

San Sadurní de Noya (Barcelona). This well-known firm is owned by the sherry-makers Gonzalez Byass, but the wines are now made for it by SEGURA VIUDAS. Light, dry and fresh and very reasonably priced, they are marketed in the U.K. under the name of "Jean Perico".

Gran-vas

Spanish name for *cuve close*. With this type of sparkling wine, second fermentation takes place in large closed tanks pressurized to 8 atmospheres, and lasts for 4–5 months according to temperature, usually −5°C. The wine is then filtered and bottled under pressure. Although the wines do not possess such a fine or lasting bubble as those made by the champagne method, they are a great deal more acceptable than GASEOSOS and make pleasant party drinking. To avoid the possibility of such wine being passed off as *cava*, Spanish regulations require that it may not be made in the same building. Corks from *cava* wine bear a star on the bottom, and *gran-vas* a small black circle.

Grapa

A metal hook used for securing the temporary cork during the second fermentation. *Grapas* and corks have now been largely replaced by crown caps.

Hill S.A., Cavas

Moja-Vilafranca del Penedès (Barcelona). Apart from its still wines (see CATALONIA), the firm produces a range of *cavas*, including "Extra Oro", "Brut", "Lord", "Espumoso", "Gran Cremant" and "Rosado" (pink).

Juve & Camps S.A.

San Sadurní de Noya (Barcelona). Sparkling wine makers of repute, selling their wines under the labels of "Reserva de la Familia", "Gran Reserva", "Gran Cru" and "Rosado"; and also under the names "De la Serra", "Oro", "Noble", "Extra" and "Bibelot".

Lavernoya S.A., Cavas

San Sadurní de Noya (Barcelona). Well known cellars whose wines, sold under the name of "Lácrima Bacus", include "Primerisimo", "Extra", "Súper", "Súper Rosado", "Gran Cremant", "Extra Rosado" and "Summum".

Lérida

The province of Lérida (Lleida) in the NW of Catalonia produces sizeable amounts of sparkling wine. See RAIMAT.

Licor de expedición

A solution of sugar in brandy and old white wine used to top up the bottles after completion of the second fermentation and removal of the temporary cork. It is the amount of sugar in the *licor* which determines the style of the finished wine. A dry *brut* will contain only some 2%, while the sweet sparklers popular in South America are dosed to the extent of 12–20%. In general, the best wines are the driest, because defects cannot be masked by excessive sweetening.

Licor de tiraje

A solution of sugar in white wine added before second fermentation. It is from the breakdown of this sugar into alcohol and carbon dioxide by the action of special yeasts that wines made by the champagne method derive their sparkle.

Mascaró, Cavas

Vilafranca del Penedès (Barcelona). Small and old-established family firm with cellars in the heart of Vilafranca, making liqueurs and an excellent brandy (see SPIRITS, AROMATIC WINES & LIQUEURS) as well as still and good *cava* wines. Its dry "Cava Reservada" and "Brut" wines contain a high proportion of Parellada and are correspondingly fresh and fruity.

See also CATALONIA/COMPAÑÍA VINÍCOLA DEL PENEDÈS.

Mestres Sagues, Antonio

San Sadurní de Noya (Barcelona). One of the smaller family firms making good sparkling wine by the champagne method, now available in the U.K. as "Brut", "Coquet", "Marajá" and "1312".

Monistrol, Marqués de NV, 75

San Sadurní de Noya (Barcelona). The *cavas* at Monistrol de Noya, just outside San Sadurní, are among the most picturesque in the area, with a flagged patio and old wine press overlooked by the parish church; and although Martini & Rossi have recently acquired a 51% holding, the company, which has been making *cava* wines since 1882, is still very much a family concern, 10 of the families who work in the *cavas* and vineyards living on the estate. Monistrol owns 300ha (742 acres) of vineyards and makes 3 million bottles of wine annually, most of it *cava* and much of it exported to Italy. The driest and most elegant of its sparkling wines is the "Brut Nature". It also makes a "Brut"; a dry and semi-dry "Rosado"; a dry, semi-dry and sweet "Extra" and a dry and semi-dry "Cremant". See also CATALONIA.

Muga, Bodegas 79

Haro (Logroño). One of the most scrupulous in its methods of the *bodegas* of the Rioja (see RIOJA), Muga not long ago revived an old Riojan tradition by making a *cava* wine. Launched under the somewhat unfortunate name of "Mugamart", it has recently been rechristened "Conde de Haro" and the 1979 vintage is a dry, fruity and characterful wine in its own right – though nobody would confuse it with champagne.

Olivella Ferrari, Cavas

Vilafranca del Penedès (Barcelona). Respected maker of *cava* wines, now incorporated with the Castillo de PERELADA. Elaboration in Vilafranca is not taken beyond the stage of clearing the wines in PUPITRES or GIRASOLS, when the bottles are taken up-ended to Perelada for *dégorgement* and labelling.

Penedès

Although some 90% of *cava* wines made by the champagne method are from the Penedès, the region is demarcated only in respect of still wines (see CATALONIA), and the official *Reglamento de los Vinos Espumosos y de los Vinos Gasificados*, specifying methods and standards, applies to Spain as a whole.

Many of the scores of *cavas* in San Sadurní de Noya and Vilafranca del Penedès are small family firms which sell direct to the visitors from Barcelona, who descend on the area in their hoardes at weekends and come to look round the estates and taste.

Firms in the district making *cava* wines and not separately listed, are:

Anglada Fernandez, E.	Llopart Mir, Josefa
Aris Casanova, A.	Llopart Vilaros, Pedro
Baques Llopart, Asunción	Masachs Juve, José
Batlle & Montserrat S.L.	Mata Casanovas S.A.
Beneit Mir, Domingo	Miró Galofre, Juan
Boado Carbo, Pablo	Mont-Ferrant S.A.
Bodega Cooperativa Vilafranca	Montserrat Carcason, M.
Bohigas Ciervo, Fermin	Nadal Giro, Ramón
Campribi Monmany, Luis	Parxet S.A.
Canals Casanova, José María	Pujol Poch, Juan
Cabals Ridora, Ramón	Raventós Castells, Josefa
Carbo Vilanova, Juan	Remosa
Cavas Raventós Catasus S.A.	Rigau Ros, Juana
Cinzano S.A.	Roca Gibert, Juan
Colome Marrugat, C.	Roig Samos, Jaime & Roig Virgili, Jaime
Colomer Costa, A.	Ros Capdevila, José
Comas Codorníu, S.	Rosell Roig, José
Domenech Ferrer, J.	Sancho Labarta, Manuel
Espumosos de Cava S.A.	Santacana Roig, Salvador
Esteve Vendrell, José	Sindicato Agrícola de Artes
Esteve Vendrell, Juana	Soler Soler, Martín
Forns Raventós, Alberto	Torrallardona, Salvador
Gibert Arissa, Jaime	Tous Gran, Juan María
Gramona Batlle, José L.	Valles Casals, Rosa
Guilera Massana, Pedro	
Lincon S.A.	

Perelada, Castillo de

Perelada (Gerona). Traditions of wine-making at Perelada, on the verges of the Pyrenees, date from the 12th century, when the Carmelite monks who settled there at the time planted the first vineyards. To this day, the cellars lie beneath the 14th-century church of Carmen de Perelada, with its delicately arcaded patio, and the crenellated castle built shortly afterwards. The old buildings house a splendid library, a museum of glassware and ceramics and an extensive wine museum. More recently, a casino has been opened in the castle – dare one suggest, to promote its excellent sparkling wines?

As distinct from the associated Cavas del AMPURDÁN, the Castillo de Perelada produces only *cava* wine. 50% of the grapes are from its own vineyards, the rest being bought from local farmers; and the wine, carefully made by the champagne method, is binned away to undergo its second fermentation in deep cellars underneath the former orchard.

The "Brut Castillo" is a deepish yellow in color with fruity nose, but, despite its name, a somewhat sweetish finish; the "Brut Natur Olivella" (made in Vilafranca del Penedès) is lighter in color, dry and very pleasant; but the best of the wines is the "Gran Claustro", which, with 5–6 years in the cellars, emerges dry, soft and flowery.

Pupitre

The traditional method of coaxing the sediment and fine suspended matter into the neck of the bottle after the second fermentation of a sparkling wine is to place the bottles, neck first, into the oval holes of a *pupitre*, a wooden frame in the form of an inverted "V". The bottles are regularly given a shake and a slight angular twist by hand, and the inclination of the *pupitre* is gradually altered, so that the bottle ends up almost on its head, with the solid matter against the bottom of the cork.

Raimat (Raymat) S.A.

Raimat (Lérida). An offshoot of CODORNÍU making *cava* wines at the Castle of Raimat in Lérida (see also CATALONIA/CONIUSA). They include "Brut", "Reserva Especial", "Rondel" and "Carta Dorada".

René Barbier S.A. 64, 66, 69, 70, 73, 76, 78, 80

San Sadurní de Noya (Barcelona). An old family concern, now part of the RUMASA group and sharing premises with SEGURA VIUDAS and the Conde de CARALT. Its sparkling wines are labeled "Brut", "Seco", "Semiseco" and "Rosado".

See also CATALONIA.

Rioja
In the full flush of the Rioja boom of the late 19th century, various of the newly founded *bodegas* set about making sparkling wine by the champagne process from the local white Viura and Malvasía grapes. The Compañia Vinícola del Norte de España (see RIOJA) was so successful that it actually started a sister establishment in Reims. Although this lasted only 3 years, CVNE for long continued to supply the French champagne makers with Rioja wine during the period when they were suffering from the after-effects of the phylloxera epidemic.

Among the few Rioja firms still making *cava* wines are Bodegas BILBAINAS and Bodegas MUGA.

San Sadurní de Noya
Now spelt on roadsigns in the Catalan form of Sant Sadurní d'Anoia, this little town W of Barcelona is the headquarters of the Spanish sparkling wine industry, with *cavas* on every street. It has no hotel, so that to visit it one must stay either in Barcelona or in nearby Vilafranca del Penedès (see CATALONIA).

Savin S.A.
This largest of Spanish wine firms, with establishments all over the country, has joined forces with FREIXENET in making *cuve close* wine through a 50% share in L'Aixertelle, a company which it formerly operated with Henkell, producers of a German *sekt*.

Segura Viudas S.A. 74, 75, 78, 80
San Sadurní de Noya (Barcelona). Flagship of the companies within the RUMASA group making sparkling wine by the champagne method. The nucleus of the modern winery is an old house picturesquely situated on the road from San Sadurní to Igualada, with Montserrat (see CATALONIA) as a backdrop. Part of the grapes are grown on the 110ha (271 acres) of surrounding vineyards, the rest being bought from local growers. The most delicate of its wines, dry, light and fresh, and one of the best of all Spanish *cavas*, is the "Reserva Heredad" – do not be put off by the somewhat pretentious bottle with its metal incrustations. Other marks are the "Brut Vintage", "Brut", "Rosé", "Dry" and "Medium Dry".

Segura Viudas also makes sparkling wine for the sister companies of René BARBIER and Conde de CARALT, and for Gonzalez & Dubosc, controled by Gonzalez Byass.

"Sunflower"
English translation of GIRASOL.

Vilafranca del Penedès
Vilafranca is primarily a center for making still wines (see CATALONIA) but a number of the *cavas* are located there; it is also the headquarters of the official regulatory body for sparkling wines, the Consejo Regulador de los Vinos Espumosos.

WINE & Food

Manufacture of sparkling wines centers on Catalonia, especially the Penedès, and details of regional cooking and restaurants are given under CATALONIA.

Spirits, Aromatic Wines & Liqueurs

Sherry is so much an image of Spain that foreigners are often surprised to learn that a great deal more of it is drunk outside the country than in, especially in Britain, the Netherlands and the northern European countries, and that in Spain itself brandy, most of it produced in Jerez, is much cheaper and more popular. Sales of sherry have, in fact, declined in recent years, a decline aggravated by the increasing fashion among the younger generation for imported spirits, vermouths and liqueurs, and brandy has been the salvation of some of the big sherry houses.

The Spanish learned about distillation from the Moors. Alcohol was first used in medicine by the Catalan-born Arnold of Vilanova, and Spanish brandy was first shipped from Catalonia in the 17th century. Until the early 19th century it was used in Jerez only for the fortification of sherry, and the first Jerez brandies were not made by the sherry houses until the mid-19th century.

The first brandies were made by what is now known as the Charentais method, perfected in Cognac, by distillation of wine in a simple pot-still, in effect a copper kettle with a coiled condenser. This takes place in 2 stages, and the raw spirit is then matured in oak casks. It is still the method employed for the best and most refined Spanish brandy; but the great bulk of inexpensive Spanish brandy is made by "continuous" distillation of wine in tall, steam-heated columns in the manner of grain whisky, a more economical and productive industrial process. The resulting *holandas*, or 65% grape spirit, made in distilleries all over Spain, are then diluted with water and aged in oak casks.

In Jerez, which produces the great bulk of Spanish brandy, maturation takes place in a *solera* (see SHERRY), with the periodic "refreshment" of the older spirit with younger; and because of the aeration and quicker maturation, this gives rise to brandies quite different in character from those made in Catalonia or France, where there is no such frequent transfer from cask to cask. Jerez brandy has an oaky charm of its own, but it is so distinctive that it is not sensible to make direct comparisons with cognac or Armagnac.

Another popular spirit is *aguardiente*, made by distilling the pips and skins remaining from the fermentation of wine. Akin to the French *marc* or Portuguese *bagaceira*, this is a somewhat fiery liquid best left to those who have learned to stomach it.

Spain also produces a gamut of liqueurs, many of them household names marketed internationally by foreign companies and made under license in Spain, by the maceration of fruits and herbs in alcoholic solution and subsequent distillation. A variety of firms in Jerez and Catalonia make very respectable gin and vodka by the traditional methods. Vermouth is made in large amounts, much of it under license, by the preparation of herbal extracts and their blending with white wine. The native *anís* (*anisette*) is first rate; and tonic wines and spirits containing quinine extract, of which the best known are "Jerez-Quina" and "Calisay", are something of a speciality and are made in Jerez, Málaga and Barcelona.

Aguardiente

Aguardiente is defined by the Estatuto de la Viña, del Vino y de los Alcoholes as "natural alcohol with a strength of not more than 80%" distiled from vegetable materials. It therefore constitutes a wide variety which includes the HOLANDAS used for the manufacture of brandy and known as *aguardiente de vino*, as well as other varieties distiled from fermented fruits and cereals.

However, over the counter of a bar, *aguardiente* means *aguardiente de orujo*, a popular and potent spirit distiled from the grape skins and pips left over from the fermentation of wine in the manner of the French *marc* or Portuguese *bagaceira*. It is made all over Spain and is not normally branded, but poured from an unlabeled bottle, a fact which, combined with its strength, intimidates many tourists.

Agustín Blazquez S.A., Hijos de

Well-known sherry firm (see SHERRY), makers of "Felipe II", one of the drier and least manipulated of the inexpensive Jerez brandies.

Alvear S.A.

Apart from making Montilla (see MONTILLA-MORILES), Alvear also produces brandy, made from HOLANDAS and matured in *solera* after the fashion of the Jerez brandies and the fortified wines of the area. The inexpensive "Secular" is fruity, with a raisiny nose and peppery finish. The more refined "Senador" and "Presidente" are oakier and more aromatic, and the finish of the "Presidente Alvear Gran Reserva" is extremely dry.

Amer Picon

The well-known orange-flavored bitters, manufactured under license in Spain.

Anís

Aniseed-flavored liqueur corresponding to the French *anisette*. The best Spanish *anís*, such as "CHINCHÓN" and "ANÍS DEL MONO", is of excellent quality.

"Anís del Mono"

One of the best and most popular brands of ANÍS, made by Bosch y Cía. in Badalona near Barcelona.

Barcelo S.A., Hijos de Antonio

Apart from making Málaga (see MALAGA), this large firm also produces *vinos quinados*, tonic or medicated wines containing quinine extract and popular in Spain.

Barceló S.A., Luis

Another Málaga firm, whose speciality is *vinos quinados*.

Bénédictine

Famous French liqueur made under license in Spain.

Bertola S.A.

Sherry firm which also makes "Tudor" and "Gran Reserva" brandies.

Bilbainas S.A., Bodegas

About the only *bodega* in the Rioja to produce that *rara avis*, a Riojan brandy to stand alongside its still and sparkling wines (see RIOJA and SPARKLING WINES). Its "Imperator" has a vinous, oaky nose, is completely dry, but tastes of little except oak, and the finish is short.

Brandy

As explained in more detail in the introduction to this section, most Spanish brandy is made from HOLANDAS, produced by distilling wine (in the manner of grain whisky) in a continuous still and maturing the raw spirit in *solera* (see SHERRY). The better Catalan brandies, as also a few of the premium Jerez marks, are, however, made by the Charentais method in pot-stills. In general, most commercial Spanish brandies are sweeter and more caramelized than the French and have therefore made less impact to date in international markets.

"Brandy 103"
Popular Jerez brandy made by Bobadilla.

Caballero S.A., Luis
Sherry concern located in Puerto de Sta. María and maker of one of the best brands of PONCHE, "Caballero", sold in eye-catching silvered bottles.

"Calisay"
Quinine-based liqueur, a speciality of the Barcelona area, which may be drunk either as a *digéstif* or, with ice and with or without fruit (such as lemon, orange and maraschino cherries), as an apéritif. A dash of "Calisay" much enlivens fruit salads. See also MOLLFULLEDA S.A., DISTILERIAS.

"Capa Negra"
Jerez brandy made by Sandeman Hnos. y Cía.

"Carlos I"
Apart from the "Marqués de Domecq", this is the most refined of the brandies made by Pedro Domecq S.A. in Jerez (see SHERRY), and though very slightly on the sweet side, it is light and spirituous, more resembling a French cognac than most Jerez brandies and more suited to northern tastes.

Chartreuse
Although many well known French liqueurs are made under license in Spain, Chartreuse is more firmly rooted, since from 1903–40, during the exile of the monks from La Grande Chartreuse, it was made exclusively in Tarragona. The distillery is still directly supervised by the 3 fathers who share the closely guarded secret of its recipe and who spend January to May in Tarragona and the rest of the year in Voiron, in the French Alps.

130 different herbs (many procured locally) are used for making Green Chartreuse, and rather fewer for the Yellow. The difference between the French and Spanish versions is minimal, though in my experience the Spanish is slightly drier – and also, of course, like all Spanish-made liqueurs, vastly less expensive.

The distillery in Tarragona – though not the *camera* where the herbs are compounded – is open to visitors, and the *salón de degustación,* where the visit ends, contains an intriguing collection, running to scores of bottles, of fraudulent imitations. After the tour, visitors may taste and buy the liqueurs.

"Chinchón"
One of the best brands of ANÍS, made in the small town of Chinchón SE of Madrid. It was named after a 17th-century Marquesa de Chinchón, wife of a governor of Peru, who in 1638 discovered the medicinal properties of quinine, giving her name to the Cinchona tree from the bark of which it is obtained and, indirectly, inspiring the fabrication of VINOS QUINADOS.

Cinzano
Cinzano, in its different varieties, is made under license in Vilafranca del Penedès and, with Martini, is the most widely drunk vermouth in Spain.

Cointreau
This famous orange-flavored liqueur was formerly made for the house of Cointreau by Cavas MASCARÓ in Vilafranca del Penedès. It is still made in Vilafranca, but by a Spanish subsidiary under the closer supervision of the French firm.

Coñac
To the legitimate discomfort of producers in Cognac, Spanish brandy is almost universally known in Spain as *coñac.* This is no fairer than labeling sherry-type wines from Cyprus and elsewhere as "sherry", a practise the Jerez houses are equally vehement in denouncing; and the makers of Spanish brandy, at least, are being more careful about referring to their product as "brandy".

"Cuarenta y Tres"
A sweet, light yellow vanilla-flavored liqueur, rather resembling "Southern Comfort" in taste, made by Diego Zamora in Cartagena. Its name means "forty-three".Sweet as it is, Spaniards often drink it as an apéritif.

"Don Narciso"
Delicate and aromatic brandy, a blend of 7- and 10-year-old spirits and one of the best from Spain, made by Cavas MASCARÓ in Vilafranca del Penedès by the Charentais method.

Dubonnet
The popular French apéritif, made under license in Barcelona and differing little from the original.

"D.Y.C."
Spanish-made whisky produced in a distillery near Segovia, where the water and grain are considered to be most like those of the Scottish Highlands. It is not of the quality of the original and has made little headway against the imported Scotch widely obtainable in supermarkets and grocers.

"Eminencia"
Jerez brandy made by Palomino & Vergara, one of the firms within the RUMASA group.

Escat
Barcelona firm making a wide range of spirits, including vodka, gin, *anís*, pastís, advokaat, kirsch, rum (known in Spain as *ron*), together with crême de menthe, cherry and apricot brandies, and a liqueur made with bananas from the Canary Islands.

"Esplendido"
The youngest of the brandies from the sherry firm of Garvey S.A.

"Felipe II"
Pleasant and inexpensive Jerez brandy made by Agustín Blazquez S.A.

"Fontenac"
Least expensive of the brandies from Bodegas Torres in Vilafranca del Penedès. It is made from HOLANDAS produced by the continuous distillation method, but is aged in French style rather than in *solera*; and is hence less oaky than its Jerez counterparts, and more along the lines of a young Armagnac.

"Fundador"
"Fundador" was one of the first Jerez brandies and was put on sale to the public by Pedro Domecq in 1874, some 20 years after Don Pedro Domecq Lustau had been so struck with the quality of a batch of HOLANDAS accidentally left in cask that he decided on systematic production of a brandy. To foreign tastes, it remains one of the most agreeable of the inexpensive brandies, since it is less sweetened and caramelized than many of its competitors. The trend in Spain has, however, been to smoother and sweeter brandies in the medium-price bracket; and Fundador, for long one of the biggest selling brand names, now occupies only 4th place in domestic sales.

García Poveda S.L., H.A.
Makers, apart from table wines from the Alicante area (see VALENCIAN AREA), of a range of "Costa Blanca" vermouths, fully flavored and spicy in comparison with those from France and Italy.

Garvey S.A.
Famous sherry house and producer, in ascending order of age and refinement, of "Esplendido", "Gran Garvey" and "Renacimiento" brandies.

Gonzalez Byass & Co. Ltd.
Apart from their sherries, Gonzalez Byass make three brandies: the best-

selling "SOBERANO", the medium-priced "INSUPERABLE" and, in very limited amount, the exquisite "LEPANTO".

Gordon's Gin
This is made under license in Spain with close supervision from London.

"Gran Duque de Alba"
Jerez brandy made by Zoilo Ruiz Mateus S.A.

Holandas
Grape spirit containing 65% alcohol and made by the continuous distillation of wine in various districts of Spain, especially La Mancha, Extremadura and Huelva. This spirit is subsequently diluted with water and aged, either in *solera* or cask, to make brandy, generally the less refined and cheaper brands.

"Imperial"
Medium-priced brandy from Bodegas TORRES in Vilafranca del Penedès and sold as either 5 or 10 years old. Made from HOLANDAS distiled from selected grapes and aged Cognac-style, it is good and aromatic Catalan brandy, less oaky and quite different in style from those from Jerez.

"Independencia"
Dark, velvety and sweet, and sold in a curious distorted bottle to emphasize its age, this is a premium brandy from the sherry house of Osborne.

"Insuperable"
The big brother of "SOBERANO" from Gonzalez Byass, smoother and more aromatic.

"Jerez-Quina"
Popular tonic wine, made with sherry, macerated cinchona bark and the peel of Seville oranges, and regularly administered to Spanish children and convalescents.

Larios S.A.
Larios makes good Málaga (see MALAGA) but in Spain it is a household word for its gin, sold in bottles with a red and yellow label with a marked likeness to that of the export Gordon's. Though not of quite the same quality as good London gin, it is entirely acceptable with mixers. The firm also produces the "1866 Gran Reserva" brandy, "Triple Seco" orange liqueur, and rum.

"Lepanto"
Soft, mellow and fragrant, but entirely Jerezano in character, this expensive brandy from Gonzalez Byass, sold in a cut-glass decanter and one of the few from Jerez to be made in pot-stills rather than by continuous distillation, is exceptional.

Liqueurs
Most of the best-known French liqueurs are made under license in Spain (see COINTREAU, BENEDICTINE, MARIE BRIZARD) and differ little from the originals – except that they are much cheaper and therefore a popular purchase with travellers. There are also numerous separately listed firms making fruit brandies, crême de menthe, kirsch, etc., and also some native liqueurs with a foreign following (see PONCHE, CUARENTA Y TRES, PACHARAN).

Lustau S.A., Emilio
Sherry firm whose brandy is sold as "Señor Lustau".

"Magno"
Made by Osborne y Cía. in Puerto de Sta. María, "Magno", which spends 4–5 years in *solera*, is dark in color, smooth, aromatic and on the sweet side, very much to the Spanish taste and a nice brandy. It currently commands some half of the domestic market in the increasingly popular medium-price range.

Marie Brizard
Perhaps the most famous of French *anisettes*, this is made under license at Pasajes in the Basque country.

Martini
Martini, especially in the sweet and bitter-sweet varieties, is extremely popular in Spain and is made in Barcelona.

Mascaró, Cavas
Mascaró, a small family concern in Vilafranca del Penedès (see SPARKLING WINES), has for long provided some of the best Catalan brandy. Made by the Charentais method and aged along French lines, it is more akin to Cognac or Armagnac than to the Jerez-style brandies. The regular "Mascaró", light, smooth and fragrant, is in my own opinion much superior to most 3-star cognacs and a great deal less expensive. The older "DON NARCISO" is produced from Macabeo, Xarel-lo and Parellada grapes vinified in the *cava* itself.

Mascaró also produces a vodka and a superior gin, made with alcohol distiled from sugar beet and juniper berries from the Penedès. For many years the firm made Cointreau for sale in Spain and now produces its own curaçao, the "Gran Licor de Naranja", a pleasant liqueur made by steeping dried orange peel from Spain, Algeria, Haiti and Italy in alcoholic solution and then distilling it.

"Ministro"
A superior Catalan-style brandy made by Bodegas TORRES.

Mollfulleda S.A., Distilerías
Large firm with its distillery in Arenys de Mar near Barcelona, specializing in the quinine-based "CALISAY". Apart from this, it also produces rum, gin, kirsch and a range of liqueurs – orange, peppermint, coffee, cocoa, and others.

Montulia S.A.
Apart from Montilla, Montulia also makes ANÍS and a range of *solera* brandies.

Orujo
Popular name for the fiery *aguardiente de orujo* distiled from grape skins and pips (see AGUARDIENTE).

Osborne y Cía. S.A.
This famous sherry firm based in Puerto de Sta. María (see SHERRY) is one of the largest Spanish brandy-makers, producing "VETERANO", "MAGNO" and "INDEPENDENCIA". All these brandies tend to be dark in color and somewhat sweetened and caramelized to the Spanish taste, and so do not usually appeal to foreign visitors. Its "Conde de Osborne" is even older and mellower than "Independencia" and is sold in distinctive white ceramic bottles designed by Salvador Dali. Osborne also makes a PONCHE and "Pitman Gin".

Pacharán
A delicious liqueur made from bilberries in Navarra. The most widely available brand is ZOCO.

Pedro Domecq S.A.
One of the first firms to make brandy in Jerez (see SHERRY), Pedro Domecq maintains a huge store for ageing its brandies in *solera* and, taking into account its vast Mexican operation, is probably the biggest manufacturer in the world. In ascending order of age and quality its labels are: "FUNDADOR", "Carlos II", "CARLOS I" and the very superior "Marqués de Domecq", available in minuscule amount and containing spirit from pot-stills. Domecq also makes an "Anís Dulce" and a sweet lime liqueur, the "Crema de Lima".

Pemartín y Cía., José
In ascending order of age and refinement, the brandies from this old-established sherry firm are "Pemartín", "Brandy 1810" and "V.O.G." It also markets a rum.

Pernod
The well-known aniseed-flavored drink is made under license in Tarragona.

Ponche
First produced by the sherry firm of José de Soto in 1888, *ponche* is a blend of brandy and herbs; often flavored with orange, it is a most satisfactory drink for those with a taste for something sweeter than brandy but less sticky than a liqueur and fills an uncluttered gap in the market. A popular brand is "Caballero", made by Luis CABALLERO S.A. in Jerez, which stands out on the shelves of a bar because of its silvered bottles. De Soto's *ponche* remains one of the best; other Jerez producers are Osborne y Cía. S.A., Jaime F. Diestro S.A., and J. Ruiz y Cía., makers of the excellent "Ponche Español".

"Presidente"
The best of the brandies from the Montilla firm of ALVEAR.

Queimada
Galician speciality made by setting alight AGUARDIENTE in a white chinaware bowl. When the blue flame subsides, the liquid is, surprisingly, stone cold. More elaborate versions are made, especially at Christmas, by pouring the spirit into an earthenware *cazuela*, adding roasted coffee beans, slices of fresh lemon and maraschino cherries, burning off some of the alcohol and ladling the potent concoction into glasses.

Quinine
Quinine-based apéritifs and liqueurs are widely produced and popular in Spain. See also "JEREZ-QUINA", "CALISAY", VINOS QUINADOS and "CHINCHON".

"Renacimiento"
Smooth and very old brandy made by GARVEY S.A. of Jerez and sold in a cut-glass decanter.

Ricard
The well-known French *pastís* made under license in Reus in Catalonia.

Rives
A good-quality Spanish gin made in Puerto de Sta. María.

"Soberano"
The biggest-selling of Spanish brandies, made by Gonzalez Byass in Jerez. Like "FUNDADOR", it is less sweetened and caramelized than many and will thus appeal to foreign visitors more than the darker and sweeter varieties popular with the Spaniards themselves. An honest-to-goodness young Jerez brandy, remarkably inexpensive, especially when bought in liter bottles, the taste for it grows!

Sol y sombra
Literally "sun and shade", a lethal mixture of brandy and ANÍS. *Aficionados* usually mix one part of brandy with two of *anís.*

Terry S.A., Fernando A. de
Among the sweetest and most caramelized of Jerez brandies, the regular "Terry", in a bottle with a yellow net, is extremely popular in Spain. The older and more refined "Solera 1900" is still on the sweet side.

Torres, Viñedos
Together with MASCARÓ, Bodegas Torres produce the best Catalan brandy, so different in style from that from Jerez and more akin to

French brandy. The range, in order of age, comprises "FONTENAC" and "IMPERIAL" 5- and 10-year-old, and "MINISTRO", but the outstanding brandy from the firm is its "Miguel Torres Black Label", made by the Charentais method on the premises and subsequently aged in oak for long periods. I have attended blind tastings where it proved extremely difficult to distinguish it from good V.S.O.P. cognac. See also CATALONIA.

Vermouth
Vermouth, much of it made under license in Catalonia (see CINZANO and MARTINI), is produced on a large scale in Spain. The only way in which these Spanish-made vermouths differ from their Italian namesakes is in the local white wine used for their manufacture – a relatively unimportant factor in comparison with the herbal extract – and in price. There is also a wide variety of purely Spanish vermouths, produced mainly in Catalonia and the Levante. These tend to be heavier and fuller in flavor.

Vinos quinados
Tonic or medicated wines containing quinine extract, drunk either for pleasure or given to children and invalids. See also "JEREZ QUINA", BARCELO S.A., HIJOS DE ANTONIO and BARCELO S.A., LUIS.

Vodka
Spanish vodka, like gin, is produced in sizeable amounts in Jerez and the Barcelona area, and is inexpensive and of acceptable quality – certainly when drunk with mixers.

"Veterano"
Jerez brandy made by Osborne y Cía. S.A. and known the length and breadth of the country, if only because of the roadside hoardings with their large black bull. Dark in color and somewhat sweetened and caramelized, it rates second in domestic sales, claiming some 25% of the market for large-selling brandies in its category.

Whisky
It is now more *chic* among Spaniards to drink whisky than sherry. Most of the best-known brands of Scotch are readily obtainable – and no more expensive than in their homeland – as also some American and Canadian whiskeys. Although attempts have been made to produce whisky in Spain, the home-made product has not caught on. See also "D.Y.C.".

"Zoco"
Best known of the brands of PACHARÁN, the bilberry liqueur from Navarra.

Valencian Area

The eastern area along the Mediterranean coast, known in Spain as the LEVANTE, comprises the five demarcated regions of Alicante, Jumilla, Utiel-Requena, Valencia and Yecla. In terms of bulk production, the Levante is second in importance only to La Mancha, producing in 1979 a total of some 400 million liters of wine, compared with 2,500 million liters from the combined regions of the center.

In general, they are of the Mediterranean type, full-bodied, spicy and high in alcohol. The alcoholic strength of the wines from Yecla and Jumilla may in part be explained by the fact that the black Monastrell grape so typical of the regions was largely unaffected by phylloxera, and the vines are not usually grafted on to American stocks as in other parts of Spain and the rest of Europe. The Monastrell is also the grape *par excellence* of Alicante, though a certain amount of white wine is made from the Verdil.

Perhaps the best of the Levante wines are the *rosados* from the upland district of Utiel-Requena, made from the black Bobal grape. Produced as a by-product of the thick and highly alcoholic *vino de doble pasta* shipped to other parts of Spain for blending, these

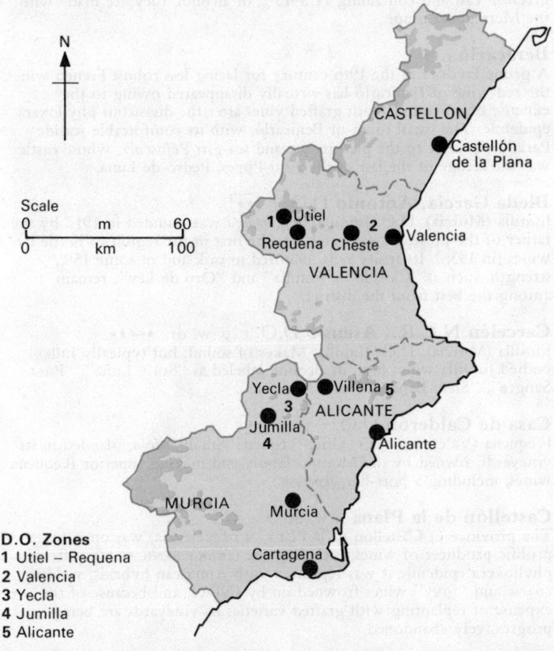

N
Scale
0 m 60
0 km 100
CASTELLON
Castellón de la Plana
1 Utiel
Requena
2
Cheste
Valencia
VALENCIA
Yecla
Villena
5
3
ALICANTE
Jumilla
4
Alicante
MURCIA
Murcia
Cartagena

D.O. Zones
1 Utiel – Requena
2 Valencia
3 Yecla
4 Jumilla
5 Alicante

are among the very best rosés from Spain, pale, very light, fruity, fragrant and refreshing. Not surprisingly, in a part of the country famous for its dessert grapes, there are also some luscious Moscatel wines from the coastal areas.

The Levante is not an area which one would visit specially for its wines, but vacationers in resorts such as Alicante, Benicasim, Benidorm, Calpe and Javea will find it worthwhile to experiment with the local growths and the house wine in the restaurants, rather than to confine themselves to Rioja.

Alicante
Alicante, with its mild climate and marble-paved promenade, lined with palms and facing the port, is the best base for visiting the *bodegas* in its area and also those of the somewhat inaccessible regions of YECLA and JUMILLA in the mountainous hinterland of Murcia. The best hotels are the 4-star Meliá Alicante and Grand Sol in the city itself, and the 5-star Sidi San Juan Palace-Sol in the vacation resort of Playa de San Juan on its outskirts.

Alicante D.O. r. p. (w. dr. or sw.) ★→★★
This demarcated region, extending to 34,221ha (85,550 acres) and producing 46.8 million liters of wine in 1979, is divided into 2 sub-regions. The maritime zone on the coast around Calpe, Javea and Denia makes sweet Moscatel. The larger and more important central zone lies in the hills around Villena, Pinoso and Monóvar and produces a light rosé, a VINO DE DOBLE PASTA, and full-bodied reds high in alcohol, made with some 90% Monastrell. Small amounts of white wine are also made from some 85% of Verdil.

Alto-Turia D.O. w. dr. ★★
Sub-division of the D.O. VALENCIA in the high NW of the province producing white wines of some quality; fruity, lightly acid with a greenish cast and containing 11.5–13% of alcohol, they are made with the Merseguera grape.

Benicarló r. ★
A prime favorite in the 19th century for lacing less robust French wines, the red wine of Benicarló has virtually disappeared owing to the expense of replanting with grafted vines after the disastrous phylloxera epidemic. The small town of Benicarló, with its comfortable seaside Parador, is close to the picturesque and sea-girt Peñiscola, whose castle was the refuge of the last of the Anti-Popes, Pedro de Luna.

Bleda García, Antonio D.O. r. [★★]
Jumilla (Murcia). D.O. Jumilla. The *bodega* was founded in 1917 by the father of the present owner and was the first in the region to bottle its wines (in 1936). Its fruity reds, matured in cask and of some 15% strength, such as "Castillo de Jumilla" and "Oro de Ley", remain among the best from the district.

Carcelén N.C.R., Asensio D.O. r. p. w. dr. ★→★★
Jumilla (Murcia). D.O. Jumilla. Maker of sound, but typically full-bodied Jumilla wines high in alcohol, labeled as "Sol y Luna", "Pura Sangre", "Siete Banderas" and "Acorde".

Casa de Calderón D.O. r. p. g. [★★]
Requena (Valencia). D.O. Utiel-Requena. Small *bodega*, islanded in its vineyards, owned by the Mompó family and making superior Requena wines, including a port-like *generoso*.

Castellón de la Plana r. w. dr. ★
The province of Castellón de la Plana, N of Valencia, was once a prolific producer of wines, including the famous BENICARLÓ. After the phylloxera epidemic it was replanted with American hybrids, yielding coarse and "foxy" wines frowned on by INDO, and because of the expense of replanting with grafted varieties its vineyards are being progressively abandoned.

Cheste w. dr. ★
Formerly a D.O. in its own right, Cheste, lying between VALENCIA and UTIEL-REQUENA, has been incorporated in the D.O. VALENCIA. It is a prolific producer of dry and somewhat earthy white wines of 12.5–15%, neutral and without a great deal of character.

Clariano r. w. dr. ★
Sub-division of the D.O. VALENCIA in the extreme S of the province bordering Alicante. It produces both red and white wines of 11–13%, the best being the reds made from the Monastrell.

Fondillón g. ★★★ 59, 68, 75, 78
Famous *generoso* from Monóvar, W of Alicante, copper-colored, aromatic and aged in cask for some 20 years. Very little is now made; the 1959 vintage is legendary.

García Carrión, Bodegas D.O. r. p. w. dr. ★→★★
Jumilla (Murcia). D.O. Jumilla. Private firm making good standard Jumilla wines, mainly red.

García Poveda S.A., H.L. D.O. r. (p. w. dr. and sw.) res. ★→★★
Villena (Alicante). D.O. Alicante. Sizeable family concern with *bodegas* at Villena in the hills behind Alicante. "Costa Blanca" red, white and rosé; "Marquesado" red, white and rosé; "Costa Blanca" Moscatel. The firm also makes a range of vermouths, full-bodied in character like the other wines.

Hybrids
The district around CASTELLÓN DE LA PLANA, BENICARLÓ and Vinaroz was a large supplier of red wine to France during the phylloxera epidemic of the late 19th century, but after it had itself been affected, the vines were replaced with American hybrids. Many survive on peasant plots, but government regulations forbid their use in new plantations.

Irrigation
Because of the low rainfall, JUMILLA and YECLA are regions where irrigation is permitted, but only on a limited scale and only during the winter.

Jumilla D.O. r. (w. dr.) ★→★★
The demarcated region extends to 17,627ha (44,000 acres) with a production in 1979 of 86 million liters of wine, most of it a dark, full-bodied red containing up to 18% alcohol. Apart from the heat of its long summers, the other reason for this high alcohol content is that, because of the high content of chalk and organic material in the soils, the region was unaffected by phylloxera, and it is one of the few areas in Spain or in Europe where vines are still grown ungrafted. The best wines are made with the Monastrell and aged in oak, and efforts are being made to reduce the high alcohol content by earlier picking and blending with white wine.

La Purísima, Cooperativa de D.O. r. w. dr. g. ★→★★
Yecla (Murcia). D.O. Yecla. An enormous concern with a capacity of 55 million liters, making 75% of the wine from the demarcated region. Its red and white "Viña Montana" shipped abroad is lighter and less alcoholic than most of the red heavyweights from the area. As well as red *reservas*, the cooperative also produces a red *solera* wine reminiscent of inexpensive port.

Levante
Name given to the strip stretching along the Mediterranean coast of Spain from the Cabo de Gato, just E of Almería, to the delta of the Ebro in the N.

Murviedro, Bodegas D.O. r. w. dr. ★→[★★]
Valencia. D.O. Valencia. A small *bodega* founded in 1927 and taking its name from the Murviedro or Saguntum of the Romans, famous for its siege by Hannibal, which makes its wines with care, mostly for export. "Viña Murviedro blanco" and "Los Monteros tinto".

Phylloxera
Certain areas of the Levante (see JUMILLA and YECLA) were wholly or partially unaffected by this insect pest of the vine and still grow ungrafted vines, while others, like CASTELLÓN DE LA PLANA, were replanted with American hybrids and have never fully recovered.

Pons Hermanos, Hijos de
Valencia. One of the large Valencian export houses, shipping everyday wine in bulk.

Poveda Luz, Bodegas Salvador D.O. r. p. g. ★→[★★★]
Monóvar (Alicante). D.O. Alicante. Family concern with *bodegas* in the hills, making some of the best Alicante wine, albeit full-bodied and high in alcohol, notably the red "Doble Capa", red and rosé "Viña Vermeta" and the outstanding "FONDILLÓN" *generoso*.

San Isidro, Cooperativa de D.O. r. (p. w. dr.) res. [★→★★]
Jumilla (Murcia). D.O. Jumilla. Huge, well-equipped and well-run modern cooperative. Apart from its big-selling "Rumor", it makes more mature wines aged in oak, mainly red, such as "Sabatacha", "Zambra" and "Solera" *reserva*, all full in body and high in alcohol.

Schenk S.A., Bodegas r. p. w. dr. and sw. res. [★→★★]
Valencia. This Spanish arm of the large Swiss concern buys wine from the whole Levante area and from as far afield as La Mancha, and apart from elaborating and shipping the ubiquitous "Don Cortez", also bottles some wines of considerable sophistication, e.g. the characterful red "Monteros" made with 100% Monastrell, a light and fruity rosé from Utiel-Requena and a luscious Moscatel.

Señorio de Condestable S.A. D.O. r. [★★]
Jumilla (Murcia). D.O. Jumilla. An outpost of the great concern of Savin S.A. making a particularly pleasant red "Condestable".

Utiel, Cooperativa Agrícola de D.O. r. ★ p. [★★]
Utiel (Valencia). D.O. Utiel-Requena. One of the best of the large cooperatives in the region making a thick black VINO DE DOBLE PASTA for blending, a normal red wine and a light, pale and fragrant rosé.

Utiel-Requena D.O. r. p. ★→★★
At the western extreme of the province of Valencia, Utiel-Requena, with an area of 49,478ha (123,415 acres) and a production in 1979 of 134 million liters, is an upland extension of the central plateau. The typical wines, made from some 90% of the black Bobal grape with smaller amounts of Cencibel (Tempranillo) and Garnacha, are of 3 types: a thick, almost black VINO DE DOBLE PASTA for blending; a pale, light and entirely delicious rosé; and a sturdy *tinto* or red wine.

Valencia
Valencia, the third city of Spain, surrounded by its orange and lemon groves, is the queen of the Levante, and despite the devastations of the Napoleonic and Civil Wars, there still remain parts of the old walls with their gates and turrets, and narrow streets flanked with balconied houses. Its *fallas*, celebrated in mid-March, with bonfires and processions of giant effigies in the streets, is one of the liveliest Spanish fiestas.

Valencia is the headquarters of numerous huge export houses, shipping wine in bulk all over the world; and its Grao ships more wine than any other port in Spain.

The natural base for visits to the neighboring vineyards and to those of UTIEL-REQUENA, it possesses numerous luxury hotels – such as the Sidi Saler Sol, Astoria Palace, Rey Don Jaime – but my own favorite is the old-fashioned and characterful 3-star Inglés, opposite the best ceramic museum in Spain, in the Palace of the Marqués de Dos Aguas.

Valencia D.O. (r.) w. dr. or sw. ★
The demarcated region, extending to 47,670ha (118,975 acres) and producing 129 million liters of wine in 1979, incorporates the former D.O. CHESTE and the sub-regions of ALTO-TURIA, CLARIANO and VALENTINO. They produce more white wine than red, mostly of typical Mediterranean type, earthy, full-bodied, strong and low in acid.

Valentino D.O. r. dr. (w.) ★
The largest of the sub-regions of the D.O. VALENCIA, to the W of the city in the center of the province and incorporating the former D.O. CHESTE. The principal white grapes are the Merseguera, Malvasía, Moscatel, Pedro Ximénez and Planta de Pedralba; and the best wines are the dry whites made from the Merseguera and Pedro Ximénez and the sweet Moscatels. Reds from the Garnacha tinta and Tintorera.

Vinival r. p. w. dr. and sw. [★]
Valencia. Vinival was founded in 1969 to handle bulk wines from various regions of the Levante from the old-established firms of Garrigos, Mompó, Teschendorff and Steiner. It operates from a huge, brick-built, cathedral-like building near the port. With its capacity of 30 million liters, it ships large quantities of sound, spicy Mediterranean-type "Torres de Serrano", red and white.

Vino de doble pasta
Much of the wine from UTIEL-REQUENA and ALICANTE is made in an entirely individual fashion. The grapes are destalked and lightly crushed, and after a few hours in the vat to extract color from the skins the must is pumped off into a fresh vat, where fermentation continues *en blanc* to produce a light, fragrant and delicate rosé. The original vat is then topped up with a further load of crushed grapes, and continued fermentation produces a *vino de doble pasta*, thick in extract, black in color, with an alcohol content of up to 18%; sold not for consumption, but for blending with thinner growths such as those from Galicia.

Yecla D.O. r. (w.) ★→★★
The demarcated region, extending to 26,207ha (65,500 acres) and producing 31 million liters of wine in 1979, neighbors that of JUMILLA in the hills of Murcia and produces very similar wines. As in Jumilla, the impact of phylloxera was far less severe than in other parts of Spain, and some 40% of the predominant Monastrell grapes are grown ungrafted. The typical wines are dark, full-bodied reds containing up to 18% of alcohol, but the Cooperativa La PURÍSIMA responsible for most of the production has recently been making lighter, less alcoholic wines.

Like all the coastal areas of Spain, the Levante offers a magnificent variety of fish and shellfish; but the region in general, and Valencia in particular, is known above all for its rice dishes, especially the world-renowned *paella*. The *huertas* or gardens of Valencia are famous for their oranges and also for their vegetables, of which good use is made in cooking. Alicante almonds are used to make nougats or *turrones*.

It is one of nature's ironies that hot regions, where one most appreciates lighter wines, produce the strongest, and colder areas the lightest. At least in its rosés from Utiel-Requena the Levante has a wine that goes admirably with fish and light food. Oddly enough, a full-bodied red wine goes better with *paella* than a white, though one of the spicy Valencian whites will also stand up to its definite flavors.

Arroz abanda
Fish and shellfish cooked with onions, bay leaf, saffron, olive oil and seasoning, and served with rice, boiled separately in the juices from the fish.

Arroz "Empedrat"
Popular with the workers in the TURRÓN *factories of Jijona, this is also known as* arroz de fábrica *("factory rice") and is made with haricot beans, garlic, tomatoes, parsley and rice.*

Bacalao a la valenciana
Dried cod cooked in the oven with rice, fish broth, tomato purée, onions, grated cheese, butter and hard-boiled eggs.

Conejo a la valenciana
Young rabbit stewed with green peppers, black peppercorns, garlic, parsley and olive oil.

Empanadillas valencianas
Small pasties filled with tuna mixed with tomato sauce, then fried crisp in olive oil or baked in the oven.

Faves al tombet
Fresh broad beans cooked with lettuce, artichoke hearts, garlic shoots, red paprika, vinegar and bread.

Guisantes al estilo valenciano
Fresh peas cooked with garlic, pepper, onions, thyme, white wine, bay leaf, olive oil and saffron.

Paella valenciana
Saffron-flavored rice, cooked simply with fish and shellfish or with a variety of other ingredients, such as chicken, meat and fresh vegetables.
It is usual in Spain to drink red rather than white wine with *paella.*

Potaje valenciano
A thick soup containing chick-peas, spinach, sweet paprika, lemon, parsley, onions, garlic and yolks of egg.

Sopa a la valenciana
Thick soup with a variety of fresh vegetables, rice, onions and parsley, cooked in ham stock.

Sopa de mariscos levantina
Valencian version of bouillabaisse *with shellfish, vegetables, saffron, bay leaf, tomatoes and garlic. It is served in 2 parts: first the broth with croûtons, and then the shellfish with a cold sauce.*

Turrón
Of two varieties, hard or soft, this nougat is a speciality of the Alicante region and is made with almonds, egg whites or yolks, and a variety of other ingredients including honey, sugar and pine kernels.

Restaurants

Alicante ★★ *Delfín* (excellent rice dishes and outstanding baked bass); ★ *Nou Manolín* (good *tapas*, reasonable prices and wonderful cellar).

Murcia ★★★ *El Rincón de Pepe* (Murcia is a goodish drive from Jumilla and Yecla, but this is quite simply one of the best restaurants in Spain).

Utiel ★ *La Abuela* (regional cooking at its best – try the *ajo arriero* with the local rosé).

Valencia ★★ *La Hacienda* (good cooking and a long wine list); ★★ *Les Graelles* (best in Valencia for its rice dishes).

Index

The following abbreviations are used in the index; for further explanation see Glossary.

Bod. *Bodega*; Cía. *Compañía*; Coop. *Cooperativa*; D.O. *Denominación de Origen* area; Hnos. *Hermanos*; (H) Entry which includes hotel recommendation; (R) Restaurant recommendation; S.A. *Sociedad Anónima*